- newspapers.
- Bolivars writings.
- personal letters

Simón Bolívar
THE HOPE
OF
THE UNIVERSE

# Simón Bolívar

# THE HOPE
# OF
# THE UNIVERSE

*Introduction,*
*selection, biographical notes*
*and chronology by*
J. L. SALCEDO-BASTARDO

*Prologue by*
ARTURO USLAR PIETRI

UNESCO

Published by the United Nations Educational,
Scientific and Cultural Organization,
7 place de Fontenoy, 75700 Paris
Typeset by Richard Clay (The Chaucer Press) Ltd, Bungay, United Kingdom
Printed by Imprimerie de la Manutention, Mayenne, France

ISBN 92–3–102103–6
French edition: 92–3–202103–X
Spanish edition: 92–3–302103–3

Simón Bolívar occupies a prominent place among those great figures of universal history whom the United Nations system recognizes as its precursors.

At the beginning of the last century, Bolívar was already trying to conceive of a future on the scale of mankind as a whole. He was not just the hero of one country, or of the group of nations which he helped to free from the colonial yoke, or even of the American continent alone; by virtue of the universal scope of his thought, he endeavoured to voice the hopes of all the peoples of the world.

The special tribute being paid to him on the occasion of the celebration of the bicentenary of his birth prompts us to evaluate the efforts made by the international community since the nineteenth century to follow the course marked out by him towards greater freedom, justice and solidarity.

*A. A. M' Bow*

AMADOU-MAHTAR M'BOW
19 January 1983

# CONTENTS

# PROLOGUE

by

*Arturo Uslar Pietri*

Two hundred years after his birth, Bolívar undoubtedly remains one of that tiny but distinguished group of people who have had something to teach mankind. He died in 1830, but the sheer magnitude of his personality is still being revealed to us and still has the power to move us. In the eyes of his contemporaries, he was the outstanding leader of the struggle for the political independence of Latin America, a charismatic figure who, virtually without resources, managed to overcome all manner of obstacles and setbacks in directing and sustaining the long-drawn-out and difficult fifteen-year offensive which was to put an end to Spanish domination over Latin America. His unyielding tenacity, his conviction that independence could and should come about in his own lifetime and his far-reaching vision of the future of the New World, set him apart from the many other exceptional leaders who emerged during the war for the emancipation of the continent.

For the Western world, he soon became the symbol of the struggle against despotism and the old monarchies. His name was synonymous with freedom. The revolutionaries of 1830 and 1848, the *Carbonari*, the liberals, the young Romantics all looked to him and his example. He was the hero who had pitted himself against 300 years of the old régime in Spanish America, succeeded in bringing it to an end, and proclaimed a new order of democracy and freedom in its stead. His admirers ranged from the restless young people in the Paris of the Bourbons, who sported the 'Bolívar hat' as though it were a battle standard, to students of world politics, and to Byron, who gave Bolívar's name to the boat in which he dreamed of bringing freedom to Greece.

Bolívar had become the eternal 'Liberator', the man who had personified a continent's determination to be free and who had striven to establish a political order founded on justice and the rights of the individual.

9

There can be no doubt that, as a military leader, he won significant victories against all odds. He sowed the seeds of destiny, in that nations were born of the battles he waged, and he secured freedom for vast numbers of people and an enormous land-mass. In 1825, when his triumph at Ayacucho put an end to the Spanish Empire and made him the arbiter of the destinies of Latin America, he conceived and attempted to give substance to the grandiose plan of uniting Latin America as he saw it, in a bid to bring about a new age of stability and justice for mankind. Indeed, his disagreement with his former followers and the growing difficulties he had to contend with stemmed from his vision of the future.

For him, independence was not so much an end in itself as a necessary step along the road to a more difficult but much more ambitious project. His aim was not merely to replace one set of rulers by another, to put Creole leaders in the seats vacated by the Spanish viceroys and governors and thereby perpetuate the political and social patterns inherited from the colonial past. He wanted something totally different: literally to create a powerful and free New World, setting an example through its institutions, intent on dispensing justice in all its forms, and laying the foundations for a new global order which Bolívar himself spoke of as 'a new equilibrium for the universe'.

Right from the start, Bolívar was distinguished for the clarity and boldness of his thinking. Had he done no more than commit to paper the ideas and judgements on the Latin American world which he bequeathed to us, he would still be considered one of the most original thinkers of his time. Moreover, he was an exceptionally gifted writer and his letters and speeches stand out among the best writings of the period. No one could equal his gift for expressing himself in terms that were robust and penetrating and charged with significance. His language faithfully reflected his temperament and his deep anxieties. He was a master of concision and of striking similes. His words were as good as his deeds.

There have been few other figures in history who combined as he did the gifts and qualities of a man of action and those of a thinker, of those who were leaders of men and also visionaries, whose political acumen did not prevent them from forming grand designs or from rising above petty day-to-day concerns. His tragedy was his inability to ensure that his vision of the future would be realized. He could not rest content with the extraordinary task he had accomplished, since he considered it merely as the necessary prelude to the new political organization of Latin America and a new world equilibrium. Only a person of his quality could have regarded the second stage as being more important than the first.

Bolívar is a figure of infinite variety. If we see him as being no more than the leader of a highly successful insurrection, we ignore one whole facet of his personality and overlook some of the most interesting and admirable aspects of his achievement. He was never merely a man of action, perpetually engaged in a struggle that must often have seemed hopeless, neither was he an ideologist unimaginatively applying doctrines and examples culled from other countries and other historical situations.

What is more, he was not just a politician, bogged down in the immediate present. A study of his life leaves us constantly amazed at the profusion and variety of talents he displayed. In his eyes, the past of the Latin American peoples was as alive as their present. He identified himself totally with the historical and cultural predicament of his fellow Latin Americans, and yet at the same time he could look forward to the future as he wished to see it and could work for a far-reaching transformation of society and its goals. He was not blinded by the various brilliant political theories of his day. He carefully examined the ideas of Rousseau and Montesquieu, comparing them with his own experience in the struggle and with the lessons of the Latin American past.

His conclusion was that the future of the Latin American peoples did not lie in merely imitating or adapting the ideas and institutions of other nations conceived in differing historical and cultural circumstances; in his opinion, only the facts, however intractable, could be the starting-point for the determined and clear-sighted effort needed, since the colonial past had in no way prepared those peoples for their difficult metamorphosis.

One fundamental theme of Bolívar's ideas on nation-building was what we, in present-day international parlance, would call the cultural constraints on development and the difficulty of adapting foreign models. He was forever alerting legislators—dazzled as they were by the examples of the institutions that emerged from the revolutions in the United States and France—to the importance of allowing for specific Hispano-American practices, traditions and experiences of the past. He ardently desired freedom, justice and democracy, but he did not lose sight of the social and political realities which 300 years of life under colonial rule had created in the America he knew.

Nor did he lose sight of the international situation hovering on the horizon. The independence of Latin America could not be envisaged and achieved as an isolated local phenomenon: it was a major upheaval establishing a new situation and a new pattern of worldwide relations. The sudden emergence of a free and sovereign Latin America would inevitably produce significant changes in political relationships all over the world. This was the exceptionally wide-ranging context within which Bolívar's action and thinking evolved and which afforded him his status and relevance as the guide of the Latin American peoples and the embodiment of their spirit.

This, moreover, is an attitude that prevailed throughout his life and in all his writings. From the outset, his vision of independence embraced the whole continent and, in this respect, he was at one with his celebrated predecessor Francisco Miranda. The issue as they both saw it was not just to win independence for a few portions of the Spanish Empire but to ensure that the whole territory it covered would become conscious of its identity and destiny, and would attain full sovereignty. This accordingly implied a form of political organization and the adoption of goals that would encompass the entire New World. From the very beginning, he spoke in the name of America rather than of Venezuela, and was not afraid to suggest ways in which political integration could come about. As he said on several occasions, 'America is our homeland.'

The question now is what he meant by 'America' and what form of integration he had in mind. His scheme of things did not rule out any significant part of the Latin America that had been subjugated by the European powers. He started with the peoples of Venezuela, New Granada and Ecuador who were close at hand and were subsequently to combine to form Colombia, but he went on to include all parts of the Empire in successive designs for co-operation.

When, in 1825, after the final and decisive victory at Ayacucho, he arrived at Potosí, that renowned centre of power and wealth, he climbed the mountain of silver that had been the symbol of colonial authority, accompanied by the representatives of Argentina, Peru and Chile. As he took in the panorama stretching out before him, as he felt—and expressed—the compelling need for integration as the only course capable of securing the future of so vast a slice of humanity and territory, he caught a glimpse of the scenario of universal history. It was at this time that he convened the Panama Congress that was to bring together representatives of the whole of Latin America in a bid to work out the practical aspects of the continent's policies, its self-defence and the joint action it would be required to take in its dealings with the rest of the world.

We need only leaf through the main documents in which his ideas are assembled to realize that his conception of the common destiny of Latin America never changed. As early as 1812, in Cartagena, when he had scarcely emerged from the ruins of the first attempt he made to set up an independent republic in Venezuela, he issued a bold manifesto sounding the alarm against the mistaken belief that any part of Latin America could achieve and preserve its independence in isolation. So long as Venezuela was not liberated, the independence of New Granada would be threatened, since an expeditionary force organized from Venezuela and setting out from the Provinces of Barinas and Maracaibo would be able to penetrate into 'the furthest reaches of southern America'.

Indeed, the huge efforts which he expected on the part of the enemies of freedom were exactly the same as those he himself had to make throughout the long hard years of his political and military career. From then on, the whole of Latin America became the theatre of operations for a single combat, the struggle for independence, only to be achieved by the integration of all its peoples in a single body that would guarantee the unity of its presence and action on the world scene.

In the astonishing letter which he wrote in Jamaica in 1815 to 'a gentleman of that island', he painted the most detailed and challenging picture of his vision of the Latin American destiny. His theme was not Venezuela but rather 'a vast, varied and unknown country, the New World'. He looked upon it as a fact of history and geography, asking impatiently whether the entire New World was not mobilized and armed to defend itself, and adding: 'On this battlefield, some 2,000 leagues long and 900 leagues wide at its extremes, 16 million Americans are either defending their rights or are being oppressed.'

In his view, an unavoidable historical phenomenon had occurred, one that was bound to have far-reaching consequences for the world. It was here that he expressed the gist of his thinking: the projected independence of Latin America was a necessary goal 'because world equilibrium demanded it'.

This, then, represented his fundamental view of things. The time had come to strike a new universal balance. The pattern of imperial domination could not continue. In the words of Virgil in his prophetic *Eclogue*, a new order was to come to pass. The Spanish Empire had to be brought to an end so that an authentic New World could come into being and engage in a dialogue on fair and just terms with the other powers of the earth.

For Bolívar, the term 'New World' did not have the restricted connotations earlier historians had given it. He did not conceive of it merely as a recent adjunct to an old world and an old order but as a heaven-sent opportunity of creating a new society that would not repeat the mistakes of the old world, but would usher in a new era in relations between all nations.

Bolívar thus became the prophet not only of the New World but of a new world order. Henceforward, he sensed and made it plain that the time had come for the emergence of new and independent nations and also that the very existence of such nations would dictate the setting up of a new pattern of relationships. Using words that are equally relevant to the struggle currently being waged by the new nations of Latin America, Asia and Africa to bring about a new order of relations, to the dramatic dialogue going on between North and South, or to the far-reaching process of the emergence of the Third World, Bolívar said: 'There is another balanced order of importance to us, and this is the equilibrium of the universe. This struggle cannot be partial for its outcome will affect vast interests scattered all over the world.'

How topical and alive his words sound today! Their subject is the key issue now being feverishly debated in the leading international forums. Two hundred years after his birth, Simón Bolívar is in the front line of the fight for the establishment of a new international order. Unesco formally acknowledged this when, in 1978, its governing bodies approved the creation of the International Simón Bolívar Prize

to be awarded every second year, starting on 24 July 1983, the bicentenary of the birth of Simón Bolívar, to those who have made an outstanding contribution to the freedom, independence and dignity of peoples and to the strengthening of solidarity among nations, or who have fostered their development or facilitated the quest for a new international economic, social and cultural order.

Caracas, September 1982

*'The freedom of the New World is the hope of the Universe'*

BOLÍVAR, 1824

JOSÉ LUIS SALCEDO-BASTARDO, born in Venezuela in 1926. Doctor of Political Science, Universidad Central de Venezuela. Dean and Professor of Sociology. Senator (1959–64). Ambassador to Ecuador, Brazil and France. President of the Instituto Nacional de Cultura y Bellas Artes (1965–66). Member of the Academies of History and Language. Was Minister responsible for the Office of the President of the Republic (1967–77). Minister of State for Science, Technology and Culture (1976–79). Author of numerous books, including *Visión y revisión de Bolívar* (thirteen editions); *Historia fundamental de Venezuela* (nine editions); *Bolívar, un continente y un destino* (awarded the Premio Continental of the OAS, and the Premio Nacional de Literatura de Venezuela (thirteen editions: French, English, Basque, German and Swedish)); *Un hombre diáfono—Vida de Simon Bolívar para los nuevos americanos*; *Andrés Bello, Americano*; *Crisol del Americanismo*; *Bolívar hombre-cumbre*. He is Chairman of the Executive Committee of the Bicentenary of Simón Bolívar. He has travelled through more than sixty countries, and has lectured in thirty nations on four continents.

# INTRODUCTION

by

*José Luis Salcedo-Bastardo*

## THE ORIGINAL CONVERGENCE

The main migration of the first inhabitants of the continent later to
be known as America started in Asia in prehistoric times. When the
first Asians crossed the ice-floes in the Bering Strait, or traversed the
chain of the Aleutian Islands, spreading through a wilderness which
became more attractive as they passed through it, they were beginning the fascinating process of creating a world which all peoples
and all cultures were finally to share.

Thus began a destiny: a home for the family of mankind; a
close-knit, mixed community with hope in its heart, the possibility
of realizing a dream of genuine, human brotherhood, living together
for justice, work, love and life, in equality and freedom. This scenario
envisioned a great world nation, which could, perhaps, emerge at
some future time, greater because of its intrinsic spiritual quality
than because of its material attributes, and whose sons would embody
the historical reality succinctly defined by Simón Bolívar in 1815:
'We are a small human race of our own' [13]. ★

But, whether because of the settlement and adaptation of the
children of Asia in their new domain, which made them a product
of the hemisphere they had reached, or whether one accepts the
hypothesis of the indigenous American man, the physical and cultural
similarities with Asians give grounds for thinking that a first interbreeding—towards the end of the Middle Ages in Europe—
produced in the indigenous population the traits of two continents,
Asia and America. Furthermore, there is reason to believe, as shown
by the recent experience of the *Kon-Tiki* expedition, that Oceania

★The figures in square brackets correspond to the numbered sections of this
anthology.

also made a contribution to American identity. If it was possible, setting out from Peru, to reach Polynesia by riding the Humboldt current, it may well have been possible to do the reverse. The 'American' Indian might thus represent a synthesis of Asia, America and Oceania.

In 1492, the glory fell to Christopher Columbus, that bold genius, to unify the whole world. He brought light to shine on the hemisphere that had lain in the shadow of its own isolation. The outstanding Genoese navigator, though having no doubt that the earth was round, believed it was smaller than it really was. He embarked upon the quest for a route to the East—to India, China and Japan—and coming upon this unsuspected and unknown part of the globe, made widespread the mistaken supposition that the inhabitants of that *terra incognita* were 'Indians'.

For the Europe of the fifteenth century, tired of sterile feudalism, the discovery of America created extraordinary possibilities. The New World was to be its great work: there the Old World, thanks to the efforts and many-sided presence of Spain, sowed its seeds. The Iberian peninsula was, in fact, an outstanding example of the mixing, confluence and combination, in body and spirit, of the different racial stocks of Europe, Africa and Asia. Spain counted among its ancestors Iberians, Ligurians, Celts, Romans, Basques, Greeks, Germans, Visigoths, Swabians and Alani. It also contained elements from Asia Minor—Phoenicians, Jews, Muslims from Arabia, and from Africa—Carthaginians, peoples from Egypt, Libya, Tunisia, Algeria, Morocco, the Congo and the Niger, all mixed together in the Muslim flood which had poured into the peninsula to settle there for eight centuries. Africa too, for its own part, shared in the great transatlantic merger of peoples, represented by its Bantu, Sudanese and Yoruba off-spring, who were snatched from their homelands by the shameful slave trade.

All races, all continents, all cultures, flow together to meet, intermingle and merge, in the splendid land Columbus discovered.

The Spain emerging from the Reconquest accepted the unforeseen finding of a new world on which to impose its Christian values as a magnificent challenge worthy of its optimism, its courage and its illusions.

With the vigour of its blood drawn from many sources, and with the drive and enterprise of a people idealistic to the highest degree, Spain devoted itself to making of the vast country, so recently discovered, another Iberia, a New Spain, a Castilla del Oro, a new Granada, Léon, Andalusia, Valencia, Extremadura, Barcelona, that is to say, an extension of itself. This dream, coupled with a sheer remorseless appetite for wealth, even conjured up a mythical, magical kingdom of supreme happiness—El Dorado. Spain gave all it could to re-create itself there. It took there all that was good and positive that it possessed, together with everything bad and negative: the lofty values of a society then in the vanguard, flexing the powerful political muscle of its all-embracing absolutism—as against the now obsolete dispersion of power of medieval times; but side by side with a promising spirit of inquiry—apparent in the rich Castilian literature—it also brought along with it prejudice and fanaticism.

## THREE CENTURIES OF COLONIALISM

Spain transferred to America her institutional structures in the political, legal, economic, social and cultural spheres, and started her enormous task. On 15 November 1533, when Francisco de Pizarro set up his standard in the Temple of the Sun in Cuzco—the holy city of the Incas in the Peruvian Andes—Spain completed the violent and cruel enterprise which concluded the American Conquest in three decades, and began the stage of colonization.

To 'create' America, three centuries were sufficient for the mother country. Was ever so much done with so little in so short a time? It should be understood that neither the territory nor the native population were, properly speaking, American. There were neither America nor Americans at the dawn of the sixteenth century. The name came by chance from Europe; Florence, through one of its gallant sons, Amerigo Vespucci, bestowed it. And Americans came forth from a fusion in which every part of the earth was involved: Asia, America, Oceania, Europe, Africa, all converged in the synthesis which produced the new man.

Moreover, if at the beginning the system of authority imposed by the conquerors was a new departure, for want of necessary adjustment, it became fossilized with the passage of time and by the end of the eighteenth century was clearly and irredeemably anachronistic.

Three hundred years after the continent's discovery, this régime, resting upon the negation of freedom, supported and maintained by means of, and by a belief in, oppression, oblivious and indifferent to rights and guarantees, and with an infrastructure of slavery and shameful inequalities became intolerable; it preached and practised the isolation of the separate colonial entities of the empire, and used fear and terror to curb imagination and restrain adventurous spirits.

The Latin America of the eighteenth century could not passively tolerate the continuation of the old structures and outdated practices, now sterile and reactionary, which nevertheless, it is only fair to recognize, had once achieved results astonishing in their range. One cannot blame those Titans, the founders and pioneers of sixteenth-century America, for the decline and rigidity which the passage of time brought and for the fact that such an organism should become petrified and lifeless.

By the start of the nineteenth century, colonialism, as an American system, was hopelessly outworn. The truth was that, from the outset and in a general way, the rejection of the Conquest became obvious in the Western hemisphere. The original inhabitants resisted the coercion which restricted their freedom and ruthlessly deprived them of their possessions. The Africans, imported against their will and enchained in the ignominy of slavery, were another explosive factor that later helped to shatter the foundations of the order which the Bourbons claimed to be perpetual and immutable.

In the end, the imagined 'New World' turned out to be nothing more than an archaic, inadequate, retrogressive, oppressive and unjust world. The half-castes, and still more the Indians and blacks, subordinate elements thereof, found themselves neglected, discriminated against and marginalized. Thus, those who were genuinely American were relegated, because of an inadmissible attitude, to the status of pariahs in their own country.

Resistance to absolutist despotism continued even though native systems of domination suicidally served to ease the consolidation of Iberian control. Struggling against that fate, the Latin American peoples generously shed their blood in the pursuit of freedom. That is the story: everywhere there were enormous sacrifices for justice and equality.

## THE HERALDS OF CHANGE

There were some precursors in the eighteenth century. Francisco de Miranda (1750–1816) of Caracas was the first. He was the first native-born Spanish American to be known internationally; never before had a man born on the other side of the Atlantic achieved such a worldwide reputation: his bravery was known in Africa, where he went to war against the Sultan of Morocco. Europe heard of his exploits: he was a Major-General of the French Revolution, and played a leading role in military affairs, from the steppes of the Caucasus to the shores of the Mediterranean, Asia Minor, Scandinavia, and Great Britain. He played a part, not without honour, in the independence of the United States. In the Caribbean—Cuba and the Bahamas—he rendered distinguished service and set an enlightened example. But his greatest achievement was his vision of Latin American unity and revolution. As early as 1781 he adumbrated the notion of a motherland to be called Colombia—as a tribute to the discoverer—whose northern frontier would be the Mississippi and which would extend to Cape Horn. He involved Europe in his ambitious project of achieving freedom for the immense country now known as Latin America (the sum of three parts, Spanish America, Brazil and the Caribbean). To this end he sought to secure help in France, Russia and England, looked for the co-operation of the United States, and referred in his programme to Asia and Africa (sepoys from India, bases on the islands of Madeira, Mauritius and Reunion, etc.), seeing independence within the overall context.

Juan Pablo Viscardo y Guzmán (1748–98) of Peru designed a vast project which also applied to Spanish America as a whole, in his famous 'Letter to the Spanish Americans', written in 1792, which became known only in 1801. His indictment of the blatant injustice of colonialism is disturbingly apt. His criticism of slavery and isolationism, and of the humiliating exploitation imposed by an insensitive mother country is totally convincing.

José Joaquím de Silva Xavier (1748–92), the brave Tiradentes, paid with his life in Brazil for his audacity in imagining a just system for our people. A sovereign republic without slavery, with schools for all, free trade, social security, economic self-sufficiency—these objectives were his mission. He lives on today in the memory of his countrymen.

In Ecuador, the harbinger was Francisco Eugenio de Santa Cruz y Espejo (1747–95), in whose veins ran the mingled blood of three races. Of outstanding intellectual calibre, he also laboured and died for the cause of Latin America. His noble aim was peaceful emancipation, without breaking the links with Spain. His ideology envisaged the co-existence of the two worlds on equal terms.

Antonio Nariño (1765-1823) was the advocate of these same hopes, in what is now Colombia, at that time the Viceroyalty of Santa Fe, or New Granada. A man of wide culture, it was he who translated from the French the text of the Rights of Man. Although severely punished, he lived to witness the triumph of the independence movement of which he had been a moving spirit in its early days.

All these have their place in history together with other valiant leaders who were not afraid of threats, persecution, danger or death: Atahualpa, Cuauhtémoc, Guaicaipuro, Lautaro, Hatuey, Andrea de

Ledesma, Túpac Amaru, Chirinos, Picornell, España, Gual, Galán, among others.

But despite these achievements, a leader to whom all could rally was still lacking. At the dawn of the nineteenth century, the intellectual man of action had not yet appeared. Latin America was then ripe for the emergence of such a man; the challenge to be taken up—and this challenge remains—was to build, on sure and sound foundations, a world that was new in the New World.

## THE BOLÍVARS IN VENEZUELA

The Bolívar family settled in Venezuela as early as 1589; natives of Vizcaya, they reached the mainland from the island of Santo Domingo. In the course of 200 years, these Iberian Basques became Spanish Americans, finally identifying themselves with the physical and psychological environment of the indigenous people, their light, their earth and its gifts, their water, their fruit and their food.

A lady of rare and dark beauty, Doña María Josefa Marín de Narváez, was Africa's contribution to the making of Simón José Antonio de la Santísima Trinidad de Bolívar y Palacios—in short, Simón Bolívar, who was born at Caracas on 24 July 1783.

He was the exemplar of that combination of peoples that is his people. He applied himself to the problem of exploring the Latin American identity and concluded:

We are . . . neither Indian nor European, but a species midway between the legitimate proprietors of this country and the Spanish usurpers. In short, though American by birth we derive our rights from Europe, and we have to assert these rights against the rights of the natives, and at the same time we must defend ourselves against the invaders. This places us in a most extraordinary and involved situation. [13]

Perplexity and confusion in this regard are quite understandable:

The greater part of the indigenous population has been annihilated, Europeans have interbred with Americans and Africans and the latter have interbred with Indians and Europeans. [The obvious conclusion is that] it is impossible to determine precisely to which human family we belong. [24]

Bolívar gives fair and due weight to the double African element in Latin America:

Our people is neither European nor North American; it is a compound of African and American elements rather than an emanation of Europe, as even Spain itself is no longer entirely European, because of its African blood, its institutions and its character. [24]

It may be noted that everywhere, in Bolivarian thought, the real, positive and forward-looking element is the idea of a mixture ready to receive a greater truth.

I consider America to be in the state of a chrysalis; there will be a metamorphosis in the physical existence of its inhabitants; the outcome will be a new breed comprising all breeds, which will bring about a homogeneous people.

Bolívar's character was shaped by adversity. Death and fate dealt hard with him: at the age of two-and-a-half he lost his father; his mother died when he was nine. As an orphan, he had to depend on guardians and relatives who tried, not always successfully, to lighten his load.

The first existing record in writing of Bolívar's words dates from his twelfth year. It is interesting to note that they relate to what were always to be his favourite subjects: selflessness and freedom. In the child's words:

the courts were free to dispose of a person's goods, and do whatever they liked with them; but not with his person; and if slaves were entitled to choose their own master, at least he should not be denied the freedom to live in whatever house he pleased.

On this, his tutor, as though speaking for the old order, added a commentary which proved to be remarkably clear-sighted. In what the pupil said he noted

the gravity and arrogance of certain works which give cause for serious misgivings ... the most unpolitic and erroneous ideas ... a maxim such that, if it gained ground and achieved credence, it could overthrow our monarchy and cause untold havoc.

Of all his teachers, Don Simón Rodríguez was the most outstanding and the best loved. Rodríguez brought out in Bolívar an independent spirit, and imbued him with the fundamental values of his heroism and excellence. Bolívar specifically recognized this: 'You formed my heart for freedom, justice, greatness and beauty. I have followed the path which you marked out for me' [56].

The young Bolívar was sixteen when he set off on his first journey outside Venezuela. He headed for Spain; the ship followed a roundabout route through the Caribbean. She dropped anchor at Veracruz; there was enough time for the youth from Caracas to visit the magnificent Mexican city. There, through his social connections, he had access to the salons of the local gentry. One day, the Viceroy Don Miguel José de Azanza inquired about events in Venezuela, where a conspiracy had been quelled shortly before. Simón Bolívar immediately but tactlessly reaffirmed his freedom-loving convictions; without turning a hair, he expressed his sympathy with the brave conspirators, and bitterly condemned the despotic regime which had martyred them. Years later, Bolívar enjoyed recalling this incident in the following terms: 'I have completely forgotten what I said, but I remember that I defended in no uncertain terms the rights of American independence.'

## THE MAKING OF THE MIND

Simón Bolívar's intellectual personality was developed in Madrid, where he lived for three-and-a-half years. He studied mathematics at the San Fernando Academy. He studied modern languages under the learned Marquis of Uztáriz and was able to speak French and Italian, and understand English fairly well. He also led an active social life, moving in the distinguished circles of Madrid.

During his three years in Europe, Bolívar became an insatiable reader. His passion for reading lasted throughout his life. Regarding his development, he was accustomed to stress that he had spent much time studying

Locke, Condillac, Buffon, D'Alembert, Helvetius, Montesquieu, Mably, Filangieri, Lalande, Rousseau, Voltaire, Rollin, Berthot, and all the classics of the ancient world—philosophers, historians, orators and poets, and all the modern classics of Spain, France and Italy, as well as a large proportion of the English classics.

As regards his intellectual side, he himself summed it up as follows: 'I am not vague. I am impetuous, careless and impatient. I pack a great many ideas into very few words.'

The adult Bolívar was said to be extremely restless. He rarely stayed still for two minutes. When speaking, he looked on the ground or lowered his eyes; when the matter in hand interested him, he kept his eyes fixed on the person to whom he was speaking. His body was lean and slender; he was five foot six inches tall. He had a high-pitched voice. He was strongly built and very agile and did not tire easily.

Before he was nineteen he married in Madrid his charming cousin, María Teresa Rodríguez del Toro, a girl of twenty. The newly-weds set off on the return journey to Venezuela. On the San Mateo estate the delicate girl from Madrid contracted malaria and died in Caracas. Their happy marriage lasted eight months.

To distract his thoughts and forget the catastrophe of this early death, Bolívar embarked for Europe. His fortune of some millions allowed him to spend freely on this tour, which was rather like the wandering of a dazed pilgrim.

There can be no doubt that his bereavement left its mark. This was to be the great turning-point in his private life. In 1828 he told Luis Perú de Lacroix, referring to the results of this distress:

If I had not become a widower, my life might have been different; I should be neither General Bolívar nor the Liberator, although I agree that it was not in my nature to become the mayor of San Mateo. . . . If my wife had not died I should not have made my second voyage to Europe . . . her death set me very early on the road to politics; it later made me follow the chariot of Mars instead of the plough of Ceres; so you may judge whether or not it influenced my destiny.

In the midst of this emotional crisis, Bolívar met again his old tutor Don Simón Rodríguez in Paris. The latter gave back to the frustrated aristocrat from Caracas his will to live. Together they went off on a journey with no planned route: France, Switzerland, Italy. Mainly on foot, they traversed highways and cities. After passing through the French countryside, they crossed the Alps, Piedmont, Lombardy, Tuscany and Umbria like wandering scholars. Never, before this excursion, had their understanding been so fully and deeply in harmony: the teacher, with his range of knowledge, was the perfect partner for his young and alert companion.

## THE CHOICE OF DESTINY

Simón Bolívar was twenty-one. It was in Paris that he chose the path he would take. Two different meetings—apart from his reunion with Rodríguez—one warmly close and the other inevitably distant though enthusiastic, left an indelible impression on his will. The first was with Baron Alexander von Humboldt, recently arrived from

South America. They talked of all sorts of things, and broached the subject of politics. Humboldt, who had not only seen and examined the natural history of the new continent, as well as the society inhabiting it, was convinced that it could soon be the scene of radical change. Bolívar asked the German scientist his opinion concerning independence: Humboldt felt it was near, but averred that he could not identify the man capable of bringing it about. This conversation stimulated the young Bolívar, and sowed in him a seed which soon took firm root.

The other encounter was not private but shared in common with multitudes of others: it was with Napoleon. The Corsican was at the peak of his power and fame. Bolívar witnessed his coronation: that in itself did not impress him much, but the joyful acclaim given to Napoleon by the vast and excited crowd stirred him to the depths of his soul:

This magnificent act or function aroused my enthusiasm, less because of its pomp than because of the affection demonstrated by a huge crowd for the hero of France; this general effusion of all hearts, this free, spontaneous popular movement excited by the glories and heroic deeds of Napoleon, acclaimed at that moment by over a million people, seemed to me to be, for him who was the object of such sentiments, the highest level of aspiration, the ultimate desire, like man's final ambition. The crown which Napoleon put on his head I regarded as a miserable thing, a gothic relic: what did appear to me great was the universal acclamation and the interest aroused by his person. This, I must confess, made me think of the enslavement of my own country, and of the glory which would belong to whoever liberates it.

Bolívar left Paris already convinced of his own destiny. Rodríguez reinforced his resolve, and encouraged him to persevere in his conviction.

In the following year the two Simóns ended their journey in Italy. In Rome this extraordinary man took another step of great importance. One sultry evening in August they—the disciple, his tutor and his friend Fernando Toro—went out to take the air; they climbed the Aventine Hill. Bolívar was inspired, his restless mind in ferment with events in Caracas and Mexico, the simple arguments about freedom which the boy imagined the slaves to hold, a nascent solidarity with the martyrs of the frustrated revolutionary attempt in Caracas, the constantly illuminating words of Rodríguez, the image of the whole of Paris acclaiming as one its leader, the encouragement of Humboldt, and in his mind's eye the vicissitudes of Roman history. There and then he made a solemn vow:

I swear before you, I swear by the God of my fathers, I swear upon my honour and by my homeland that I shall not let my arm rest, nor my soul repose until I have broken the chains laid upon us by the Spanish oppressors. [1]

On his way back to Venezuela, Bolívar spent several months in the United States. What did he think of it? His response: 'For the first time in my life I have seen rational liberty.' This was another motive and a powerful argument to strengthen further his resolve.

As his personality took shape and reached maturity, the situation in Caracas was also changing. The gentry in the Venezuelan capital were laying separatist plots to seize political power, the only sphere of authority which they lacked—they already held economic, social and cultural power—for complete dominance. The toppling of the Spanish Crown by Napoleon was to become the spark which would set off the revolutionary explosion. A king like Charles IV was certainly not capable of coping with the profound crisis which was at hand. The throne passed to Ferdinand VII and, after much political juggling, Joseph Bonaparte became the King of Spain.

The Cuadra Bolívar, a country house belonging to the brothers Juan Vicente and Simón, was used for conspiratorial meetings in favour of a Creole committee or council to take the place of the colonial authorities. What in the past would have been enough to merit exemplary punishment, even the death penalty, merely led to a mild disciplinary measure involving confinement far from the city.

## THE PROCESS BEGINS

On Holy Thursday, 19 April 1810, complying with the police measure against him, Bolívar was away from Caracas. That was the day when the revolution broke out. Venezuelans at last took over the executive power. The City Council of Caracas inspired the move: the Governor and Captain-General, the Intendant of the Army and of the Royal Treasury, the *Auditor de Guerra*, the General Adviser to the Government and Lieutenant Governor, the Chief Justice and members of the High Court and Council were all deposed. In order not to alarm the people—still loyal to the King, whom they preferred to the ambitious local oligarchy—the government which assumed power that day adopted an inoffensive and neutral title, Junta Suprema Conservadora de los Derechos de Fernando VII (Supreme Council for the Maintenance of the Rights of Ferdinand VII).

The final goal was independence, but caution suggested that the pitfalls of previous occasions when action was taken precipitately be avoided. This time, a cautious approach succeeded. The Creoles assumed political power with the support of the masses, who were staunch royalists.

The Supreme Council sent four diplomatic missions abroad. Juan Vicente Bolívar and Telesforo de Orea were sent to the United States. Simón Bolívar, newly designated colonel, and Luis López Méndez, accompanied by Andrés Bello were sent to London, Vicente Salias and Mariano Montilla to the West Indies and José Cortés Madariaga to New Granada.

The meeting of the three distinguished sons of Caracas who were also to become three outstanding personalities of the Americas, Miranda, Bolívar and Bello, took place in the British capital. During his stay in London, Bolívar's thoughts on integration, the idea of Latin American unity as postulated by Miranda, were published for the first time. They appeared in the *Morning Chronicle* of 5 September 1810. Three days later, Bolívar himself signed a clearly revolutionary manifesto, calling on the Supreme Council of Caracas to break off relations with the Spanish Crown:

We are committed in the eyes of the world and, without discrediting ourselves forever, we cannot deviate in the slightest degree from the glorious path that we have opened up for America. . . . We are pledged to bring about universal liberation. The firmness and resolve with which we have advanced should not fail to bring about its coming. [2]

Further revealing evidence of Bolívar's developing personality at that time is provided by Joseph Lancaster, the great British educational reformer who, in 1824, recalled that at General Miranda's house, in Grafton Street, Piccadilly, London, on 26 or 27 September 1810, Bolívar showed 'a strong and keen interest' in education. There is also documentary evidence of contact, during this trip to Great Britain, with the inventors of a new warfare and fortification system: Messrs Holmes and Atkins.

We can thus put specific dates to his policies on unity and culture and his policies for war and peace. Under the expert guidance of Miranda, his precursor and master, already in his sixties, the young Bolívar, twenty-seven years old, would, when the time was right and the circumstances propitious, make his entry into history, with the world wide open to him.

Bolívar returned to Caracas, followed immediately by Miranda. The latter returned in time to be elected a member of the First Congress of Venezuela which solemnly declared independence on 5

July 1811. Bolívar was not interested in parliamentary matters [3]. Although first ignored, Miranda came to prominence when, because of a crisis created by armed reaction against the new government, he was given powers as a 'dictator' when the situation became desperate. There was widespread disorganization and confusion. The eminent statesman could do nothing and the Republic collapsed.

Bolívar escaped abroad, not without great difficulty. After a brief stay in Curaçao, he passed through the painful period of his first exile. During this exile, he was to show the strength of his personality. Beaten but unbowed, he was tough, steadfast and strong. He never thought of surrender, however adverse the circumstances.

## ONCE MORE INTO THE BREACH

From Cartagena, he explained the unfortunate events in Caracas, in a profound and well-argued manifesto. The fearless fighter proved to be also a shrewd political observer, an analyst of complex situations which few could grasp so clearly.

Reiterating his integrationist beliefs, as always in favour of unity, he called on the people of New Granada not to remain indifferent to the fate of their brothers in Venezuela.

He succeeded in his purpose, and entered his country from the west, and, after moving from triumph to triumph in the 'admirable' campaign, the former fugitive from Caracas arrived in his native city to widespread acclaim. He brought with him the new glory of his title 'the Liberator'. This was the name given to him by Mérida, then by the whole of Venezuela and finally confirmed by Caracas. Thanks to the military successes of this victorious march, the Second Republic was established.

On his way, as he passed through Trujillo, Bolívar was moved to make an awesome decision: to declare the 'War to the Death' [5]. His aim was clearly to differentiate the parties, to let the enemies of liberty know that their fate when they fell into the hands of the patriots would be the same as that meted out to the patriots themselves [7]. In his anger, he promised death to Spaniards and Canary Islanders alike while sparing the lives of even guilty native-born Americans. The upper-class leading groups (the Creoles) wanted only to break the country's political submission to the metropolis; this was clearly demonstrated by the experience of 1810–12. The revolution went no further than the political surface. There was nothing done specifically for the people, neither against slavery nor with regard to the distribution of land. Declarations on liberty and justice were mere words. The Creoles thus attained full power by acquiring the right to self-government and, indeed, to govern, the capacity to make laws and have the higher offices of the emergent state open to them.

The 'War to the Death' was a mistake and did not bring about the results expected. The royalist forces were still sustained by the people. The poorest and most humble sectors of the population, especially the *llaneros* (plainsmen), led by José Tomas Boves, soon struck another fatal blow at the revolution. Once more, terror proved fruitless. The King or his name, with the support of the Church, which was subject to him by virtue of the right of ecclesiastical patronage, enjoyed a favourable image, in strong contrast to the antipathy aroused by the local oligarchies. The people were not fools, they chose knowingly, guided by their instinct and reason in their own interests: they saw in the King a more understanding and protective power, and felt he was more well disposed towards them.

Fleeing from Boves, then master of the situation, a fearful band of refugees departed from Caracas, Bolívar with them. This was the 'Evacuation to the East'. They set off, mourning their dead, for days of exhausting travel over difficult and almost impassable roads. Again it seemed to be the end.

Bolívar reached the port of Carúpano, whence he departed for his second period of exile. All seemed lost, but he possessed an undying faith. For the outstanding characteristic of this leader was precisely his tenacity in his struggles. He grew with defeat. It was at Carúpano itself that he framed one of his slogans: 'God rewards constancy with victory' [11].

When he escaped this time, Bolívar made an observation which was clearer in his mind than ever before. Public opinion was won over by the royalists: the vast, and indeed crucial, mass of the people did not feel that the revolution was their affair, they did not defend it and were not interested in it. They were fighting against it. The struggle was a civil one, since the fight was between brothers; the 'foreign' (peninsular Spanish) force in Venezuela was insignificant. The 'army' worthy of such a name and which Spain was to send the following year under General Pablo Morillo had not yet arrived.

In the Carúpano Manifesto, Bolívar made a commitment—it was the expression of unbending conviction:

I swear to you, dear compatriots, that this august title, given me by your gratitude when I came to strike off your chains will not be an empty one. I swear to you that, Liberator or dead, I shall always deserve the honour you paid me; and there is no power on earth which can stop me in the course I propose to follow until I can return to free you for the second time. [11]

Unbreakable in exile, he led a pitiful existence in the West Indies. It was merely by chance that he did not fall at the hands of a paid assassin in Jamaica. All doors seemed closed. However, he took advantage of this inactivity to meditate. Bolívar reflected on the future and on Latin America. The reflection led to another of his basic documents, the 'Jamaica Letter' [13].

It was written in reply to an Englishman, Henry Cullen, who had asked the Liberator for his impressions of the current situation. Once again he reflected—mainly on the basis of reports, studies and intuition since he lacked the direct experience which he was soon to acquire—on the complex overall Latin American situation. Bolívar propounded judgements and predictions whose accuracy posterity was to view with admiration and astonishment.

His continental vision stands out firmly and clearly in the Jamaica Letter. In it, he indicated the reasons which argued in favour of union: language first of all, religion, customs, history, suffering and hopes. He also pointed to the obstacles: enormous distances, different temperaments and local interests.

In the evaluation of all these factors, it is the positive ones which are affirmed, and the emphasis on the Latin American spirit which is underlined.

Bolívar thought of that great nation—spread over 30 million square kilometres—which might constitute Latin America at some time in the future. This was also one of Miranda's visions. It should be recalled that at the time the United States was a strip of thirteen former colonies along the North Atlantic coast, which in its expansionary thrust had already reached the Mississippi, which his great precursor had determined would be the northern boundary of 'Colombia', as he called the other great America. Canada, at the time, was an icy waste of lakes and forests. Reflecting on the boundaries demarcated by Miranda, Bolívar said, 'More than anyone, I desire to see America fashioned into the greatest nation in the world, greatest not so much by virtue of her area and wealth as by her freedom and glory' [13]. There is the precise text which points to history—liberty and glory—as the basis of greatness. Size was not what really mattered. It was the new thought, the real possibility of attaining justice and equality, the solidarity which produces strength, morality and culture which elevate a society, the supreme values of education, science, the arts and letters, etc.

During his meditations in Jamaica—recorded in several basic documents [14, 15]—Bolívar finally succeeded in providing a true, positive, brief and accurate explanation of why efforts to win the people over to this new cause had failed. His diagnosis was that the champions of independence did not offer absolute liberty, as the Spanish guerrilla bands did. He, therefore, made a resolution: next time it would be different!

## THE THIRD AND FINAL ASSAULT

Towards the end of 1815, when the possibility of assistance for the revolution from the British possessions faded, Haiti became his last hope. And the Liberator's hope was not misplaced.

The magnanimous Alexandre Pétion, president of the hospitable Caribbean nation, was understanding and attached to Bolívar [16]. With the complete moral and economic support of Admiral Luis Brion and of the merchant Robert Sutherland, the hero of Caracas rebuilt his forces for liberty.

The Haitian government was poor but it helped generously: eight schooners, adequate munitions, the most diverse resources and, above all, moral support to sustain the good cause. Bolívar set forth from the cays of San Luis with his expedition of salvation. He soon arrived at Margarita, an island off eastern Venezuela, where he proclaimed his new policy of receptivity to the interests of the people: slavery would be abolished.

At Carúpano, where the odyssey of his second exile started and where it now ended, Bolívar announced substantial reforms: 'absolute freedom for the slaves who have suffered under the Spanish yoke for the past three centuries' [17]. Henceforth, there was to be only one class of men in Venezuela; all men were to be citizens.

But there was a new and unexpected setback. When he was about to announce additional measures for carrying out the revolutionary plan, the Ocumare disaster struck in July 1816. This meant his third departure into exile. Determined not to allow himself to be captured, he was preparing to shoot himself when Juan Bautista Bideau, a Haitian, rescued him from the beach. Where would he go? Anywhere, 'even to the pole', wherever he could secure the means to resume the struggle.

Again in Haiti, Bolívar dared not request anything further from the man who had helped him so generously shortly before. He hardly dared to ask for the least help simply to move on elsewhere, to raise there the resources he needed.

Pétion was sublime in the measure of his kindness towards the unfortunate fighter, to whom he said:

If fortune has mocked you twice, perhaps she will smile on you the third time. I have a presentiment that she will do so, and if there is anything I can do to lighten your pain and grief, you can count on me to the limits of my power. Make haste and come to the city. We will talk together.

Thanks to the Port-au-Prince agreement, the final expedition set sail from Jacmel. Bolívar praised Pétion to all posterity:

My gratitude knows no bounds. I can say from the bottom of my heart that you are the greatest benefactor on earth! One day, America will proclaim you its Liberator.

Egalitarianism was reaffirmed by Bolívar on his arrival in Venezuela. Slavery had to be abolished. The people were beginning to understand and want the revolution. It would no longer be a matter of abstractions and legal formulae that the common people could not understand—Constitution, State, powers, legislation, Republic. The burning issue was now equality: all men brothers and equal. And these social goals were soon to be linked with an economic revolution as determined by the people themselves: land, and justice in the enjoyment of national resources.

José Antonio Páez, an energetic leader, had succeeded during the years of adversity in attracting the same masses of plainsmen who had followed Boves, the scourge of the patriots. The change here was because Páez, himself a plainsman who understood them well, promised them farms and guaranteed free pasture in the savannahs.

It was in this way that the mass of the plainsmen were won over to the revolutionary cause. The offer of land was the only condition which Páez imposed on Bolívar to accept his authority. The Liberator agreed and from that time on, the idea of agrarian justice was one of the priorities of his comprehensive revolutionary programme.

The contents of the revolutionary programme were thus already defined. The old order which had been formed over 300 years was complete and harmonious, despite its outdated nature. Politically, it was rooted in the absolutism of the Bourbon monarchy, the colonial system, dependent and oppressive, with no liberty, rights or guarantees. Socially, inequality was the rule—slavery and privilege, classes, estates and castes, and many other distinctions. Economically, there was injustice in the distribution of property—a small power-ful class with the majority of the people lacking the basic necessi-ties. Legally there were many restrictions and divisions in Latin America, with isolation, distrust and suspicion generally fostering self-seeking individualism. Culturally, it was extremely backward; the mind was shackled.

## SYSTEMATIC AND CO-ORDINATED REVOLUTION

Bolívar did not invent, in the strict sense of the word, the various elements comprising the vast scheme of change and progress with which he was going to replace the old order. He created a sig-nificant number of them, drawing on a rich, historical legacy. He inherited a strong tradition shaped by centuries of unfulfilled dreams.

His wisdom and his merit lay in the fact that he gave shape to it all in a living, genuine and workable order. Simón Rodríguez wrote correctly that Bolívar 'gave America many of his own ideas while propagating those foreign notions which were most likely to make free societies of slave societies'.

Already in 1819, the systematic and coherent revolutionary programme for Venezuela, and ultimately Latin America and the world, was clear. It was a five-pronged programme to bring happi-ness to Latin America. Politically, it aimed at independence, emanci-pation or autonomy; the establishment of a democracy, and of a constitutional, representative, pluralist and popular republic. Liberty would be the key value, the 'sole goal worthy of the sacrifice of human life' [9, 12, 49]. Socially, it enlarges the rule of absolute free-dom—'the law of laws'—the abolition of slavery [17, 31, 39], the repeal of privileges and the removal of all barriers and divisions between citizens. Economically, the goal was clearly justice in the distribution of national resouces [20, 77] especially land, in addition to national ownership of mineral wealth [96]. Legally, particularly in the sphere of international law, everything was concentrated on Latin American unity; the effective and real union of our countries in a vigorous, strong and triumphant entity [62]. From a homeland thus constituted, one could look to the other continents in terms of justice and national harmony. This was the key idea of integration in the service of world peace, 'the hope of the Universe'. Culturally, this many-sided programme concluded with a magnificent scheme for education. Morality and enlightenment, in Bolívar's opinion, were 'our prime needs' [24]. He thought the government's first duty to be to provide education for the people [76].

The taking of Guayana, south of the Orinoco, in 1817 gave the Republic which had come into being for the third time the effective base which it required. The city of Angostura became the seat of government. This time, the eternal light of South American—today Latin American—liberty, was to be lit more successfully than in 1810, 1813 and even 1816. This fact was to redound to the glory and happiness of mankind as a whole, for, although the world was waiting for liberty in South America, the outcome of the revolution in the hemisphere depended on liberty in Venezuela.

The country finally came into being on the banks of the Orinoco; it was born well accustomed to changing fortunes, alive and prepared, and with a clear view of its objectives. The river was a bulwark protecting the capital. The province of Guayana, which until then had been spared destruction, possessed all kinds of resources: people, livestock, gold, supplies, exportable fruits and trading potential.

The executive power became established in Angostura: the Presidency of the Republic and the secretariats, including the very important Ministry of Foreign Affairs. The Court of Justice, the supreme organ of the judiciary, and a Council of State with interim legislative functions were also set up there. Furthermore, to make complete a genuine state of law and culture, Bolívar founded the national newspaper, *El Correo del Orinoco*.

From Angostura, this eloquent, brotherly and cordial message was sent to the Rio de la Plata:

When the victory of the Venezuelan forces has secured that country's independence, or when more favourable circumstances allow us to communicate more frequently and maintain closer relations, we will hasten, on our part, to draw up an American Pact, which, by forming a single political body of all our republics, will show America to the world in a light of majesty and grandeur unrivalled by the nations of antiquity. This united— if Heaven should grant this fervent wish—America could truly call herself the Queen of Nations and Mother of Republics. All Americans should have only one home country. [22]

The connection was thus made between the two ends of South America: one cause, one sentiment, one stance.

Bolívar's desire for stability and resolution of the political problem culminated, in February 1819, with the opening of the Congress. In addressing this body, Bolívar made a speech which was

the most important and extensive of all his intellectual output [24].
He welcomed the national representatives who made his office and
all the institutions legitimate. He disclosed for their guidance a draft
constitution and he outlined the proposed legal and political framework, thus showing his level of culture, maturity and wisdom.
Finally, in order to link together the past, present and future, he
summarized past events, laying special emphasis on the fact that the
recent past should be borne in mind for the future.

Bolívar also laid emphasis on the distribution of land, which he
begged for in recompense of his services, and on the abolition of
slavery for which he pleaded as he would plead for his life and the
life of the Republic. In addition, he referred to Venezuela's commitments to its benefactors—the national debt; he established the Order
of the Liberators and reaffirmed the decision 'homeland or death' as
an irrevocable and conscious commitment. The speech at Angostura
is the greatest, most profound, thoughtful and best written of
Bolívar's pronouncements.

In further fulfilment of his duty, Bolívar crossed the Andes. He
crossed the icy summits from the warm plains with his soldiers at
an unexpected time and place. The outcome of such great daring
was the freeing of New Granada at the Battle of Boyacá.

## THE CONTINENTAL PROJECT

The triumph of New Granada strengthened Simón Bolívar's resolve
to make unity a reality. He submitted the Bill on the Constitution of
Colombia to the Congress at Angostura [28]. Venezuela merged
with New Granada under a new name, a name denoting 'justice and
gratitude', not chance. It honoured Columbus, the Discoverer, the
father and creator of the New World.

The Liberator viewed Colombia as the nucleus of unity, as the
driving force which would give impetus to integration [29]. A good
indication of the prestige of the republic was that it soon succeeded
in incorporating Quito, Panama and Guayaquil. There were soon
signs of similar affinity and enthusiastic solidarity in Santo Domingo
and Costa Rica. The people of Santo Domingo and the Costa Ricans
expressed the wish to join in Bolívar's political undertaking—Great
Colombia—through two leaders, José Núñez de Cáceres and Rafael
Francisco Osejo, both teachers and exemplars of a wide-ranging view
of Americanism.

Two other Spanish American countries, Cuba and Puerto Rico,
were included in the Liberator's plans. 'Are not the people of these

islands Americans? Are they not maltreated? Do they not desire a better life? [13]' he asked in his Jamaica Letter. Concrete plans were to be made to liberate these islands, which in the end were to comprise the ten countries which now, on the eve of the twenty-first century, are unquestionably 'Bolivarian': Venezuela, Colombia, Ecuador, Peru, Bolivia, Panama, Costa Rica, the Dominican Republic, Cuba and Puerto Rico.

The Liberator wanted his Colombia to be, and to a certain extent it was, the first nation of its time, the most advanced, ranking first in political repute: first, in having the most concise and complete set of goals for the dignity of mankind and the effective enjoyment of justice, equality, liberty and democracy. No nation in Europe or in the other continents surpassed Colombia in these respects. The United States, pursuing its magnificent industrial development and enjoying a high level of stability and civil liberty, was, nevertheless, afflicted by the cancer of slavery and racial hatred. At that time, only Colombia offered liberty, democracy, justice, equality, unity and culture all together. It was, in sum and in synthesis, the triumph of the logical mind, which, based on his mathematical training during his youth in Madrid, reached such a level of clarity and form with Simón Bolívar.

The Liberator knew what he was saying when he declared that revolution in Latin America was 'the hope of the Universe' [59]. For mankind, the true era of social justice was about to begin, starting right there in Latin America.

Colombia was to realize the aspirations of Latin American man, the long-held hopes of all men who had everywhere suffered humiliating oppression and cruel injustice.

While Europe was cultivating liberal individualism, Bolívar was seeking to establish effective justice and equity in Latin America, promoting true equality and heeding the just claims of the oppressed. When Great Britain implemented the 'freedom of contracts' policy (with effect from 1813–14), leaving the economically weak unprotected and renouncing state intervention in the community, Bolívar strove to give the Latin American revolutionary movement a collective dimension, speaking of 'supreme social liberty', 'social security', 'social guarantees', and 'social rights'. The abolition of guilds in Europe from 1791 and the penalizing of all attempts to reintroduce them meant that at the beginning of the nineteenth century, there were no legal or corporate rules or conventions to govern working conditions. The situation, which had become unbearable by the middle of the 1820s, was worse for the rising industrial proletariat in Europe than for Roman slaves or medieval serfs;

but in Latin America, Bolívar was passing obviously interventionist and protective legislation on Indian labour: this legislation was no mere isolated expression of humanitarianism but an important element of the key question of cultural and political dignity. While in Europe the goal was illusory individual liberty, where it was thought that society itself or any kind of association restricted personal freedom and negated the rights of man and the citizen, and the state was considered to be an archaic, despotic entity which should fade away, resulting in a return to a kind of pre-social era marked by the re-emergence of *Homo homini lupus* and the idea that might is right, Bolívar, on the premise that 'there is nothing more dangerous where the people is concerned than weakness of the executive', was striving for an active, centralist, democratic, civilian republican system, a 'strong system which can communicate its aspirations to the entire society'.

Such was Bolívar's zeal in his decrees for native workers that, at times, he included in them an unusual prescription:

The present decree will not only be published in the usual form, but the authorities will also specifically inform the Indians, urging them to insist on their rights even if these affect those authorities who will be accountable for any breach of them.

## THREE ASPECTS OF HIS CONCERN FOR DETAIL

Bolívar became the key personality for the three phases or stages in the building of Latin America; being, action and perseverance. Liberation, growth and relevance. The main thrust of Bolívar's action was to break the fetters of servitude, then to provide nationhood with structure, identity and permanence and, finally, to link and bind the result to the world context. He thus gave preferential attention to three main issues: war, education and diplomacy. He had to attend to everything concerning the existence of Latin America, but his meticulous zeal and concern had to be applied to the most minute details of the matters in question over the three areas of politics, adult education and the international community.

Bolívar was the champion of peace. He went to war as a necessity, imperative and inevitable in pursuit of the goal of peace as was fully proved in the first stage of the revolution. Despite his true feelings, it was his lot to become a warrior: to experience and be the leading actor in a tragic period, marked by a very long and bloody confrontation—Venezuela lost 30 per cent of its population during the twelve years of the South American war of liberation. There is no need to repeat that his ideal of brotherhood and creation needed a peaceful environment, the only valid environment for the constructive efforts of peoples.

He became skilled in the art of war. His campaigns in Venezuela, New Granada and subsequently in the south, and the battles at Carabobo, Boyacá, Bomboná and Pichincha, Junín and Ayacucho were the pillars of his military glory. He reached Potosí, near Argentina, after a fifteen-year march, flying the flag of free America in 1825 [75]. Pasto, Quito, Guayaquil, Peru and Upper Peru were aware of his efforts and of his ability to conquer, to convince and to overcome the resistance of three centuries of colonial absolutism and imperialism to liberty and the rights of the new nations.

Bolívar's daily life meant doing much with very little. His iron personality was used to rising from the lowest depths to the utmost heights. Tough, inured to hardship, fearless in the face of adversity, struggling against combined opposing factors, his was an example hard to emulate. He called himself 'a man for all difficulties'. There is reliable proof of his tactical skill even before 1819. He wrote to General Bermúdez:

As a general rule, if there are no unsurmountable obstacles in the battlefield and if we are not in a very advantageous position, the enemy must be constantly observed from afar so that we may attack, using the same formation which they have been using; we should, however, always be ready to follow their movements as quickly as possible, striving very carefully to oppose them with an equal or a wider front; even though we have fewer resources than our enemy, one advanced wing is very likely to outflank the enemy. Make sure that the leading ranks are composed of chosen men placed in the forefront, so that the fate of the column and even victory may depend on the first three lines of troops. The rest of the column will follow the thrust of the leading troops.

In his general conception of the continental campaign for liberation and in providing for a possible and massive retaliatory attack by the joint forces of the Holy Alliance, he stands out as a talented strategist.

He was also meticulous with regard to a thousand and one logistical problems: food and care for the troops, attention to the horses, munitions, stores, ships, foreign volunteers, nails for horseshoes, paper, uniforms, transportation, communications, the speed and safety of mail, the health and morale of the forces, in short everything [21, 27].

# EDUCATION, SCIENCE AND CULTURE

The civilizing work carried out in Latin America under the guidance of the great son of Caracas was unprecedented and unrivalled. There was a certain logical order in his untiring efforts: war was indispensable if an independent America were to be 'possible'. But education was also absolutely fundamental to the identity of the New World.

Even in 1810, he avidly inquired into the system of 'mutual schools' established by Joseph Lancaster [63, 65]. In 1814, he showed interest in a public library for the newly freed Caracas and he instructed his diplomatic agents in Great Britain to recruit 'artists skilled in those sectors of industry needed by Venezuela and to send us the machines and instruments which to our great detriment we lack'.

The history of his administrative actions is, moreover, illustrated in the very diversity of the matters he considered, a thousand and one different aspects of a single, central concern.

He set up a school for the education of poor and abandoned orphans in Santa Fe in 1819 [26]. In May 1820, he passed legislation for the education of native children and made 'the rights and duties of men and citizens in Colombia, in keeping with the law' part of the curriculum [32].

He established a nautical school in Guayaquil in 1823 [50]; he had previously founded a similar institution in Cartagena. Its shores washed by two oceans, Colombia had more than a maritime vocation, as underlined by the fact that it derived its name from the most famous of admirals.

He set up the University of Trujillo (Peru) in May 1824 [58]. By December, he had made the Colegio de Santa Rosa de Ocopa into a school for public education. In Peru, on 5 May 1825, he made primary education compulsory. He also promulgated several decrees on education for women [70].

Of the many measures he took, an outstanding one is the decree promulgated in 11 December 1825 at Chuquisaca, based on the conviction that the government's first duty is to provide education for the people [76]. It covered the responsibilities and functions of the Director-General of Public Education, resolutions for the establishment of a graded primary school in the capital of each department, a military academy in the capital of the republic, a college of arts and sciences in Chuquisaca and a commitment to put into education all the savings which could be made in the other sectors of public administration. On that same day he referred to a long-cherished concern: the adoption of war orphans by the state. He also gave attention to military education at various levels and regulated religious education.

Bolívar was a precursor in his ideas on education [35, 67]. He did not share the prevailing grim and repressive idea of education whereby the school was considered to be a harsh reformatory with excessively rigorous discipline. He stressed the social nature of education, which should not be identical for all communities, or for all time. It should not be the same for all children either, but should always be adapted to their age, aptitudes, intelligence and temperament [79]. Institutions of learning should not, in his opinion, be merely a means of learning to read and write: he attributed many more functions to the school. He said that, in addition to intellectual, moral and civic training, 'the first maxim to be inculcated is that of hygiene. When the importance of respecting this principle is thoroughly examined, no one will doubt its value' [79]. The Liberator also wanted children to practise democracy from early childhood. His writings contain observations of unquestionable significance on language teaching, leisure, holidays, methods of teaching reading, methodology for the study of history, the learning of geography and cosmography, mathematics and Roman law, and the exercise of memory and comprehension.

In his consciousness of the cultural integration of mankind, Bolívar hoped that communication between wise and learned men would be extremely fruitful for Latin America. He was also aware that rapid growth alone could not be depended on for spiritual fulfilment. He never made the mistake of considering it in a theoretical situation of isolation and self-sufficiency.

The scope of Bolívar's view was universality, in which all peoples give the best of themselves to a common spiritual heritage. The question of translations and the value of the dissemination of books were also given attention. The Education Chamber, in his draft plan for the Moral Power [25], was to be responsible for the publication of foreign books on education in Spanish, with appropriate observations and corrections, as well as for encouraging writers and publishers to produce and disseminate 'original works on this subject, in conformity with our traditions, customs and principles'. The chamber itself was to compile and issue a publication aimed at encouraging others in this task and for the enlightenment of all.

Bolívar gave first priority to teaching and instructional methods and all that concerned them. He stressed that the chamber shall use every possible means and shall not spare any expense or sacrifice to obtain this knowledge. For this purpose, it shall commission zealous and educated persons without any other commitment to travel throughout the world, make inquiries and collect every kind of knowledge on this subject. [25]

With regard to translations, Bolívar, in reforming the University of Caracas [87], introduced a positive measure of promotion in the years of service required for advancement: a university professor could gain two years' advancement if he translated foreign works and eight years' if he were the author of an original work. A professor could obtain these two awards only once.

The Liberator regarded scientists as the true discoverers of the country's resources who should be encouraged by the government [41, 53]. He thought that science was one of the four powers which were the soul of the physical world, together with courage, wealth and virtue. He invited Europeans to come to South America and bring their knowledge with them to construct the New World [23].

Bolívar's administrative methods gave priority to science. University institutions, faculties and teaching posts, colleges and institutes for the sciences were all given his close attention [67, 71, 89, 91]. And, true promoter of knowledge that he was, he carefully supervised everything. He tilled all fields with equal enthusiasm. In a statement on human concern and culture, he wrote from Lima to the Rector of the University of Caracas as follows: 'After relieving the anguish of those who still suffer from warfare, nothing concerns me more than to spread knowledge of the sciences.'

A perceptive intellectual, sensitive to the presence of leading academies, he declared, in addressing the assembled doctors at San Marcos in Lima, a prestigious university and one of the oldest in the Americas, together with those of Santo Domingo and Mexico:

I shall forever remember this honoured day in my life. I shall never forget that I belong to the venerable Academy of San Marcos. I shall endeavour to bring myself closer to its worthy members and shall employ whatever moments are mine after I have accomplished the duties to which I am now bound in striving, if not to arrive at the peak you have attained, at least, to copy you. [85]

Scientific knowledge, Simón Bolívar was convinced, as he stated even under such difficult circumstances as in 1815, is instructive, significant and conclusive. 'The sciences have always immortalized the countries where they have flourished.'

## DIPLOMATIC ACTIVITY

Bolívar was also intimately involved in diplomacy. His public career indeed began and ended in diplomacy. It started in 1810 with his mission to London. It was a difficult mission because of the ambiguity of the situation: he was seeking support for an independence movement which could not really speak its name but was disguised as a movement to preserve the very situation which was being firmly but cautiously challenged. Twenty years later, before his death in 1830, he was again made a diplomat through a gesture by General Andrés Santa Cruz, President of Bolivia, who appointed him to be that republic's ambassador to the Holy See. The Liberator died before this news reached him; but he might otherwise have ended his life occupying the same function as when his public career began. Under his guidance, Venezuelan diplomacy soon achieved a memorable success, the 1820 Trujillo treaties, which like other very significant undertakings fell to Antonio José de Sucre, the faithful interpreter of Bolívar's plans and ideas. The *Tratado de Regularización* concluded the 'War to the Death' and is one of the first agreements in the world seeking to alleviate, as far as possible, the human effects of devastating violence. Bolívar described it as 'the finest monument of piety applied to war'. At that time the Liberator approached his inveterate enemy, General Pablo Morillo, head of the Spanish forces and, thus, for the first time, won recognition for Colombia from the former motherland. On 27 December 1820, Bolívar drank with Morillo to

the heroic constancy of the combatants on both sides: to their unrivalled firmness, suffering and courage. To those meritorious men, who through terrible times, upheld and defended Liberty. To those who died gloriously in defence of their homeland or its government. To the wounded of both armies who showed fearlessness, dignity and character. Eternal hatred to those who thirst after blood and spill it unjustly.

At Angostura, he had voiced true affection for the nation of the Río de la Plata which he was soon to reiterate: 'I can assure the Argentine government of my cordial support for that sister republic which shall forever be one of the most important parts of America.'

In 1824, he convened the Amphictyonic Congress of Panama. 1825, 1826 and 1827 were particularly active years for foreign policy.

Bolívar well understood all the subtleties of diplomacy. His advice to General Heres contained the following lesson:

I will give you a good maxim for diplomatic matters: calm, calm, calm; delay, delay, delay; compliments; vague words; consultations; examinations; twisting of arguments and requests; references to the new congress; digressions on the nature of the issue and the documents ... and at all times, be very slow, be very laconic so as not to give anything away to your opponent. Make the excuse that you are a military man; that you are unaware of the nature of matters entrusted to you [sic]; your post is a temporary one and the Peru affair is very sensitive. Above all, be always firm where good principles and universal justice are concerned. . . . Let us conduct ourselves properly and let time work miracles.

Another proof of his perspicacity is found in the brilliant instructions to Sucre during his difficult mission to Ecuador:

General Sucre shall amplify all these reasons, with all those which he considers appropriate in the light of his own caution and his talents, the circumstances in the country which he is visiting, and public opinion, reinforcing them with the advantage which the republic expects to derive from his zeal: but be moderate, prudent and circumspect so as not to alarm or displease, which can easily be done in such matters by a mere gesture or expression.

Thanks to Bolívar, Colombia became a haven for democracy, a bastion of hope for liberals all over the world. In Colombia, Bolívar was patiently and conscientiously establishing a network of diplomatic contacts to prepare for the dawning of Latin America's great day.

Relying on the co-operation of the enlightened minds of this time who had been recruited, without prejudice, wherever it was necessary, in Caracas, Popayán, Mexico, Tucumán, etc., he built up the diplomatic machinery which would work for integration at the right time. The Liberator, his Foreign Minister, Don Pedro Gual, and the efficient José Rafael Revenga worked for the success of missions by Joaquín Mosquera, Miguel Santa María and Bernardo Monteagudo. Bilateral treaties signed between Colombia and Peru, Chile and Mexico stipulate: 'Both parties pledge to offer their good offices to the governments of the other states of former Spanish America so as to enter into this pact of union, alliance and eternal confederation.'

## BREADTH OF VISION

The Liberator had the magnetism to attract from every part of Latin America leading figures representing the diverse sectors and interests composing the whole Latin American scene. From Venezuela came Sucre, Páez, Urdaneta, Mariño, Arismendi, Bermúdez, Anzuategui, etc. From New Granada, the Nariños, Santander, Mosqueras, Arboledas, Retrepo, etc. From Mexico, the congressman and plenipotentiary, Santa María. From Panama, José Domingo Espinar. From Ecuador, the poet and diplomat Olmedo. From Peru, Unanué, Sánchez Carrión, Vidaurre, etc. From Bolivia, Santa Cruz. From Chile, the illustrious O'Higgins, and from Argentina, the celebrated San Martín, Pueyrredón, Monteagudo, Alvear, etc. From Cuba, Commander Rafael de las Heras. Pétion from Haiti, Brion from Curaçao, José Félix Bogado from Paraguay. The enlightened José Ignacio de Abreu y Lima came from Brazil. Quite a number came from Canada, the United States and Europe—England, Scotland, Ireland, France, Prussia, Spain, Poland, Italy—all drawn by his fame. His will expressed that of many, and countless observers testify to the validity of his title to renown.

His programme for the Panama Congress was the first in the annals of history and, since then, the only one to consider a dynamic and effective union on a basis of solidarity among equal, autonomous, democratic nations, invited to confer, free of any hegemonic pressure and free to decide on matters of mutual general interest:

The strength of all would contribute to assisting any one in need on account of an external enemy or anarchic factions within. . . . None would be weak in respect of another; none would be stronger. [86]

Bolívar wanted the Panama congress to discuss great New World matters, to formulate supranational laws and to focus efforts on mutually agreed goals. Latin America was to decide on its essential unity for the future; his wish, expressed in 1822, was to be fulfilled:

America's great day has not yet dawned. We have driven out our oppressors, broken the tablets of their tyrannical laws and founded legitimate institutions: but we still have to lay the foundations for a social pact which shall make of this world a nation of republics.

Bolívar even thought that Latin America, the land of good men, liberty and love, could pass on the breath of revolutionary justice to Africa and Asia so as to break the yoke of slavery imposed by Europe on the world at that time: 'This is what I call the balance of the whole world, and it should enter into the calculations of American policy' [8]. The Liberator hoped for a more positive and effective worldwide alliance than the previous weak, ephemeral associations of states. He even thought of a world federation in which the principles which had given life to Latin America would hold full sway. 'With the passage of the centuries, perhaps a single nation—the federal nation—may cover the whole world' [86].

His ideas on the encouragement of immigration, totally devoid of racial preference, give proof of the breadth of his humanity. Never were the doors of any country so absolutely and freely opened as when he called on 'foreigners from all nations and of all professions' to come and settle. His only requirement of such immigrants was probity. Bolívar was aware of the beneficial effects of interbreeding. Latin American man was the product of dissimilar inputs; all human groups were involved. We are moving towards the 'new breed comprising all breeds, which will bring about a homogenous people'. He uttered an enthusiastic slogan in Angostura: 'Different blood flows in the veins of our fellow citizens; let us mix it to make it one' [24].

Bolívar's geopolitical concepts were in keeping with his universalist outlook. Here again, Latin America was serving mankind. With regard to the states in the isthmus of Central America, he thought that their 'magnificent position between the two mighty oceans' could in time make them 'the emporium of the world'.

Their canals will shorten distances throughout the world, strengthen commercial ties between Europe, America and Asia, and bring to that happy areas tribute from the four quarters of the globe. There someday, perhaps, the capital of the world may be located—reminiscent of the Emperor Constantine's claim that Byzantium was the capital of the ancient world. [13]

He again referred to canals between the two oceans in writing about Colombia, which included the Isthmus of Panama. Here was this great nation which he had created as 'the centre of the world, spread between its extensive coasts and between those oceans which nature has separated but which our homeland unites with long, broad canals' [24].

## THE ROLE OF THE PRESS
## IN SOCIAL COMMUNICATION

During his brief but fruitful stay in England, Bolívar was able to appreciate how important the press was as a vehicle of ideas. Miranda's connections with the London journals and newspapers favourably prepared public opinion for the mission which he undertook with Lopez Méndez and Bello. On 5 September 1810, he published his first newspaper article. From that summer in England until his death, he firmly recognized the press as a powerful medium of communication, 'as useful as stores and ammunition' [19].

It is surprising that a man who was neither a man of letters nor exclusively devoted to intellectual work should have been brought by his political capacity to work actively in journalism, aware of the significance of social communication and particularly, of the possibility of using this medium to win over public opinion, a force 'worth even more than armies'.

Bolívar is now rightly considered a journalist and one of the best in the Latin America of his time. His clarity, attention to detail, precision and accuracy can be seen in his work. He conducted press campaigns and was a resourceful polemicist. One of his adversaries, the blind José Domingo Diaz, recognized that the press was Bolívar's main weapon.

Despite the burning passion which he displayed during the continuous political struggle, in war and peace, Bolívar preached equanimity [10]. Truth, he maintained, should be the raw material for journalism. Not even when there were unjust diatribes against him, to which he was particularly sensitive, were justice and calm forgotten. One day in August 1825, he became angry over an attack in the press and ordered a riposte. He proclaimed, however:

Do not dwell on trivialities, say things out loud and clear and always tell the truth, which is what really hurts and not the falsehoods which they are trying to use as weapons against me. If I say anything which is not the pure and simple truth, do not repeat it since I do not want untruths to be said.

On another occasion, he uttered the unanswerable dictum: 'Falsehoods are always very weak.'

Pétion, who had valiantly sponsored Bolívar's main expeditions, extended his generosity to Latin America, as it awoke to liberty, when he gave Bolívar a printing press as a gift. This press was lost during the Ocumare disaster. Afterwards, the Liberator crowned his dream in Angostura by founding *El Correo del Orinoco* (1818–21). He declared to his friend Don Fernando Peñalver:

For the time being we need only the articles which I requested before, since without them, much precious time is being wasted. . . . Above all, send me, by some means or other, the printing press which is as useful as stores and ammunition. [19]

He made many comments on the *Gaceta de Bogotá*. He was concerned about matters of form: 'Our *Gaceta* is unpresentable because of its typography'; he recommended that full use should be made of paper—then in short supply—by 'using the smallest types available'. With the immediacy of an experienced journalist, he gave equal attention to content and presentation:

The comments can be improved with a bit more salt and some body; but they must be included in the text so as to have maximum effect. . . . The form of all things must match their inherent structure and these forms must be as pleasing as possible so as to gratify and enchant. It is very important that this newspaper, which has such good editors, deal with matters in a proper journalistic manner.

He made similar remarks in early May 1824 to his efficient secretary, José Gabriel Páez. His journalistic recommendations to General Heres in August 1825 were among his most detailed. He even went into questions of layout, now a specialized field of modern journalism, indicating the way in which columns were to be arranged:

The entire paper should be divided into different sections so that, say, financial matters and income come under 'finance'. If it is about Ferdinand VII, 'tyranny' or 'fanaticism', as the case may be. If it is a rare or unheard-of event: 'extraordinary', 'strange' or 'scandalous' as appropriate.

His conclusions had the value of specific guidelines:

Articles should be short, spicy, pleasant and cogent. The government should be spoken of respectfully, and legislation, wisely and seriously. I want the newspaper to be protected but it would be better for you not to appear as the principal, but rather the government or Larrea or a friend; but let it be organized elegantly, tastefully and properly.

With regard to the appropriate tone, he stressed that 'nobility and propriety are necessary for the most cruel satire as well as for the most exalted words of praise'.

Bolívar, the statesman and governor, was consistent with Bolívar the journalist. His respect for freedom of expression was total and sacred. In the 1819 draft constitution, he proposed that

the right to express one's thoughts and opinions by word of mouth, in writing or in any other way, is the most important and invaluable gift of nature. Not even the law itself could ever prohibit it, and the law can only refer to it in just terms, making those who abuse it to the detriment of public order and the life, honour, esteem and propriety of each citizen responsible for their speech and writings.

In the draft constitution for Bolivia, he stipulated that 'everyone may communicate his thoughts by word of mouth or in writing and publish through the press without any prior censorship, while retaining responsibility as provided for by the law'.

## HOPE AND CONFLICT

Formidable tasks awaited Bolívar in the south. In February 1824, the Peruvian Congress gave him full powers consonant with his official status as 'dictator' there, which he held for one year within carefully established constitutional limits. He scrupulously accounted for his government in February of the following year through his minister, the Peruvian José Faustino Sánchez Carrión. This ideologist and political leader was not only an effective aide, but also the driving force at Bolívar's side, of the great events which occurred during those months, from Trujillo to Huamanga and from Huamanga to Lima. The creation of the Liberation Army of the North, the establishment of the Supreme Court and of the Universidad de la Libertad in Trujillo, the liberation campaign, ending in success for Latin America at Ayacucho, the organization of civilian administration in the country and the convening of the Amphictyonic Congress in Panama from the Casa de la Magdalena; all these events brought Bolívar and Sánchez Carrión together early in the history of the Republic of Peru.

The most pleasant of the fateful years of Bolívar's career were spent in Ecuador, Peru and Bolivia. With the end of the war against absolutism a period of undisturbed and uninterrupted peace ensued, though the much desired stability remained a dream. The people, especially the downtrodden indigenous masses, lined the roads to acclaim their redeemer. Bolívar, the avenger of the neglected peoples, was the object of deep affection and sincere emotion from the crowds as was Napoleon in Paris.

By a just law of recompense, while on the high plateaux, he reaped the reward for sacrifices made in Venezuela, New Granada and the Caribbean.

Ecuador will be for ever proud of its unflinching loyalty to the Father of the Nation. In the period of base ingratitude that followed, that country would take pride in offering its liberator the quiet refuge perversely refused by others. Bolivia was also to express similar filial sentiments.

Peru proved a fruitful environment for his vigorous mind. There he wrote his best letters—the Pativilca letter to his beloved teacher Don Simón Rodríguez [56], the Cuzco letters to his uncle and godfather, Don Estéban Palacios [72], and his essays in literary criticism for the poet Olmedo [68].

All Latin America made its way to Peru. Under the orders of Antonio José de Sucre, commander of Bolívar's troops and of his entourage, there were officers from Argentina, Bolivia, Chile, Colombia, Cuba, Ecuador, Panama, Paraguay, Peru, Puerto Rico, Uruguay and Venezuela, and from England, Germany, Holland, Ireland and Spain. They were the decisive factors at Ayacucho on 9 December 1824. Forty-eight hours before the beginning of the battle, the Liberator signed a circular to the governments which were to lay the foundations of Latin American unity in Panama. Death was overcome, life was about to begin. From the summit of the Andes, Bolívar shone forth as the arbiter of Latin America, at the zenith of his glory.

At Cuzco, Sucre had the honour of striking Pizarro's flag which had been there for three centuries. The trophy was handed to Bolívar who sent it to his native Caracas.

Indicative of the complex and painful circumstances in which Bolívar always lived is the fact that at the very moment when he was devoting his efforts to Latin American unity within the Union of Gran Colombia, the forces of dissolution were unleashed. 'Whatever I do with my hands, others destroy with their feet' was how he spoke of his work, a labour like that of Sisyphus condemned to roll a heavy rock up a hill only to have it roll down again as it neared the top. As quickly as communications at that time allowed, Bolívar left Lima in September 1826 for Colombia, 'a horrible labyrinth . . . an edifice like the Devil's, with fire everywhere'.

His arrival in Colombia temporarily halted the divisions there. General José Antonio Páez and General Francisco Paulo de Santander were the leaders of the challenge to the stability of the republic. For a while, Bolívar had the situation under control. However, his health was failing and, at the age of forty-six, weakened both physically and spiritually by the battles waged over a vast area of 5 million square kilometres during two decades, Bolívar already had the appearance of an old man.

In 1827, he gave what remained of his life to his homeland, Venezuela, which had nurtured him and made him what he was. He went there to promote unity and brotherhood, placing his experience and administrative skill at the service of the country. More convinced than ever that the prime needs were 'morality and enlightenment', he devoted himself particularly to education. He adopted effective measures for the manumission of slaves. He reorganized fiscal matters by means of regulations on revenue and customs. On many occasions, he repeated his precepts on integrity and honesty.

This journey was one of sad disillusion. A century seemed to have passed between the optimism of Angostura in 1819 and his now diminished circumstances of broken hopes, reflected in his anguished message to the Convention at Ocaña [90]. Soon, he was to bid the country farewell, his bones and ashes to return in a leaden casket in 1842.

## FOR THE UNIVERSITY

In the history of Bolívar and Latin American culture, the final visit of the great son of Caracas to his native country will be remembered because of its great impact on the university. Caracas, like Trujillo, Bogotá, Quito, Arequipa, Cali, Medellín or San Cristóbal de Ayacucho received, through its university, the civilizing touch of the statesman who knew full well that 'nations march towards greatness at the same pace as education advances. They fly if it flies' [79].

On 24 June 1827, exactly six years after the Battle of Carabobo which set the seal on Venezuelan liberty, the Liberator, in conjunction with José María Vargas and José Rafael Revenga, issued new statutes for the Universidad Central de Caracas [87]. This is the second longest of Bolívar's decrees, comprising almost 300 articles. It repealed outdated rules, updated and appropriately refurbished that great institution, and laid the foundations for a new arrangement which, without doubt, could be seen as the beginning of a major university reform, many of the principles of which are still fully applicable.

An open-door policy for the university was encouraged, with a view to the genuine dissemination of culture. The right of the student body to take part in the running of the institution was recognized. Students were exempted from military service and any duties that prevented them from giving full attention to higher education. A system of equivalences and examinations allowed for full co-operation between the universities. It was stipulated that teaching posts were to be filled by open competition, and examining boards were enjoined to perform their duties fairly, leaving aside personal considerations and emotional factors.

Bolívar wanted teachers to be masters in the full sense, telling them not only to transmit their knowledge but also to become 'a model for the youths entrusted to their care—decency, decorum, urbanity, refined language—everything a teacher should embody, whereby they might train good pupils with practical examples' [87]. Bolívar had the greatest respect for educators. He affirmed that 'the noblest aim of all men is to enlighten their peers'. He personally embodied 'love and respect' for his teachers. Years later he recalled his connection with Andrés Bello: 'I recognize the superior quality of my fellow citizen of Caracas and my contemporary; he was my teacher when we were of the same age and I loved and respected him.'

He envisaged and himself embodied the role of a teacher as a loving and patient gardener. He was happy to say to Don Simón Rodríguez, when at the pinnacle of his power and glory:

You must constantly have reflected 'all this is mine, I sowed this plant, I watered and tended it, nourished it when it was young and weak, and now that it is healthy, strong and fruitful, I reap those fruits. They are mine, I shall savour them in the garden I planted. I shall enjoy its friendly shade, for I have a prescriptive and exclusive right to everything.' [56]

In the new rules for the University of Caracas, Bolívar also took care of social security for teachers. A 'full income' retirement system after twenty years of service was devised. As a democrat wishing to see republican renewal, he set the term of office for the rector at three years.

He never thought of the university as a school writ large or as a federation of professional schools. On the contrary, he saw it as an organic, high-level body to which he assigned lofty responsibilities, beyond mere instruction. His plan for the university included the establishment of four academies: literature, natural science, political science and ethics, and divinity. Each one was to focus on the study of local realities with a view to concrete solutions and social benefit. The Faculty of Medicine was entrusted with tasks in the field of national health. It was instructed to 'prepare and publish the most appropriate methods for curing epidemic and contagious diseases. To publish these methods so as to put the people on guard against the diseases which are most common or peculiar to these countries.' It was also the responsibility of the Faculty of Medicine to set up one or several museums, to promote the publication of manuals and to consider the ways of protecting and making better use of the forestry resources of the republic.

Bolívar's interest in the university can be seen in a series of thirteen decrees promulgated during the five years between 1824 and 1829. In the last decree promulgated at Popayán on 5 December 1829, he ascribed to the universities the major role of managing and administering the education sector, in other words, the duties corresponding to the Subdirecciones de Estudios in places where there were universities.

Bolívar's enthusiasm for education at the highest levels of excellence does not in any way imply any élitist leanings on his part. In an exemplary manner, he criticized and fought misguided aristocratic ideas on leisure and the rejection of manual labour as being unfit for gentlemen. With regard to the career of his nephew Fernando, the son, so to speak, that he never had, he emphatically stated that if the young man were to decide 'to learn a craft or trade, I should be delighted, since we have plenty of doctors and lawyers, but lack good mechanics and farmers, who are the keys to the country's progress, prosperity and well-being' [42].

At the end of his life, one week before he died, Simón Bolívar's thoughts turned to the University of Caracas, to which he had granted adequate funds and property to ensure its autonomy and, in his will, declared:

It is my wish that the two works presented to me as a gift by my friend General Wilson, which formerly belonged to the library of Napoleon, namely Rousseau's *Social Contract* and Montecuccoli's *Military Art*, be given to the University of Caracas. [61]

Referring to these books of 'inestimable value' which symbolize and illustrate the complementary halves of his personality—warrior and statesman, thinker and soldier—Bolívar had said:

These works will give me great pleasure in all respects. Their authors are highly regarded both for the good and the harm that they have done; their first owner is the honour and despair of the human spirit, and the second, who honoured me by giving them to me, is worth more than any other, for he has traced with his sword the precepts of Montecuccoli, and the Social Contract is engraved on his heart, not with theoretical characters but with deeds in which heroism and beneficence have an equal share. [61]

## THE FINAL ACT

Bolívar left Venezuela in July 1827 on the last stage of his life's journey, which was also to see the collapse of his political creation. The years he was forced to stay in the south were the greatest sacrifice of his life. He was faced with an unavoidable dilemma: if he remained in Colombia and abandoned Peru, he would lose everything, since his enemies there would gather strength for a retaliatory attack against Colombia; if he went to Peru, he would lose power, as he in fact did, in Colombia. He could scarcely hope that his compatriots would not return to a course which had cost so much. He accepted the challenge. His crusade took him as far as Potosí: he was paid the homage of being considered the Protector of America's Liberty, invited by the Argentines and respected by the people as the living guarantor of the Revolution.

Leaders such as Paez and Santander and many other narrow-minded upholders of the *patriecita* (little homeland) concept took advantage of those years to pervert revolutionary ideals for the mere satisfaction of their personal interests. Bolívar wanted an examination of the bases of the republic, with a view to thorough-going corrective measures. This was why the Convention of Ocaña was called.

The desired agreement did not materialize. The situation developed quickly, culminating in an act of force, the 1828–30 'dictatorship'. This painful and tragic stage of the Liberator's political career has been the subject of a legend representing his emergency rule as being comparable with the undemocratic dictatorships and despotism which have since plagued Latin America.

The nature and rationale of Bolívar's dictatorship were the same as those of dictatorships under the Roman republic. It was a system within the law; he willingly declared it to be temporary, set a date for its termination and convened the national representatives on the due date, 2 January 1830. Moreover, the Liberator did not assume full powers: the Council of State frequently imposed its collective will, even in sensitive matters which were strictly the personal responsibility of Bolívar himself.

Basically, during this brief period of disruption, Bolívar's revolutionary spirit was not diminished. He did not repudiate, dilute, compromise or reject any of his main ideas. On the contrary, his clear-cut and unchanging position, against slavery in particular, was expressly reiterated. His position in favour of the indigenous peoples became clearer, as did his attitude towards the affairs of Colombia and the continent: all these goals were reaffirmed through his decrees and actions during this crucial period. Careful consideration and impartial judgement of the dictatorship, which was never tyrannical, shows that, rather than a slide into reaction, it was Bolívar's final attempt to give impetus to the revolution, to move it out of the quagmire and make it viable.

In early 1830, the new congress, known as the 'Admirable Congress' because of the quality of its members, began its meeting as duly required. Bolívar handed over power and, in practice, ended his public career. There is a pathetic note in his utterances [97]. He left for his final exile but did not fulfil his aim of travelling to Jamaica and later settling in Europe like San Martín. Because of transport difficulties, he stayed on the Caribbean coast of Colombia, where he learnt of the foul murder of his most faithful companion, the selfless Marshal Antonio José de Sucre [99] and heard that Colombia had ceased to exist, splitting into the three former parts of Venezuela, New Granada and Ecuador. His native country denounced and officially banished him.

He was unspeakably embittered. On 17 December 1830, at one o'clock in the afternoon, he passed away. At the very end, he became even greater through his forgiveness: his last wishes were for the well-being of his homeland [100].

## ETHICAL AWARENESS

It is fitting to consider Simón Bolívar, citizen of Venezuela, Caracas and Latin America, as a lasting and fixed point of moral reference. He is the historical, spiritual and ethical heart of a nation which could have been the greatest in the world—a Latin America stretching from the Mississippi to the Straits of Magellan and comprising Spanish America, Portuguese America or Brazil, and the Caribbean mosaic which, despite the English, French, Dutch, Danish, Papiamento and Creole or Patois spoken there, is a living part of one and the same basic reality.

The story of Bolívar is instructive in many respects. His conduct as a public figure was particularly upright and blameless. He once responded to a proposal by Santander that they both support a company which planned to open a canal in Panama by saying:

After reflecting at length about what you said to me, not only do I think it inopportune to take part in this affair, I would also advise you not to become involved in it.... I am personally determined not to become involved in this or in any other commercial transaction.

He was extremely honest in administering national finances. He described 'the sacred duty of a republican to account for one's administration to the representatives of the people [as an] agreeable necessity'.

Bolívar wanted the Constitution expressly to include among civic duties the responsibility of

ensuring that public revenue is legitimately invested for the good of the society and of denouncing any who defraud it to the representatives of the people, whether such fraud is committed by the taxpayer or by the administrators or by the government which controls it.

He also steadfastly maintained that the citizen should not merely refrain from breaking the law; he should also see to it that laws are observed and do his utmost to have them kept, for example, by using persuasion or representation to the authorities, if all other methods fail.

He was a forthright champion in the campaign against administrative corruption [51, 88]. He was always firm and unyielding in his struggle against this disgraceful blemish. He continuously supported morality in public administration. In 1813, imposing the ethics of the new order and defending the only sector which could then provide funds for the new nation, he decreed:

Anyone found guilty of defrauding the treasury of the National Tobacco Revenue, or of selling clandestinely outside the state monopoly, or of robbing the treasury by theft or other unlawful means shall be shot, and his property shall be seized to offset the losses and damage incurred. [6]

And, he added severely,

the same penalty shall be applicable to all judges or other persons responsible for enforcing this law, summarily as indicated ... should they mitigate it in favour of the offenders, through connivance, partiality or on any other grounds. [6]

Vested with supreme power in Lima, he unhesitatingly ruled that any public servant convicted of having misappropriated, or appropriated to his own use, ten pesos or more of public funds should be liable to capital punishment [55]. On that same occasion, underlining the severity asserted in Caracas, he went on to stipulate that any judge failing to act in accordance with the decree should be condemned to the same penalty [55].

Bolívar started his political career a rich man, for in 1804 his fortune was estimated at 4 million pesos. His wealth was lost in the vicissitudes of war. The following lapidary phrase dates from 1828: 'I wish I had material wealth to distribute to each man in Great Colombia, but I have nothing: I have only my heart with which to love you and my sword to defend you.' For fifteen years he was in charge of the national finances of Venezuela, Colombia and Peru, the only check on him being his own strict principles, yet he died a poor man. In his will he declared: 'My only assets are the mines and the land in Aroa (bought by his forefathers) in the province of Carabobo and a few jewels which are listed in an inventory which should be among my papers.'

## STRENGTH IN UNITY

On the bicentenary of his birth, we see that one of Bolívar's most significant lessons to mankind was his resolute and absolute commitment to liberty, to the glory of which he brought all people together, and, with this, his firm conviction of the unique value of unity, solidarity and integration.

The agreement between the two great leaders of the struggle in South America, the liberators Simón Bolívar and José de San Martín [36, 43] was a high point in American history, compelling and instructive in its simplicity. The Guayaquil meeting took place on 26 July 1822. Despite their differences on minor matters, they called each other 'brothers in arms, in aims and in opinion'. Joining their forces and their prestige, they together gave South America an unequalled opportunity of uniting. There was a common and fruitful understanding, as the events were to reveal. On his return from the meeting, San Martín told the Peruvians, 'I had the pleasure of embracing the hero of South America. This was one of the happiest days of my life. Let us all pay a tribute of eternal gratitude to the immortal Bolívar.' Bolívar stressed the major points agreed upon with the hero of the battles of San Lorenzo, Chacabuco and Maipú which led to the independence of Argentina and Chile: eternal friendship between their countries, settlement of border problems, complete federation, a common diplomatic approach to Spain and agreement on the vital Latin American issues. San Martín's desire was that 'all our actions should be accomplished in unity, without which there can be neither peace nor stability'. The outcome of the meeting satisfied both men. There was no intransigence, no rancour, no frustration, no obstruction and no sabotage. The way was clear to reach the highest goal of unity in liberty [44, 45].

Bolívar's worth in the eyes of all people lies, we must repeat, in his unfailing and constant commitment to unity. He fought against selfishness. He was a soldier for unity, the key thought underlying each of his major documents. In the Cartagena Manifesto he declared: 'Our own disunity, not Spanish arms, made slaves of us' [4]. In the Carúpano Manifesto he asserted: 'It seems that Heaven for our humiliation and our glory has allowed our conquerors to be our brothers, and that only our brothers may triumph over us' [11]. In the Jamaica Letter he stated: 'Surely unity is what we need to complete our work of regeneration' [13]. In the Angostura speech, he repeated: 'Unity, unity, unity should be our slogan' [24]. He told the Congress of Bolivia that their two most fearful enemies were tyranny and anarchy [83]. To the Convention of Ocaña, he declared: 'No nation ever made itself worthy of respect unless it was fortified by unity' [90]. His farewell to the Admirable Congress was a moving one:

Countrymen, listen to me for the last time as I come to the end of my political career: in the name of Colombia, I beg you, I beseech you to stay united so that you will not destroy our nation and become your own executioners. [97]

In his final statement, he proclaimed that as a common obligation 'You must all work for the inestimable good of the union' [100].

In accordance with Simón Bolívar's forecast and his metaphorical but truthful view that 'we are a small human race of our own', Latin America should draw closer to other regions of the world, tending towards his vision of a new balanced world order. His words uttered in 1814—allowing for the changed circumstances—are still appropriate as we approach the twenty-first century:

The ambition of the European nations [for which today read: imperialist centres of all types and origins] has placed the yoke of slavery on the shoulders of the rest of the world; and the rest of the world must try to establish a balance between itself and Europe, so as to destroy the domination of the latter. This is what I call the balance of the whole world and it should enter into the calculations of American policy. [8]

## NEW HORIZONS

Bolívar is a living exemplar, especially for the Third World which has emerged midway between the mutually exclusive and polarized

blocks. While warning us of the need for a lifelong struggle to protect ourselves from the danger of subjection, he enjoins us to make
our experience available to this third part of the world, with which
we are in solidarity as a result of the difficulties we have shared, and
on account of our similar ideals and unfulfilled aspirations.

Bolívar's almost photographic description in the Jamaica Letter
of the monopoly exercised by Spanish absolutism in this part of the
world clearly and with visionary foresight applies to any former
colony in Asia or Africa.

The role of the inhabitants of the American hemisphere has for centuries
been purely passive. Politically they were non-existent. We are still in a
position lower than slavery. [Their position was] no better than that of serfs
destined for labour or at best they have no more status than that of mere
consumers. Yet even this status is surrounded with galling restrictions. . . .
Do you wish to know what our future held? Simply the cultivation of the
fields of indigo, grain, coffee, sugar cane, cacao and cotton; cattle-raising
on the broad plains; hunting wild game in the jungles; digging in the earth
to mine its gold which can never sate that greedy nation. [13]

The current Latin American situation, within a worldwide system
marked by increasing interdependence but also by conflict, turbulence, rapid change at almost supersonic speed, in which man has
acquired an unforeseen capability to control nature through science
and technology, makes it our duty to devise a coherent and comprehensive plan of action and development for all our countries.

Bolívar's thinking and the example he set for the noble cause of
Latin American man and suffering humanity as a whole could help
these fellow countries to find themselves. No one indeed has surpassed this man of vision in breadth of outlook, in comprehensive
fulness of approach or in the determined pursuit of sure and feasible
goals.

In his highly expressive writings, he recorded, for all peoples
and for all times, a blunt message shaped by the harsh reality of
experience:

We were abandoned by the whole world. No foreign nation guided us
with its wisdom and experience, or defended us with its arms or protected
us with its resources. This was not the case of the United States during its
struggle for freedom: though possessing all kinds of advantages over us, the
three most powerful European nations, all owners of colonies, helped it to
attain independence; and yet Great Britain did not retaliate against that
very same Spain which waged war against her to deprive her of her colonies.
. . . Even the victories of the great and immortal Wellington have been
indirectly harmful to us, since the Spaniards, ignorant in the art of war-

fare, learnt it from the heroic British commanded by the illustrious captain who, at one time, was to liberate South America. These are the singular facts which will go down in history along with others too numerous to mention. The United States, which by its trade could have provided us with the necessities of war deprived us thereof because of its dispute with Great Britain. Otherwise, Venezuela would have triumphed alone and South America would have been spared the devastation of Spanish cruelty and the destruction of revolutionary anarchy. We have no weapons with which to confront the enemy but our arms, our breasts, our horses and our lances. The weak need a long battle to triumph; the strong, as at Waterloo, need to wage a single battle and an empire disappears. [14]

For those who truly heed the voice of history and draw from it lessons for their lives, such disappointments teach an unsurpassable lesson: that of faith in one's own strength and security only in unity with one's kinsmen.

His teaching on liberty was insistent. Our countries, selfless and generous by nature, romantic and idealistic in their very being, account freedom a precious heritage which no one is prepared to surrender. And each and every effort for effective justice must be made conditional on liberty, that 'necessary and splendid breath of the soul' as Borges poetically puts it.

Bolívar, the Liberator, neither a conqueror nor an oppressor, sacrificed himself for liberty. His revolution was meant to be the first grand attempt in the world at a movement for full freedom, with a concomitant economic and social content. He rebelled against absolutism, especially in its worst form—colonialism—with a view to establishing a positive and democratic system which would respect the rights of the individual, while recognizing the higher collective interest.

Bolívar's struggle and sacrifice for true independence will have borne fruit if, in the face of today's aggressive forms of neocolonialism, which exploit and speculate upon the accidental technological inferiority of the Third World, the various peoples belonging to the great universal family of the dispossessed are warned and made aware of their duty to choose freely their own methods and determine their own objectives without aping foreign models of development which are only relevant to, and suitable for, countries that are already developed.

Today, more than ever, we need true independence of judgement, spiritual sovereignty, hard work, solidarity in our action and clarity in our aims so as to realize 'the hope of the Universe'.

Puerto de Hierro, Venezuela
16 August 1982

# AN ANTHOLOGY OF BOLÍVAR'S WRITINGS

## 1

# The oath of freedom taken in Rome

*On 15 August 1805, on the Aventine Hill, in the presence of his tutor, Don Simón Rodríguez and his friend Fernando Toro, Bolívar swore that he would devote himself to the cause of freedom. This text, reconstructed years later from memory by Don Simón Rodríguez, is well known.*

This country has produced everything—severity in antiquity, austerity under the Republic, depravity under the Emperors, catacombs in the time of the Christians, valour to conquer the whole world, ambition to make all the states of the globe its tributaries, women capable of letting their sacrilegious carriage-wheels pass over the mangled bodies of their fathers, stirring orators such as Cicero, lyrical poets to enchant us such as Virgil, satirists such as Juvenal and Lucretius, unsound philosophers such as Seneca, and citizens of integrity such as Cato. This country has produced everything, except in the cause of humanity: corrupt Messalinas, heartless Agrippas, great historians, distinguished naturalists, illustrious warriors, rapacious proconsuls, licentious sensualists, sterling virtues and gross crimes; and yet, for the cause of spiritual growth, the banishment of care, the betterment of man and the ultimate perfectibility of his intellect, it has produced little or nothing. This civilization which rose in the East has revealed all its aspects and characteristics here; but, as for solving the great problem of human freedom, it would seem that this has been ignored, and that the identity of this mysterious stranger, freedom, will come to light only in the New World.

I swear before you, I swear by the God of my fathers, I swear by them, I swear upon my honour and by my homeland that I shall not let my arm rest, nor my soul repose until I have broken the chains laid upon us by our Spanish oppressors!

2

# 'We are committed in the eyes of the world. We are pledged to bring about universal liberation'

*From a note sent from London on 8 September 1810 to the Government of Caracas. Drafted by Andrés Bello, inspired by Francisco de Miranda and signed by Bolívar and Luis López Méndez, it associates the three greatest figures from Caracas—the Precursor, the Humanist and the Liberator—in a sufficiently clear declaration on behalf of independence, already perceived in Latin American terms.*

A few days ago the iniquitous and scandalous decree, in which the Council of the Regency declared us rebels, imposed a strict blockade on our coasts and ports and warned the other American Provinces to cut off and intercept any form of communication with us, was officially received in this Court.

The published papers enclosed will give you an indication of the state of affairs in Spain and Portugal and the ideas held until now concerning current events in Venezuela and in other parts of the continent. Our cause has many friends in this country and cannot conceivably lose them so long as reason and justice find supporters. We are committed in the eyes of the world and, without discrediting ourselves forever, we cannot deviate in the slightest degree from the glorious path that we have opened up for America. Let the cold gratitude of tyrants be the reward of those countries which have not had the courage to tread this path, or which, instead of following in our footsteps, have sunk so low as to disparage us, while we, unflagging, continue our efforts and propagate sound thinking, for we are pledged to bring about universal liberation. The firmness and resolve with which we have advanced should not fail to hasten its coming, and, until that happy day, our tender concern for justice and philanthropy will console us for the blindness or ingratitude of our fellow men.

3

# 'Fearlessly let us lay the foundation stone of South America's freedom'

*Bolívar's first speech. Delivered at the Sociedad Patriótica, Caracas, a political association to further the revolutionary cause, on 4 July 1811. He encourages the political process in Venezuela and defines it in terms of the general interest of Latin America.*

There cannot be two Congresses. How can those most aware of the need for unity foment a split? Our aim is to make that unity a reality and an inspiration in our glorious pursuit of our freedom: uniting to do nothing, sunk in apathy, was a weakness in the past; today, it is treason. The National Congress is deliberating on what should be done. And what are they saying? That we should begin with a federation, as if we were not all united against foreign tyranny. What are we to expect of the results of Spain's policy? What does it matter to us whether Spain sells its slaves to Bonaparte or whether it keeps them, if we are resolved to be free? These misgivings are the unfortunate result of the fetters of the past. Great plans should be made in tranquillity? Are not 300 years of tranquillity enough? The Junta Patriótica respects, as it ought, the Congress of the nation, but the Congress must heed the Junta Patriótica, a centre of enlightenment and the focus of all revolutionary concerns. Fearlessly let us lay the foundation stone of South America's freedom: he who hesitates is lost.

I propose that a deputation from this body convey these sentiments to the Sovereign Congress.

4

# Analysis of failure and useful suggestions for the progress of the revolution

*Bolívar's first fundamental document, known as the 'Cartagena Manifesto'. He examines and explains the causes of the fall of the First Republic of Venezuela, 1810–12. Cartegena de Indias, 15 December 1812.*

To save New Granada from the fate of Venezuela and to relieve the latter of its sufferings are the aims that I set myself in this document. Fellow citizens, I beg you to accept it as a tribute to such laudable aims.

People of Granada, I was born in the unfortunate city of Caracas. I have miraculously escaped from its material and political ruin and, ever faithful to the liberal and just system proclaimed by my country, I have come here to follow the banners of independence that are flying so gloriously in these states.

Allow me, fired by the patriotic zeal that has moved me to address you, to indicate briefly the factors that brought Venezuela to its destruction: I am confident that the terrible and exemplary lessons to be learnt from that fallen republic will persuade America to mend its ways and make good the lack of unity, resolution and energy apparent in its governments.

The greatest mistake Venezuela made when it entered the political scene was undeniably its fatal adoption of a tolerant system—a system rejected ever since, because of its weakness and inefficiency, by all sensible people, but stubbornly maintained to the end, with a singular lack of perspicacity. . . .

The statutes consulted by our law-givers were not those from which they might learn the practical science of government, but those which have produced certain idealists who, imagining Utopian republics, have endeavoured to achieve political perfection, assuming that the human race is perfectible. As a result, we have taken philosophers for leaders, philanthropy for legislation, dialectics for tactics, and sophists for soldiers. Such topsy-turvy principles and events severely disrupted the social order, and the state naturally slid rapidly downhill into general dissolution.

Hence the absence of punishment for crimes against the state, blatantly committed by malcontents, and particularly by our implacable born enemies, the European Spaniards, who, with evil intent, remained in our country in order to keep it in a continual state of unrest and to foment whatever conspiracies they were allowed to organize by our judges, who always pardoned them, even when their crimes were so outrageous as to threaten public welfare.

The doctrine on which this attitude was based originated in the philanthropic maxims of certain writers who claimed that nobody was entitled to deprive a man of life, even if he had committed an offence against his country. Protected by this pious doctrine, every conspiracy was followed by a pardon, and every pardon was followed by another conspiracy and another pardon, for liberal governments have to prove how merciful they are. Criminal clemency, which contributed more than anything else to the collapse of the edifice whose construction was not yet even completed!

*Faulty organization*

Hence the decision to attempt to muster disciplined veteran troops, already trained and capable of going into battle to defend liberation with victory and glory. But, instead, countless bodies of undisciplined militia were set up which, apart from draining the public funds with their pay, destroyed agriculture by causing the country-dwellers to leave their homes, and made those people hate a government which compelled them to take up arms and abandon their families.

'Republics do not need paid men to maintain their freedom', said our statesmen. 'All citizens will be soldiers should an enemy attack us. Greece, Rome, Venice, Genoa, Switzerland, Holland, and recently North America—all triumphed over their adversaries without the aid of mercenary troops, always ready to support despotism and gain control over their fellow citizens.'

With such anti-political and fallacious arguments they impressed the gullible. However, they did not convince the more discerning, who were aware of the tremendous difference between the peoples, times and customs of those republics and those of our own. It is a fact that those republics did not maintain standing armies; but that was because in antiquity it was not customary to do so, the defence and glory of states being vested in their political virtues, austere customs and military character, qualities that we are very far from possessing. And as for the modern republics that have shaken off the yoke of tyranny, it is well known that they have maintained sufficient numbers of reserves for their security, with the exception of North America, which, being at peace with the whole world, and protected by the sea, has not found it necessary in recent years to maintain the full complement of reserve troops that would be needed to defend its borders and its cities.

. . . . . . . . . . . . . . . . . . . . . . . . . . . . . . . . . . . . . .

The outcome brought it cruelly home to Venezuela that it has mis-calculated, for the militia who went into battle, untrained in the handling of weapons and unaccustomed to discipline and obedience, were overwhelmed at the beginning of the last campaign, despite the remarkable and heroic efforts made by their chiefs to lead them to victory. This caused general loss of morale among officers and men, for it is a military axiom that only hardened troops are capable of recovering from the initial setbacks of a campaign. The raw recruit believes that all is lost as soon as he suffers his first defeat, for he has not learnt from experience that with bravery, skill and perseverance a reverse can be overcome.

The subdivision of the province of Caracas, planned, discussed and approved by the Federal Congress, aroused and fomented bitter feelings of rivalry with the capital in the cities and smaller towns; according to members of Congress anxious to gain control over their districts, it represented 'the tyranny of the cities and the bane of the state'.

. . . . . . . . . . . . . . . . . . . . . . . . . . . . . . . . . . . . . .

The dissipation of public funds on unnecessary and detrimental items, and in particular on the salaries of countless clerks, secretaries, judges, magistrates, provincial and federal legislators dealt the Republic a mortal blow, obliging it to resort to the dangerous expedient of issuing paper money without any guarantee except the strength and assumed revenue of the Federation. This new money seemed to many people to be a flagrant violation of the right of ownership, for they considered that they were being dispossessed of objects of intrinsic value in exchange for others of doubtful, not to say illusory, value. The paper currency brought to a head the discontent of the stolid people of the inland areas, who appealed to the Spanish command to come and liberate them from a currency which appalled them more than servitude.

However, the Government of Venezuela was weakened most of all by the adoption of the federal system, in accordance with extravagant maxims concerning human rights. By authorizing self-government, this broke down social contracts and created anarchy in the nation. Such was the true state of the Federation. Every province was autonomous and, taking this as an example, every city laid claim to equal powers. . . .

The federal system, although the most satisfactory and the most conducive to human happiness in society, is, none the less, the system most contrary to the interests of our new-born states. Generally speaking, our fellow citizens are not yet ready to stand alone and exercise their rights to the full; they lack the political virtues characteristic of the true republican—virtues that are not acquired under totalitarian governments, which ignore the rights and obligations of the citizen.

Moreover, what country in the world, law-abiding and republican though it may be, can be governed by such a complicated and weak system as the federal one when it is up against factions at home and war abroad?

A government must come to terms, so to speak, with the circumstances, the times and the people with whom it has to deal. If the latter are prosperous and calm, the government should be moderate and protective; but if they are in a disastrous situation and agitated, it should strike awe in them and rule them with a rod of iron commensurate with the dangers, without waiting for laws or constitutions, until the reign of happiness and peace is restored.

. . . . . . . . . . . . . . . . . . . . . . . . . . . . . . . . . . . .


## THE NECESSARY CHANGES


I feel that so long as we do not centralize our American governments our enemies will take full advantage of the situation: we shall inevitably be involved in the horrors of civil strife and suffer humiliating defeat at the hands of the crew of desperadoes infesting our regions.

The general elections held by country-dwellers and by the scheming inhabitants of the cities raise yet another obstacle to our federation, since the former are so ignorant that they vote indiscriminately and the latter so ambitious that they attempt to turn everything to their own advantage, so that the reins of government are placed in the hands of men already disloyal to the cause, inept and lacking in integrity. Party politics prevailed throughout and, consequently, threw us into greater disarray than did the circumstances. Our own disunity, not Spanish arms, made slaves of us.

The earthquake of 26 March was, without a doubt, both physically and mentally destructive, and it can rightly be called the immediate cause of Venezuela's downfall, but this occurrence would not have had such fatal effects if, at the time, Caracas had been governed by a single authority, which, acting quickly and energetically, could have repaired the damage without hindrance or rivalry, whereas, in fact, interference with the measures to be taken compounded the disaster to such an extent that it became irremediable.

If Caracas, instead of a weak and insubstantial federation, had established a straightforward government, as the political and military juncture required, you would exist today, Venezuela, and enjoy your freedom!

After the earthquake the Church played a very considerable part in the rebellion of small towns and villages, and in allowing our enemies to enter the country, sacrilegiously abusing the sanctity of its ministry to the advantage of the ringleaders of civil war.

However, we have to admit quite frankly that these traitorous clerics were moved to commit the execrable crimes of which they are justly accused because they could do so with total impunity.

. . . . . . . . . . . . . . . . . . . . . . . . . . . . . . . . . . . . .

## STRATEGIC SUMMARY

From the foregoing, it may be concluded that, among the causes of Venezuela's downfall, the nature of its contribution should be placed first on the list. I repeat that it was as contrary to Venezuela's interests as it was advantageous to those of its adversaries. In second place comes the spirit of misanthropy which possessed those who governed us. Third, the unwillingness to establish a military force which could have saved the Republic and repulsed the attacks of the Spaniards. In fourth place, the earthquake, together with the fanaticism which led to this phenomenon having the most serious consequences. Lastly, the internal factions which were in reality the poison that brought the country low.

These examples of mistakes and misfortunes will not be entirely useless to the countries of South America which aspire to liberty and independence.

New Granada has seen what happened to Venezuela. Consequently, it should avoid the pitfalls which to the latter proved fatal. To that end, I submit that the recapture of Caracas is essential to the security of New Granada. At first sight, this project may seem unlikely to succeed, costly and perhaps impractical. However, if it is examined carefully, thoroughly and with foresight, its necessity will become obvious, and, once its utility is acknowledged, it must be carried into effect. . . .

It is characteristic of human fortune that it is not always the numerical majority which decides; it is superior moral strength that tips the political scales. For this reason, therefore, the Government of

Venezuela ought not to have failed to extirpate an enemy who, though apparently weak, had the support of the province of Maracaibo, and of all those who obeyed the Regency; gold, and the cooperation of our eternal adversaries, the Europeans who live among us; the clerical party, always inclined to aid and abet despotism; and, above all, the fixed opinions of so many ignorant and superstitious people who live in our states. So, as soon as a traitor officer went over to the enemy, the political machinery started to fall apart, and the unparalleled patriotic efforts exerted by the defenders of Caracas were unable to prevent its final collapse as a result of the blow dealt by just one man.

. . . . . . . . . . . . . . . . . . . . . . . . . . . . . . . . . . . .

So, we have no choice in guarding against such disasters but to be prompt in pacifying our provinces in revolt, then to raise forces to combat our enemies and in this way to train soldiers and officers worthy of being called the backbone of their country.

Everything conspires to push into this course of action: besides the urgent need to shut out the enemy, there are other powerful reasons for us to take the offensive, such weighty arguments that it would be an unpardonable military and political error not to do so. We have been invaded, and hence we are obliged to drive the enemy far beyond our borders. It is a principle of the art of war, moreover, that all defensive wars are ruinous and prejudicial to those who wage them, since they are weakened and have no hope of reparation, whereas offensive hostilities in enemy territory are profitable through the gain derived from the enemy's losses; so we must on no account engage in a defensive war.

. . . . . . . . . . . . . . . . . . . . . . . . . . . . . . . . . . . .

It is an encouraging fact that, when we show ourselves in Venezuela, thousands of brave patriots flock to our side, patriots longing for us to appear so that they may cast off the yoke of the tyrants and join forces with us in the fight for freedom.

. . . . . . . . . . . . . . . . . . . . . . . . . . . . . . . . . . . .

5

# Proclamation of war to the death

*A radical and clear-cut political act, an attempt to identify the conflict-ing parties and hasten a military solution that would consolidate independence within a short time. Published in Trujillo on 15 June 1813.*

## SIMÓN BOLÍVAR
Brigadier of the Union,
Commander-in-Chief of the Army of the North,
Liberator of Venezuela

TO HIS FELLOW CITIZENS

Venezuelans,

An army of brothers, sent by the sovereign Congress of New Granada, has come to liberate you and is already among you, having driven the oppressors out of the provinces of Mérida and Trujillo.

We have been sent to destroy Spaniards, to protect Americans and to reinstate the Republican Governments that made up the Federation of Venezuela. The states protected by our forces are once again governed by their former constitutions and magistrates, in full possession of their freedom and independence, for our sole mission is to break the chains of servitude with which some of our countries are still burdened, and we have no intention of laying down laws or exercising the authority to which our supremacy in war might entitle us.

Moved by your misfortunes, we could not remain indifferent to the sufferings brought upon you by the Spanish barbarians, who have wrought destruction on you with their rapine and murder, who have violated the sacred law of nations, who have infringed the most solemn treaties and agreements and who have committed all manner of crimes, reducing the Republic of Venezuela to the most appalling desolation. Justice, therefore, demands revenge, and we are driven by necessity to take it. May the monsters that have infested the soil of Colombia and covered it with blood disappear for ever! May their punishment fit the enormity of their crimes, and may it thus remove the stigma of our shame and show the nations of the world that America's sons are not wronged with impunity!

Despite the justifiable resentment we bear towards the cruel Spaniards, we are willing, in generosity of spirit, to extend for the last time the hand of reconciliation and friendship. They are still welcome to live at peace among us if, rejecting their crimes, and genuinely repentant, they work with us to destroy the usurping Government of Spain and to re-establish the Republic of Venezuela.

Any Spaniard, without exception, who does not take action against tyranny on behalf of the just cause by the most active and effective means will be regarded as an enemy and punished as a traitor to the country and, consequently, will be executed. Conversely, a general and unconditional pardon will be granted to those who come over to our army, with or without their weapons, and to those who lend assistance to the good citizens who are striving to throw off the yoke of tyranny. The military staff and civil magistrates who publicly recognize the Government of Venezuela and join us will remain in office. In short, those Spaniards who render signal service to the State will be considered and treated as Americans.

And you Americans who have strayed from the path of justice and have been misled or corrupted, learn now that your brothers forgive you and sincerely regret your aberration, convinced that you cannot be held responsible, that only the state of blind ignorance in which you have been kept until now by the instigators of your crimes could have induced you to commit them! Do not fear the sword that has come to avenge you, and to sever the shameful bonds with which your executioners have fettered you to your fate! You may be sure that there is no threat to your honour, lives or property. The title of American will suffice as a pledge and safeguard. Our forces have come to protect you and will never turn on one of our brothers.

This amnesty is extended even to those same traitors whose crimes are recent, and it will be so scrupulously respected that no reason, cause or pretext will make us break our promise, however substantial or unexpected are the grounds we may have to bear you ill will.

Spaniards and Canary Islanders, death shall be your fate, even if you are neutral, unless you contribute actively to the liberation of America! Americans, life shall be yours, even if you are not blameless!

Trujillo Headquarters, 15 June 1813

*Simón Bolívar*

6

# The utmost severity in cases of fraud

*Committed to building up a system of absolute honesty, Bolívar intro-duced capital punishment for persons guilty of fraud in respect of the Republic's principal source of income, at that time the Tobacco Revenue. Law enacted at Puerto Cabello on 11 September 1813.*

### SIMÓN BOLÍVAR
Brigadier of the Union,
Commander-in-Chief of the Liberation
Army of Venezuela, etc.

Considering that income from the Tobacco Revenue is steadily fall-ing from day to day and that the yield is not equivalent to the revenue that ought to be obtained under this head, owing to fraudu-lent practices: either clandestine sales of tobacco by individuals, or criminal misappropriation on the part of some of the employees of the Department; and considering that this offence is particularly serious inasmuch as the common defence of the Fatherland and of Liberty requires that all good citizens make sacrifices, particularly in respect of their profits and their property, to help support the Liber-ation Army, and that, if they refuse to do so, these execrable robbers are attacking the state as they might attack an enemy, and depriving it of the assistance required for its defence, which virtually places them in the category of traitors; I have therefore decreed and decree as follows:

1. Any person found guilty of defrauding the treasury of the National Tobacco Revenue, or of selling clandestinely outside the state monopoly, or of robbing the treasury by theft or other unlawful means, shall be shot, and his property shall be seized to offset the losses and damage incurred.

2. The Director-General of the National Revenue, in strict compliance with this law, may order the appropriate judges to curtail or omit, if need be, the ordinary processes of law and confine them-selves to making summary judgements.

3. The same penalty laid down in Article 1 shall be applicable to all judges or other persons responsible for enforcing this law, summarily as indicated in the previous Article, should they mitigate it in favour of the offenders, through connivance, partiality or on any other grounds.

Countersign and put into effect: communicate to all concerned, print and publish in the usual form.

Issued at the Puerto Cabello Headquarters on 11 September 1813, third year of independence and first year of the war to the death, signed by my hand, sealed with the seal of the Republic and countersigned by the Secretary of State and of the Exchequer.

Simón Bolívar

*Antonio Muñoz Tebar*
Secretary of State and of the Exchequer

7

# Record of the enemy's crimes and reasons for total war

*Reasoned reply to His Excellency the Governor and Field Marshal of the Island of Curaçao and its dependencies—under British occupation at the time—from the Headquarters of Valencia, 3 October 1813.*

The courtesy I owe to a high representative of the British nation and to the glory of the American cause make it a sacred duty for me to explain to Your Excellency the painful reasons for the attitude which, to my regret, I take towards the Spaniards. They have, in the course of this year, reduced Venezuela to ruin and committed crimes that should condemn them to eternal oblivion, if the need to justify in the eyes of the world the war to the death that we have declared did not oblige us to drag them down from the scaffolds and out of the terrible dungeons which hide them, and bring them before Your Excellency.

This continent is separated from Spain by the wide ocean, has a larger population and greater wealth than Spain, and has endured for three centuries a state of degrading dependence under tyranny. On learning in 1810 that the governments of Spain had been dissolved because the French Army had occupied the country, it took immediate steps to ward off a similar fate and avoid impending anarchy and confusion. Venezuela was the first country to set up a junta to defend the rights of Ferdinand VII, pending the final outcome of the war: it offered any Spaniards who wished to emigrate a fraternal refuge, gave administrative posts to many of them and kept in their positions many who were influential and highly placed. Here was tangible proof of the Venezuelans' desire for unity: a desire which met with a disappointing response from the Spaniards, who for the most part betrayed the trust and generosity of the people in the most perfidious manner.

Venezuela took such a step of dire necessity. In less critical circumstances, Spanish provinces of less moment than Venezuela had set up governing juntas to protect themselves from disorder and turmoil. And should not Venezuela, likewise, have shielded itself from so many disasters, and assured its continuing existence, despite the rapid changes affecting Europe? Did it wrong the Spaniards of the Peninsula, left vulnerable to the upheavals caused by the fall of the recognized government? Ought they not to have appreciated the sacrifices we made to offer them a safe refuge? Could anyone have anticipated that a strict blockade and outrageous hostilities would be the response to such generosity?

Venezuela believed that Spain had been utterly defeated, as did the rest of America, when it took that step, which it might have taken long before, fired by the example of the Spanish provinces, to which it had been declared equal in rights and political representation. Then the Regency was instituted, and established its disorderly rule in Cadiz, the only place not under the French flag; from there it thundered its destructive decrees against free countries which, though not obliged to do so, had maintained relations with, and remained a part of, a country of which they were by nature independent.

Such was the generous spirit that inspired America's first revolution, a bloodless revolution, undefiled by hatred or revenge. In Venezuela, Buenos Aires and New Granada, they might well have given vent to the justifiable resentment aroused by so many wrongs, so much violence; they might have massacred those viceroys, governors and regents, and all those high officials, butchers of their own kind, who, in their delight at the massacre of Americans, threw the most illustrious and virtuous of men into horrible dungeons to perish, despoiled honest citizens of the fruits of their labours and in general persecuted industry, the arts and anything that might have made more bearable the horrors of our slavery.

For three centuries, America suffered under this tyranny, the most severe ever to have afflicted the human race: for three centuries it regretted its fateful wealth that held such magnetic attraction for its oppressors; and yet, when wise Providence gave it an unexpected opportunity to cast off its chains, far from thinking of revenge for these outrages, it offered its own enemies refuge and a share in its heritage.

*General destruction*

When we see today almost all parts of the New World engaged in a cruel and destructive war, when even those who dwell in hovels are inflamed by the furies of discord, when the devouring fire of war is kindled by sedition even in remote and isolated villages, and when the American countryside is stained with human blood, we must seek the reason for such an appalling upheaval on this peace-loving continent, whose mild and benevolent sons have always set a rare example of gentleness and submission, unparalleled in the history of any other people in the world.

The fierce Spaniard, defiling the coasts of Colombia, and turn-ing the most beautiful natural site into a huge and horrible empire of cruelty and rapine—here, Your Excellency, is the vile originator of those tragic scenes over which we weep. His entry into the New World blazed a trail of murder and desolation; its original inhabitants were wiped off the face of the earth; and, when his raging fury found no other living beings to destroy, he turned upon those of his own sons who had settled on the land that he now occupied.

See him, Your Excellency, on fire with bloodlust, desecrating what is most holy, and sacrilegiously breaking those covenants which the world honours and which have received the inviolable sanction of all states and all peoples. Last year, an agreement delivered into his possession the entire independent territory of Venezuela; total and peaceful submission on the part of the inhabitants seemed to indicate that the country had been pacified and had completely abandoned its past political claims. But while Monteverde swore to the Venezuelans that he would scrupulously keep the promises made, we were scandalized and appalled to see the most barbarous and pitiless violations—towns sacked, buildings burnt down, women raped, the larger cities reduced *en masse*, so to speak, to the caverns of hell. What hitherto would have seemed impossible—the enslave-ment of an entire population—actually came to pass. Only such wretched creatures as managed to escape the eye of the tyrant pre-served some semblance of freedom, reduced to living in isolated shacks in the wilderness where wild beasts roam.

How many elderly and respectable people, venerable priests among them, were chained in dungeons and other infamous prisons, along with common criminals, and exposed to the derision of the brutal soldiery and the vilest elements of all classes! How many of them died, crushed by the weight of their afflictions, suffocating and starving in squalor! At a time when the Spanish constitution was being promulgated as the escutcheon of civil liberty, hundreds of victims weighed down with chains and fetters were being dragged off to filthy, lethal dungeons, without any reasons being given; indeed, the origins and political opinions of these unfortunate people were not even known.

This, Your Excellency, is the plain, unadorned and yet unprecedented truth about Spanish tyranny in America. It is a picture that arouses both indignation against the tormentors and righteous compassion for the victims. And yet, sensitive souls have not interceded on behalf of their suffering fellows, nor have they demanded fulfilment of a pledge that affects all mankind. Your Excellency is now acting as a respectable mediator for these ferocious monsters, answerable for so many evils. Your Excellency must believe me: when the troops of New Granada rose on my orders to avenge these crimes against nature and society, neither the instructions issued by that benevolent government, nor my intentions, were to exercise the right of retaliation on the Spaniards, who condemned as insurgents all Americans worthy of the name and were causing them suffering or even more terrible and cruel tortures. But on seeing these savage monsters make a mockery of our clemency and, sure of impunity, pursue even in defeat the same bloody course, I then took up the sacred mission entrusted to me: to save the endangered lives of my compatriots, I strove to overcome my natural sensitivity, and thrust aside all pernicious feelings of mercy, for the sake of my country.

Allow me, Your Excellency, to recommend that you read the letter of the brutish Zerveriz, idol of the Spaniards in Venezuela, to General Monteverde, published in the *Gaceta de Caracas*, No. 3; here, Your Excellency will discover the bloodthirsty intentions that were put into effect by these depraved men. Being apprised beforehand of his sacrilegious intentions, which dire experience was presently to confirm, I resolved to wage a war to the death, and so put an end to the overwhelming advantage held by the tyrants as a result of their destructive system.

Indeed, when the liberation army launched its campaign in the province of Barinas, Colonel Antonio Nicolás Briceño was, alas, captured along with other high-ranking officers, and the barbarous and cowardly Tizcar put to death as many as sixteen of them. Similar scenes took place at the same time in Calabozo, Espino, Cumaná and other provinces and in such inhuman circumstances that I deem it unworthy of Your Excellency and of this document to describe such abominable deeds.

*Lest we forget*

Your Excellency will find an outline of the ferocious acts in which Spanish bloodlust indulged in the *Gaceta*, No. 4. The general massacre conducted unsparingly in the peaceful town of Aragua by that most brutal of men, the detestable Suazola, was one of those fits of bloodthirsty madness which have only rarely degraded mankind.

Men and women, old people and children, with their ears cut off, flayed alive and then flung into poisoned pits or put to death in slow agony. Crimes were committed against nature in its innocent beginnings, and the unborn foetus was bayoneted or battered to death in its mother's womb.

In San Juan de los Morros, a simple farming community, the barbarous Antoñanzas and the bloodthirsty Boves also pandered to the Spaniards' taste for such scenes. In those unfortunate villages corpses can be seen hanging from the trees. There, it seems, the spirit of crime holds its murderous sway, and no one can approach the place without feeling the urge to exact implacable vengeance.

Venezuela was not the only luckless scene of such horrible carnage. Wealthy Mexico, Buenos Aires, Peru and ill-fated Quito resemble vast cemeteries, in which the Spanish Government heaps up the bones cloven asunder by its homicidal axe.

Your Excellency will find the pedestal on which a Spaniard places the honour of his country in the *Gaceta*, No. 2. Brother Vicente Marquetich states in a letter that Regules' sword has put to death 12,000 Americans, on the battlefield and by torture, in a single year; and he glorifies the seaman Rosendo Porlier for his principle of *giving no quarter, even to saints if they appear in the guise of rebels.*

I shall refrain from afflicting Your Excellency with further descriptions of the dreadful sufferings inflicted on mankind by Spanish savagery in the attempt to establish an unjust and humiliating dominion over the gentle Americans. Would that an impenetrable veil might conceal forever from men's gaze the excesses of their fellow men! Would that cruel necessity had not imposed on us the inescapable obligation to exterminate such treacherous killers!

Your Excellency, for a moment please put yourself in our position, and say what action we should take against our oppressors! Decide, Your Excellency, whether it is even possible to secure America's freedom while so many implacable enemies draw breath! Terrible disappointments urge us every day to be unstinting in enforcing the harshest of measures, and I can tell Your Excellency that humanity itself commands us to do so, gently but sternly.

Inclined by my strongest feelings to be lenient with many Spaniards, I have generously allowed them to remain among us in complete freedom; but scarcely had their throats been saved from the avenging knife, when they caused commotion among the unfortunate people, and their new atrocities were the most appalling of all.

In the valleys of Tuy and Tácata and among the communities of the West, which might, it seemed, escape the ravages of civil war, their evil doings have increased, leaving a lamentable record of their raving cruelty. Defenceless women, children of tender age, helpless old men, have been found flayed, their eyes gouged out, disembowelled; one might will begin to think that America's tyrants do not belong to the human race.

It will be useless to plead for passports to this or that colony, or some other place outside Venezuela, on behalf of those held in gaol. At great cost to peace, we have experienced the dire consequences of such measures; for you may be sure that, despite the promises by which they were bound, almost all those who obtained passports changed their destination so as to disembark on enemy territory and joined the ranks of the murderers who are molesting defenceless people. Even in gaol they are hatching subversive plots, which will doubtless do more harm to themselves than to the government, obliged, as it is, to use greater force in checking the fury of zealous patriots against the rebels who threaten their lives than in frustrating the devilish machinations of these same rebels.

So Your Excellency will decide; either the Americans must patiently let themselves be exterminated or they must destroy an iniquitous race which, as long as it draws breath, will not cease to work for our destruction.

Your Excellency was not mistaken in crediting me with feelings of compassion; they are shared by all my compatriots. We might show lenience to the Kaffirs of Africa; but the Spanish tyrants, though it goes against our deepest feelings, force us to retaliate. American justice will always, notwithstanding, distinguish the innocent from the guilty, and Your Excellency may be sure that the former will be treated with the humanity due even to the Spanish nation.

I have the honour to be, Your Excellency, with the highest consideration and respect, your attentive and devoted servant,

*Simón Bolívar*

8

# Firm in the principles of freedom and liberation, subject to justice and the law. A new world order

*Speeches in the popular assembly of the Second Republic, in the church of San Francisco, Caracas, on 2 January 1814.*

Citizens,

Hatred of tyranny took me away from Venezuela when I saw my country in chains for the second time; and from the far borders of the Magdalena River the love of liberty has brought me back to her, overcoming whatever obstacles stood in my path as I came to save my country from the terrors and harassments of the Spaniards. My forces, with triumph at their heels, have occupied the whole country and have destroyed the monstrous enemy. Your chains now bind your oppressors; and the Spanish blood spilled on the battlefield has avenged your slaughtered compatriots.

I have not given you freedom. You owe it to my comrades in arms. Look at their noble wounds, still bleeding; and remember those who have perished in battle. The glory of leading their military exploits was mine. Neither pride nor ambition for power inspired me in this undertaking. Liberty lit this sacred flame in my breast; and the sight of my fellow citizens dying in the outrage of torture, or moaning in chains, made me take up my sword against the enemy. The justice of the cause rallied the most courageous soldiers to my banners, and just Providence granted us victory.

To save you from anarchy and destroy the enemies who tried to uphold the oppressors' faction, I accepted and kept the power of a sovereign. I have given you laws: I have organized the administration of justice and revenues: I have, finally, given you a government.

Citizens: I am not a king. Your representatives should make your laws; the national treasury does not belong to the man who governs you. All those to whom you have entrusted your interests should account to you for the use they have made of them. Judge impartially whether I have used power as a means to my own advancement, or whether I have sacrified my life, my feelings and all my time in order to make you into a nation, and to increase your resources; or, rather, to create them.

I long for the moment when I can hand over this power to the representatives you must designate; and I hope, citizens, that you will relieve me of a responsibility that some of you could worthily assume, allowing me the only honour to which I aspire, that is, to continue to fight your enemies; for I shall never sheathe my sword until the freedom of my country is fully assured.

The glory that you won in driving out your oppressors was eclipsed; your honour was compromised; you lost it under the yoke of the tyrants. You were the victims of pitiless vengeance. The interests of the state were in the hands of rogues. Decide whether your honour has been restored; whether your chains have been broken; whether I have exterminated your enemies; whether I have administered justice; and whether I have organized the funds at the disposal of the Republic.

I offer you three accounts substantiated by those through whom I have exercised supreme power. The three secretaries of state will enable you to see whether you can again appear on the world stage, and will show you how all the nations, which thought you already lost, are once again turning their gaze upon you in admiration as you fight to ensure your continued existence; how these same nations will not be slow to protect and recognize your national flag; how your enemies have been destroyed whenever they have opposed the armies of the Republic; how I, at their head, have defended your inviolable rights; how I have used your funds in your defence; how I have issued regulations to husband and increase them; and how, even in the midst of battle and the heat of the struggle, I have thought of you and of laying the foundations on which to build a happy and honourable nation. I urge you to say, finally, whether the plans adopted are capable of raising the Republic to glory and happiness.

*The Secretary of State, Antonio Muñoz Tebar, then read this text written by Bolívar:*

As ever, with regard to New Granada, it is evident that Your Excellency's policy has been not only to strengthen the bonds of our alliance with her. It has tried for something more: to unite the two regions as one nation. Reasons of the highest importance call for this essential step. The interests of New Granada, which are also our own, and the oft-expressed ideas of other cabinets on this issue oblige Your Excellency to press on with such a measure. Our strength will be the fruit of this union. The enemies of the American cause will tremble before such a formidable force, which, united, will resist them on all sides. Out internal strength and prosperity will reach their peak, when all their component parts are directed by the same impulse to form a great and harmonious whole. As we thus work for our national greatness, let us extinguish all sparks of discord, among ourselves, and prevent what has already once afflicted New Granada, when its constituent regions engaged in a mutually destructive war, to the delight of the savage Spaniard, as he saw his enemy weaken without risk to himself.

During those centuries of ignominy, a continent with a larger population and greater wealth than Spain was the victim of treacherous plotting by the Cabinet in Madrid; if that Cabinet, at a distance of 2,000 leagues and without huge armies, could hold America, from New Mexico to the Magellan Straits, under its harsh despotism, why can there not be a stable union between New Granada and Venezuela? Indeed, why should not the whole of South America be united under a single central government?

We should take care to learn from experience: the sight of Europe, awash with blood in its efforts to redress a balance that is constantly upset, should make us correct our policies and steer clear of such bloody dangers. If our Continent were to be divided into nations, as in Europe, and if the American Government were led by the principles which guide cabinets there, we, too, should suffer the swings of the continental balance and should spill the blood that Europe sacrifices on the altar of its policy.

We now find ourselves in the happy position of being able to steer our policy in the most appropriate direction with no obstacles in the way. You, Your Excellency, to whom America looks up in your victory as the hope of your fellow citizens, are the most suitable person to unite the votes of all the Southern states, and simultaneously to devote yourself to building the great American Nation and guarding it against the evils which the system of separate nations has brought to Europe.

Apart from the balance of power which Europe is seeking where it is least likely to be found, in the midst of war and turmoil, there is another balance, Excellency, which matters to us: the balance of the whole world. The ambition of the European nations has placed the yoke of slavery on the shoulders of the rest of the world; and the rest of the world must try to establish a balance between itself and Europe, so as to destroy the domination of the latter. This is what I call the balance of the whole world, and it should enter into the calculations of American policy.

It is essential that the forces of our nation be capable of successfully resisting any aggression that may be attempted by European ambition; and such giant-like strength, which must oppose that other giant, can be attained only through the union of the whole of South America as one national body, so that one central government can concentrate its great abilities on one single end, that is, to resist with all its might any attacks on it from outside, while within its confines mutual co-operation should increase and flourish, raising us to the heights of power and prosperity.

*Bolívar closed the proceedings with the following words:*

I have always felt confusion and embarrassment when I am called a hero and heaped with so much praise. To risk my life for my country is a duty, and that duty has been done by your brothers on the battlefield: to sacrifice all for liberty, this you have done yourselves, generous compatriots. The feelings that inspire my soul inspire yours likewise. It is Providence, not my heroism, that has worked the miracles you admire.

When madness or cowardice delivered you to the tyrants, I tried to go far away from this unhappy country. I was the traitor who ensnared you and left you to languish in chains. I witnessed the first killings which raised the general alarm. In my indignation I resolved to die of despair or poverty at the ends of the earth rather than witness the violence of the despot. I fled from tyranny, not to save my life or to hide in obscurity, but to risk my life on the battle-field in the quest for glory and liberty. Cartagena, sheltered by the Republican banners, became my refuge. This heroic town was fighting to defend its rights against the oppressor's army which had already crushed almost the whole of the state. I arrived with some of our compatriots at the moment of conflict, and when the Spanish troops were closing in on the capital and calling for its surrender, the forces of Caracas did much to drive our enemies back at all points. Thirst for battle and the desire to avenge the outrages suffered by my compatriots made me enlist then in those ranks, which went on to win resounding victories. New expeditions were undertaken against other provinces. At that time, in Cartagena, I was colonel, inspector and counsellor; nevertheless, I had enlisted as a simple volunteer under the orders of Colonel Labatut, who was marching against Santa Marta. I set no store by rank and distinctions. I aspired to a more honourable destiny: to shed my blood for the liberty of my country.

9

## 'The liberty and independence of the American continent are inevitable'

*Newspaper article by the Liberator, published in the* Gaceta de Caracas *on 28 April 1814. It contains a lively description of his views on political events in Europe and America.*

Reflections on the present state of affairs in Europe and America.

Great events have followed hot upon one another's heels. The northern powers which were dominated or threatened by southern Europe have thrown off the yoke, and we have witnessed the rebirth of those fine examples of policy which had been reduced to nothing because a conqueror had conceived the ambition to rule half the world. Germany, Prussia, Switzerland, Holland, Spain, the Republics of Venice and Genoa, the Papal States—all these had ceased to exist or were under the influence of the overlord. A simultaneous movement by all these powers, encouraged by Great Britain, and much helped by the Emperor of Russia, who was also threatened, mobilized great forces which resisted the onslaught of the conqueror, and at Leipzig the freedom and independence of Europe were finally secured. That memorable event brought a complete change of policy on the part of all cabinets. Those same peoples who had recovered their freedom did not believe they could take advantage of it; the most experienced politicians never thought that, at a stroke, twenty years of glorious conquests could be destroyed; and yet the whole of Europe awoke from the state of lethargy into which it had been sunk by the legions of the warlord; all the people remembered their former political institutions, and once again they had begun to love glory and that state of freedom and independence that is the summit of human happiness. Spain itself has made glorious sacrifices for the freedom and independence which the nations of Europe are defending at such great cost, and which is also dearest to the hearts of all the peoples of Spanish America. History seldom affords such a striking contrast as that to be seen in the policies of the Spanish nation; she wants to be free; she fights for her independence and yet at the same time tries to subjugate peoples who are defending the same sacred rights. Her fruitless efforts have failed in America, for justice prevails on both sides of the world. And this is not the only contrast that distinguishes Spain in Europe. Six years of bloody battles, extraordinary sufferings, unprecedented devastation and alternating humiliation and glory have cost this nation a king, whom it will no longer allow to enter its territory except under conditions and agreements impossible to implement. No longer is he dearly beloved Ferdinand, heaped with the highest praise and so much lauded by the Spanish nation; now he is that stupid idiot Ferdinand, who wants to bring it under French influence; now the most bitter sarcasm is openly directed at the idol they used to adore. That same Ferdinand, whose name has echoed across America in the midst of the horrors of the fiercest fighting, is now none other than the friend of Bonaparte and nothing but a tool for dividing into opposing factions that same nation which has made use of this magic name in America to set the peoples at one another's throats.

But it seems that the age of calamities has come to an end. A most agreeable prospect is now opening before the eyes of the impartial observer. However much the newspapers of the continent of Europe may shout about the re-establishment of the Bourbons in France, not politics, nor the welfare of Europe, nor the cleverness of Bonaparte, nor his influence, can make this fanciful idea a reality. At a general congress the interests of the world are under discussion. The ministers of the warring nations expedite the proceedings; peace is sincerely desired by all the powers; all people are tired of a war to the death, which had spread desolation, hardship and weeping, and left orphans throughout that unhappy continent. All demand it, all desire it, and England itself lends its good offices for the sake of world peace. Favourable results may be expected. But in the midst of all these transactions, what fate will befall America? This problem, which in the past presented immense difficulties, no longer seems difficult to solve. Let us cast a glance at the present situation in Spanish America; let us draw a brief outline of its noble efforts to win independence, and we shall arrive without difficulty at the fairest and most accurate conclusions.

Throughout the vast territory of America, from New Spain to the banks of the River Maule, from the impenetrable mountains of Arauco to the southernmost parts of the continent, we shall find Americans making valiant efforts and sacrifices without number to win their independence. American blood has everywhere been shed, mingling with that of its oppressors, and, in thousands of battles, justice has always triumphed over tyranny. In New Spain, Florida, Venezuela, the Provinces of La Plata, Peru, Chile, Santa Fé—throughout America, the tricoloured banner is triumphant, Americans are victorious, and their military ability should prevail over Spain and prove to the nations of Europe, as they fight for their freedom, that the same divine fire that inspires their self-defence is burning equally fiercely even in these remote countries.

Shall the fine and plentiful resources of this continent, its mines and treasures, continue to be the exclusive possession of an ignoble power which, with its barbarous laws, has made so many millions of its inhabitants miserable for three long centuries? This cannot be, nor would it suit the aims of the trading nations, which will find in America a market for their goods, the respect of the peoples, and immense riches which, freed from the restrictions dictated by the most short-sighted avarice, will improve the lot of both continents.

For centuries we have been waiting for this happy moment— for the hopeful dawn that is now breaking over Spanish America. The end of a disastrous war seems near. Will those powers in whose interest it is to preserve it allow the horrific devastation of this continent to continue? This is equally unthinkable. Spain itself, realizing that it is powerless to subdue America, will abandon its insane undertaking; and thus will save the lives of so many victims whom it sends across the ocean to their deaths on Colombian soil. No, there can be no more expeditions sent to fight against New Spain, Buenos Aires and Venezuela. Other attempts will be doomed to failure. What should we conclude, then, from these great events, as regards the outlook for Europe and America's ability to fight? That peace in Europe is inevitable, as are the liberty and independence of the American continent.

10

# Awareness of the value of social communication. A lesson in journalism and impartiality

*From a letter to the doctor and poet Vicente Salias, editor of the Gaceta de Caracas, written from the army headquarters at San Mateo on 22 February 1814.*

Numbers 39 and 40 of the newspaper you edit contain both official and individual items which have displeased the Liberator; in particular, a note and a letter from a foreigner in which His Excellency the Governor of the island of Curaçao is unjustly insulted, regardless of the consideration due to a leader of his calibre and to a British citizen. The assertion made by the foreigner in his letter is that the Governor helped the besieged town of Puerto Cabello; and as you have been so harsh as to censure him in your columns, when real events—no matter how inopportunely—provide you with material for comment, it would seem that impartiality should oblige you in the same way to give the lie to other slanders, whose falsehood can be seen at a glance.

The accusation to the effect that the Governor of Curaçao greeted Monteverde with salvoes of artillery is not only couched in improper terms, but is also an offensive absurdity. Throughout the civilized world, it is a requirement of protocol and the general custom of nations to greet foreign military leaders and diplomatic ministers with the honours due to them; and in this respect the Governor of Curaçao did no more than his duty in honouring a Spanish general. To insinuate that, instead of being honoured, he should have been court-martialled for his failure to defend Venezuela, is a rebuke that would be better directed at Spain, which should be the judge of Monteverde's conduct, rather than at a leader of the British nation, who was merely under an obligation to pay due respect to a general.

You also inform the public that Marshals Soult and Suchet together routed the Duke of Wellington, a news item as unfounded as it is absurd, since it would be impossible for these French marshals to join forces and, at best, they could only act in association. Other errors and improprieties found in the above issues led the Liberator to consider the withdrawal from circulation of a newspaper which, should it continue in this strain, would be doing more to destroy us in the eyes of the public than to publicize the true spirit of the government. However, he has resolved on the following: (a) that no official document shall be published in the newspaper unless you have received it from the Secretary of State, under strict orders from the Liberator concerning its publication; (b) that no news shall be printed concerning the war on either continent, unless it has been extracted from official documents and not derived from rumours or individual accounts of a situation; (c) that no comments shall be made on action taken by other governments without consultation with the Secretary of State to obtain prior approval from the Liberator, unless they attack the very customs or principles by which nations are governed.

The aim is not to restrict the freedom of the press, nor is the government challenging you regarding the ownership of your newspaper. You may publish in it any opinions you like, as long as you do not threaten the reputation of the Republic by disparaging comments on the authorities of the most highly respected nations.

Besides, we have only this newspaper in which to make ourselves known to the world; it is therefore essential that it represent us faithfully and not distort our views to the detriment of our position.

11

## 'Fight and you will conquer.
## God rewards constancy with victory'

*'The Carúpano Declaration' of 7 September 1814, when Bolívar left Venezuela for his second exile in the West Indies. It is a crucial document, called 'very important' by Bolívar himself. In some ways it foreshadows the Angostura Speech.*

### SIMÓN BOLÍVAR
Liberator of Venezuela and
Commander-in-Chief of its armies

#### TO HIS FELLOW CITIZENS

Citizens:

Unhappy the ruler who is the originator of disasters afflicting his country or crimes committed by it, and who is forced to defend himself in the public forum against the accusations that his fellow citizens have brought against him concerning his conduct; but most fortunate he who, avoiding the pitfalls of war, politics and public disgrace, keeps his honour intact and steps forward, guiltless, to demand from his companions in misfortune a just decision on his innocence.

I have been chosen by the fortunes of war to strike off your chains, and I have also been, as it were, the tool of Providence in filling to the brim your cup of suffering. True, I have brought you peace and freedom, but in the wake of those priceless benefits I have brought war and slavery. Victory led by justice was our constant guide, until we tore the ruins of the great capital of Caracas from the hands of its oppressors. The laurels of New Granada's warriors never withered while they fought against the tyrants of Venezuela, and the soldiers of Caracas were crowned with equal good fortune as they resisted the cruel Spaniards who again tried to subjugate us. If inconstant fate gave victory alternately to our enemies and ourselves, only American peoples were seized by an inconceivable madness that made them take up arms to destroy their liberators and restore the sceptre to their tyrants. Thus, it seems that heaven, for our humiliation and our glory, has allowed our conquerors to be our brothers, and that only our brothers may triumph over us. The

liberating army exterminated the enemy hosts, but could not exterminate people for whose happiness it had fought in hundreds of
battles, and it would have been wrong to do so. It is unjust to
destroy men who do not wish to be free, neither is freedom to be
enjoyed under the sway of arms, contrary to the opinion of fanatics
whose depraved minds make them love chains as if they were social
bonds.

Weep, then, only for your compatriots who, spurred on by the
frenzy of discord, have plunged you into this sea of disasters, the
mere sight of which makes nature tremble, and which it would be
horrible as well as impossible to describe. Your brothers, not the
Spanish, have rent your bosoms, spilt your blood, burned your
homes and condemned you to exile. You should cry out against
those blind slaves who tried to impose on you the chains with which
they themselves are bound; do not rail against those martyrs, ardent
defenders of your liberty, who have spilt their noble blood in every
battle, have faced every danger, and have acted with utter selflessness
to save you from death or shame. Be just, even in your grief, as the
cause which provokes it is just. Citizens, let not your torments
madden you to such a point that you believe your protectors and
friends to be accomplices in imaginary crimes, whether of deliberate
commission or of omission. The leaders of your destinies, as much as
their collaborators, have had no other purpose than that of winning
your lasting happiness, which for them would be everlasting glory.
However, if events have not turned out as they had hoped, and if
unparalleled disasters have frustrated such a praiseworthy undertaking, this has not been through ineptitude or cowardice, but has,
indeed, been the inevitable consequence of a vast project beyond the
strength of any human power. To destroy a government whose
origin is lost in the mists of time; to overturn established principles;
to change customs, to stir up public opinion, and, finally, to establish
liberty in a country of slaves is an ambition as impossible to achieve
quickly as it is beyond the reach of all human power; so that the
reason for our failure to attain our goal is inherent in the nature of
our cause; for, even as justice warrants our audacity in undertaking
this task, so the inadequacy of the means at our disposal renders it
impossible of fulfilment. To vindicate nature outraged by tyranny is
praiseworthy, noble and sublime: nothing is comparable to the grandeur of such an act, and even when desolation and death are the
reward of that glorious endeavour, it should not be condemned. We
should be guided not by what is attainable, but by what is right.

In vain have unparalleled efforts won countless victories, dearly
bought with the blood of our heroic soldiers. A few successes on the

opposing side have toppled us from the pinnacle of glory, while the majority of the people have been led astray by religious fanaticism and seduced by the blandishments of devouring anarchy. Against the torch of liberty, which we have held up to America as the guiding light and end of our endeavours, our enemies have raised the blazing axe of discord and devastation, together with the powerful incentive of usurping the honours and fortune that rightfully belong to men debased by the yoke of servitude and brutalized by the indoctrination of superstition. How could mere political theory prevail, without any support other than its truth and naturalness, against depravity coupled with unbridled licence, limited only by its own powers and suddenly converted, by religious prestige, into a semblance of political virtue and Christian charity? No, common men cannot conceive of the value of the reign of freedom, to the extent of preferring it to blind ambition and vile greed. On this great choice has our fortune depended; it lay in the hands of our compatriots, who, corrupted, have failed us; for the rest, everything else has been the consequence of a decision more dishonourable than fatal, that is to be deplored more for its essence than for its consequences.

It is both wrong and foolish to blame public figures for the vicissitudes which the order of things produces in certain states, for it is not within the power of a general or other leader to hold in check, in one moment of turbulence, collision and clashing opinions, the torrent of human passions which, stirred up by revolutions, increases in proportion to the force resisting it. And even when serious errors or violent passions on the part of the leaders cause repeated damage to the Republic, that same damage should, nevertheless, be judged fairly and its origin looked for in the basic causes of all misfortunes: human frailty, and the rule of chance over all events. Man is the flimsy plaything of Fortune, with whom he can often gamble and win; but he can never rely upon her, for our sphere is not in contact with hers, which is of a much higher order than our own. To pretend that politics and war progress in accordance with our plans, as we grope blindly along, sustained only by the strength of our intentions, and with the limited means at our disposal, is to lay claim to god-like achievements by human methods.

I am very far from holding the mad belief that I am guiltless of the catastrophe afflicting my country; on the contrary, I suffer and am deeply grieved at the thought that I am the unhappy instrument of its dreadful misfortunes; and yet I am innocent, for I have never consciously taken part in voluntary or malicious error, although, on the other hand, I may have acted wrongly and unwisely. I feel in my heart that I am innocent, and this, for me, is the most genuine plea, arrogant and nonsensical as it may seem. For this reason I scorn to answer every accusation that may be levelled at me, in good or bad faith, and defer such a judgement, that my own vindication requires, until I can appear before a tribunal of wise men, who will judge my conduct on my mission to Venezuela honestly and in full knowledge of the facts. I speak of the Supreme Congress of New Granada, of that august body which sent me with its troops to help you, as they did heroically until all perished on the field of honour. It is just and necessary that my public life be carefully examined, and judged with impartiality. It is just and necessary that I satisfy any whom I have offended, and that I be compensated for the erroneous charges of which I am blameless. This great judgement should be pronounced by the sovereign whom I have served: I assure you that it will be done with all due formality, and that my actions will be borne out by indisputable documents. Then you will know whether I have been unworthy of your trust, or whether I deserve the name of Liberator. I swear to you, dear compatriots, that this august title, conferred upon me by your gratitude when I came to strike off your chains, will not be an empty one. I swear to you that, as Liberator or in death, I shall always be worthy of the honour that you bestowed on me; and no human power on earth can stop me in the course I propose to follow, until I can free you for the second time, by that western path drenched in so much blood yet bedecked with so many laurels. Wait, compatriots, for the noble and great people of New Granada who will fly to help you again, to gain new triumphs and to bring you freedom once more, if your own courage has not already won it. This will come to pass, if by your valour alone you can successfully withstand that host of madmen who are ignorant of their own interests and honour; for liberty has never bowed to tyranny. Do not compare your physical strength with that of the enemy, for the fire of the spirit brooks no comparison with material weapons. You are men, they are beasts; you are free, they are slaves. Fight, then, and conquer. God rewards constancy with victory.

Carúpano                                                                          *Bolívar*
7 September 1814

12

# 'Liberty, the only aim worthy of the sacrifice of men's lives'

*A vigorous declaration of political philosophy in an address delivered in Bogotá on 23 January 1815 on the establishment of the Government of the United Provinces of New Granada.*

Your Excellency, President of the Union:

Twice the collapse of the Republic of Venezuela, my country, has forced me to seek refuge in New Granada, which I have twice helped to save. When, during the first civil war, in the midst of the tumult of anarchy and the terror of a savage invasion which menaced these states on all sides, I had the good fortune to find myself among brothers, I paid for their hospitality with my services.

Now, fresh disasters in Venezuela bring me here, and I find the interior of the country again ravaged by dissension. Your Excellency has done me the honour of sending me to put down the insurrection in Cundinamarca, and peace follows division. Dreadful, dreadful division! But pardonable. . . . Allow me, Your Excellency, to trace this calamity to its unhappy origins.

Since the New World was created under the fatal sway of servitude, it has not been able to strike off its chains without breaking its own limbs; such is the inevitable consequence of the evils of servility and the errors of ignorance, the latter state being all the more persistent in that it is based on the most fanatical superstition ever to have disgraced the human race. Tyranny and the Inquisition had reduced to the state of brutes both native Americans and the sons of the Conquistadors who brought them these ill-fated gifts. Thus, what enlightened reason, what political virtue, what uncorrupted morality could be found among us to break the sceptre of oppression and replace it at once with the rule of law, which would be required to establish the rights and duties of the citizens of the new republic? The habit of unquestioning obedience had so stupefied our spirit that it was not possible for us to discover the truth or to know what was right. Our only duty had always been to give way to force; similarly, it was the greatest crime to seek justice and to inquire into natural and human rights. To speculate in science, to work out what was useful and to practise virtue were assaults against tyranny: it was easier to commit them than to be pardoned for

them. Disgrace, exile and death often dogged the talents which our
unfortunate great men acquired, to their own detriment, despite the
mountain of obstacles placed in the way of enlightenment by the
tyrants of this hemisphere.

Never, sir, never has any nation in this world, so generously
endowed with land, wealth and population, suffered such ignominious custody for three centuries, spent in a total absence of awareness,
cut off from world trade or involvement in politics, and plunged in
chaotic darkness. All the nations of the earth have governed themselves, with despotism or freedom; systems both just and unjust have
ruled the great societies, but always imposed by their own citizens,
so that they reaped the good or the evil that they had sown. Glory
or dishonour have rebounded upon their children; but we, have we
been the masters of our country's destiny? Even slavery—have we
been responsible for it? We cannot even claim to have been the
instruments of oppression. Everything on this soil was foreign. Religion, laws, customs, food, clothes—all were from Europe, and we
were not allowed even to imitate anything. We were passive beings,
condemned only to bear with docility the burdens that our masters
heaped so mercilessly upon us, and reduced to the level of wild
beasts. Only the irresistible force of nature has been able to return us
to the world of men: and although our intellect is still weak, we
have taken our first tentative steps on the path of destiny.

Yes, Your Excellency, we have mounted the political stage to
act out the great scene which we, as owners of half the world, are
entitled to perform. Great vistas are opening before us, inviting us to
act for our own sake; and although our first steps have been as timid
as those of an infant, the harsh school of tragic events has strengthened our advance, for by falling we have learned the pitfalls, and
through shipwreck the position of the reefs. We have groped our
way along, for we were blind; but blows have opened our eyes; and
with the experience that we have gained, and our new clearsighted-
ness, why can we not overcome the dangers of war and politics and
win the freedom and glory that await us to crown our sacrifices?
The latter were unavoidable; the road to victory has always been
strewn with sacrifice. The whole of America is red with American
blood. This was necessary in order to wash away such an ancient
stain on our reputation! It is the first blood to be shed with honour
in this unhappy continent, forever the scene of desolation, but never
of liberty. In Mexico, Venezuela, New Granada, Quito, Chile,
Buenos Aires and Peru, heroic and triumphant action has been seen;
everywhere in the New World the blood of its sons has been shed,
now at last for liberty, the only aim worthy of the sacrifice of men's

lives. For liberty, I say, the earth is bristling with weapons, where only a short time ago it was a resting-place for slaves; and if dreadful disasters have befallen the most beautiful provinces and even whole republics, this has been through our fault and not through the power of our enemies.

Our inexperience, Your Excellency, in all departments of government, has depleted our resources and considerably increased the precarious advantages of our enemies, who, profiting by our mistakes, have sown the poisonous seeds of discord among us, so as to destroy those regions that they can no longer hope to possess. They have annihilated the race of original inhabitants to replace it with their own, and to dominate it. . . . Now they are laying waste even inanimate things as, unable to conquer, they give free rein to their innate will to destroy. They want to turn America into a desert and a wilderness; their aim is to exterminate us, but without risking their own safety, since their weapons are the vile passions that they have handed down to us as an inheritance: ruthless ambition, despicable greed, religious prejudice and political error. In this way, without taking any risks themselves, they are deciding our fate.

In spite of such mortal enemies, we see the splendid Republic of Buenos Aires subduing the Kingdom of Peru, Mexico overcoming the tyrants, Chile triumphant, eastern Venezuela free, and New Granada calm, united and threatening its foes.

Today, Your Excellency, you complete your arduous tasks by establishing here in this capital the fatherly government of New Granada, and receiving as a reward for your constancy, honesty and wisdom the blessings of the people, who are indebted to Your Excellency for peace at home and security abroad.

By the justice of the principles that you have adopted, and by the moderation of your blameless conduct, you have not conquered but won over your domestic enemies, who have received more benefits from those opposing them than they hoped to receive from their friends. These wished to set up an isolated republic in the midst of many others, which viewed with horror such a separation, since, by dividing the heart from the rest, it would kill the whole body. You, Your Excellency, have more than answered the prayers of your enemies by making them members of the great family which, bound by ties of brotherhood, is stronger than our oppressors.

You have dispatched your troops and turned your gaze in all directions: the north has been strengthened by General Urdaneta's division; Casanare is awaiting the reinforcements marching towards it under Major Lara; Popayán will be helped in generous measure; Santa Marta and Maracaibo will be liberated by the magnificent army of Venezuelans and Granadians that Your Excellency has done me the honour of placing under my command. This beneficent army will, on its way, strike off the chains that shamefully weigh down all Americans in the north and south of South America. I swear it on the shining honour of the liberators of New Granada and Venezuela; and for you, Your Excellency, either I will give my life, as a final tribute in gratitude, or else I will hoist the flag of New Granada even in the remotest corners of tyranny. In the meantime, Your Excellency will face the world with the majestic attitude of a nation to be respected for the unshakeable solidity of its foundations. By forming a whole of all the hitherto fragmented parts, it can be recognized as a body politic by foreign states which could not negotiate with that freak republic, since its legal authority could not be enforced while the effective power of the provinces had no legality. As these represented none but themselves, they were as divided sisters who did not make up a family.

Although my untimely zeal has carried me away in this address, which should have been only inaugural, I will compound my fault by daring to add that the establishment of supreme courts which will not give their own interpretations of the laws, but will obey them unquestioningly in dispensing justice and so safeguard the honour, lives and fortunes of the citizens, will, I am happy to say, be one of the finest monuments that Your Excellency will raise to the glory thereof. Justice is the queen of the republican virtues, which are the foundation of equality and freedom, and these in turn are the pillars of this establishment.

The organization of the national treasury, which requires from citizens a very small part of their private fortune to augment the public funds that maintain the whole of society, occupies a prominent place in Your Excellency's thoughts; for without revenue there can be no armies, and without armies honour must perish—honour, for which we have already made countless sacrifices, to keep burnished the splendour bought by the lives of so many martyrs and so much material deprivation.

But, Your Excellency, the most important matter calling for your attention is public opinion; it needs the protection of an enlightened government which knows that opinion is the source of the most significant events. Through opinion, Athens guarded her freedom against the whole of Asia. Through opinion, the companions of Romulus conquered the world; and through opinion, England influences all governments, ruling the great oceans like Neptune himself.

Let us tell the people that heaven has given us freedom in order to preserve what is good and honourable, to build a home country where justice will prevail; that this half of the globe belongs to those whom God caused to be born on its soil, and not to the transatlantic deserters, who fled from the blows of tyranny only to establish it here, to our cost. Let our love be a bond uniting all the children of the New World; let hate, vengeance and war depart from us; and let war be waged on our frontiers only against those who deserve it; that is, against tyrants.

Your Excellency, the civil war is ended; peace now reigns in our land; the citizens live in peace, calm under the protection of a just and legal government, and our enemies tremble.

## 13

# A comprehensive and prophetic view of Latin America *

*Bolívar's masterpiece, the 'Jamaica Letter', written in answer to an inquiry from Mr Henry Cullen, in Kingston on 6 September 1815. Published in* The Jamaica Quarterly Journal and Literary Gazette, *Vol. 3, No. 1, July 1818, without mention of the addressee.*

My dear Sir:

I hasten to reply to the letter of the 29th ultimo which you had the honour of sending me and which I received with the greatest satisfaction.

Sensible though I am of the interest you desire to take in the fate of my country, and of your commiseration with her for the tortures she has suffered at the hands of her destroyers, the Spaniards, I am no less sensible of the obligation which your solicitous inquiries

---

*The present English text is substantially that reproduced in the sesquicentennial commemorative edition published by the Ministry of Education of the Republic of Venezuela in 1965, which is taken from *Selected Writings of Bolívar*; compiled by Vicente Lecuna; edited by Harold A. Bierck, Jr; translation by Lewis Bertrand. Published by the Bolivarian Society of Venezuela. New York, The Colonial Press, Inc., 1951. Vol. 1, pp. 103–22. Subheadings have been added within the text by the compiler of the present volume.

about the principal objects of American policy place upon me. Thus, I find myself in conflict between the desire to reciprocate your confidence, which honours me, and the difficulty of rewarding it, for lack of documents and books and because of my own limited knowledge of a land so vast, so varied, and so little known as the New World.

In my opinion it is impossible to answer the questions that you have so kindly posed. Baron von Humboldt himself, with his encyclopedic theoretical and practical knowledge, could hardly do so properly, because, although some of the facts about America and her development are known, I dare say the better part are shrouded in mystery. Accordingly, only conjectures that are more or less approximate can be made, especially with regard to her future and the true plans of the Americans, inasmuch as our continent has within it potentialities for every facet of development revealed in the history of nations, by reason of its physical characteristics and because of the hazards of war and the uncertainties of politics.

As I feel obligated to give due consideration to your esteemed letter and to the philanthropic intentions prompting it, I am impelled to write you these words, wherein you will certainly not find the brilliant thoughts you seek but rather a candid statement of my ideas.

'Three centuries ago,' you say, 'began the atrocities committed by the Spaniards on this great hemisphere of Columbus.' Our age has rejected these atrocities as mythical, because they appear to be beyond the human capacity for evil. Modern critics would never credit them, were it not for the many and frequent documents testifying to these horrible truths. The humane Bishop of Chiapas, that apostle of America, Las Casas, has left to posterity a brief description of these horrors, extracted from the trial records in Seville relating to the cases brought against the *Conquistadores*, and containing the testimony of every respectable person then in the New World together with the charges, which the tyrants made against each other. All this is attested by the foremost historians of that time. Every impartial person has admitted the zeal, sincerity and high character of that friend of humanity, who so fervently and so steadfastly denounced to his government and to his contemporaries the most horrible acts of sanguinary frenzy.

With what a feeling of gratitude I read that passage in your letter in which you say to me: 'I hope that the success which then followed Spanish arms may now turn in favour of their adversaries, the badly oppressed people of South America.' I take this hope as a prediction, if it is justice that determines man's contests. Success will crown our efforts, because the destiny of America has been irrevocably decided; the tie that bound her to Spain has been severed. Only a concept maintained that tie and kept the parts of that immense monarchy together. That which formerly bound them now divides them. The hatred that the Peninsula has inspired in us is greater than the ocean between us. It would be easier to have the two continents meet than to reconcile the spirits of the two countries. The habit of obedience; a community of interest, of understanding, of religion; mutual goodwill; a tender regard for the birthplace and good name of our forefathers; in short, all that gave rise to our hopes, came to us from Spain. As a result there was born a principle of affinity that seemed eternal, notwithstanding the misbehaviour of our rulers which weakened that sympathy, or, rather, that bond enforced by the domination of their rule. At present the contrary attitude persists: we are threatened with the fear of death, dishonour, and every harm; there is nothing we have not suffered at the hands of that unnatural stepmother—Spain. The veil has been torn asunder. We have already seen the light, and it is not our desire to be thrust back into darkness. The chains have been broken; we have been freed, and now our enemies seek to enslave us anew. For this reason America fights desperately, and seldom has desperation failed to achieve victory.

Because successes have been partial and spasmodic, we must not lose faith. In some regions the Independents triumph, while in others the tyrants have the advantage. What is the end result? Is not the entire New World in motion, armed for defence? We have but to look around us on this hemisphere to witness a simultaneous struggle at every point.

The war-like state of the La Plata River provinces has purged that territory and led their victorious armies to Upper Peru, arousing Arequipa and worrying the royalists in Lima. Nearly one million inhabitants there now enjoy liberty.

The territory of Chile, populated by 800,000 souls, is fighting the enemy who is seeking her subjugation; but to no avail, because those who long ago put an end to the conquests of this enemy, the free and indomitable Araucanians, are their neighbours and compatriots. Their sublime example is proof to those fighting in Chile that a people who love independence will eventually achieve it.

The viceroyalty of Peru, whose population approaches a million and a half inhabitants, without doubt suffers the greatest subjection and is obliged to make the most sacrifices for the royal cause; and, although the thought of co-operating with that part of America may be vain, the fact remains that it is not tranquil, nor is it capable of restraining the torrent that threatens most of its provinces.

New Granada, which is, so to speak, the heart of America, obeys a general government, save for the territory of Quito which is held only with the greatest difficulty by its enemies, as it is strongly devoted to the country's cause; and the provinces of Panama and Santa Maria endure, not without suffering, the tyranny of their masters. Two and a half million people inhabit New Granada and are actually defending that territory against the Spanish army under General Morillo, who will probably suffer defeat at the impregnable fortress of Cartagena. But should he take that city, it will be at the price of heavy casualties, and he will then lack sufficient forces to subdue the unrestrained and brave inhabitants of the interior.

With respect to heroic and hapless Venezuela, events there have moved so rapidly and the devastation has been such that it is reduced to frightful desolation and almost absolute indigence, although it was once among the fairest regions that are the pride of America. Its tyrants govern a desert, and they oppress only those unfortunate survivors who, having escaped death, lead a precarious existence. A few women, children and old men are all that remain. Most of the men have perished rather than be slaves; those who survive continue to fight furiously on the fields and in the inland towns, until they expire or hurl into the sea those who, insatiable in their thirst for blood and crimes, rival those first monsters who wiped out America's primitive race. Nearly a million persons formerly dwelt in Venezuela, and it is no exaggeration to say that one out of four has succumbed either to the land, sword, hunger, plague, flight or privation, all consequences of the war, save the earthquake.

According to Baron von Humboldt, New Spain, including Guatemala, had 7,800,000 inhabitants in 1808. Since that time, the insurrection, which has shaken virtually all of her provinces, has appreciably reduced that apparently correct figure, for over a million men have perished, as you can see in the report of Mr Walton, who describes faithfully the bloody crimes committed in that abundant kingdom. There the struggle continues by dint of human and every other type of sacrifice, for the Spaniards spare nothing that might enable them to subdue those who have had the misfortune of being born on this soil, which appears to be destined to flow with the blood of its offspring. In spite of everything, the Mexicans will be free. They have embraced the country's cause, resolved to avenge their forefathers or follow them to the grave. Already they say with Raynal: The time has come at last to repay the Spaniards torture for torture and to drown that race of annihilators in its own blood or in the sea.

The islands of Puerto Rico and Cuba, with a combined population of perhaps 700,000 to 800,000 souls, are the most tranquil possessions of the Spaniards, because they are not within range of contact with the Independents. But are not the people of those islands Americans? Are they not maltreated? Do they not desire a better life?

This picture represents, on a military map, an area of 2,000 longitudinal and 900 latitudinal leagues at its greatest point, wherein 16 million Americans either defend their rights or suffer repression at the hands of Spain, which, although once the world's greatest empire, is now too weak, with what little is left her, to rule the new hemisphere or even to maintain herself in the old. And shall Europe, the civilized, the merchant, the lover of liberty, allow an aged serpent, bent only on satisfying its venomous rage, to devour the fairest part of our globe? What! Is Europe deaf to the clamour of her own interests? Has she no eyes to see justice? Has she grown so hardened as to become insensible? The more I ponder these questions, the more I am confused. I am led to think that America's disappearance is desired; but this is impossible because all Europe is not Spain. What madness for our enemy to hope to reconquer America when she has no navy, no funds, and almost no soldiers! Those troops which she has are scarcely adequate to keep her own people in a state of forced obedience and to defend herself from her neighbours. On the other hand, can that nation carry on the exclusive commerce of one half of the world when it lacks manufactures, agricultural products, crafts and sciences, and even a policy? Assume that this mad venture were successful, and further assume that pacification ensued, would not the sons of the Americans of today, together with the sons of the European *reconquistadores* twenty years hence, conceive the same patriotic designs that are now being fought for?

### The general worth of American liberty

Europe could do Spain a service by dissuading her from her rash obstinacy, thereby at least sparing her the costs she is incurring and the blood she is expending. And if she will fix her attention on her own precincts she can build her prosperity and power upon more solid foundations than doubtful conquests, precarious commerce, and forceful exactions from remote and powerful peoples. Europe herself, as a matter of common-sense policy, should have prepared and executed the project of American independence, not alone because the world balance of power so necessitated, but also because this is the legitimate and certain means through which Europe can acquire overseas commercial establishments. A Europe which is not moved by the violent passions of vengeance, ambition and greed, as is Spain, would seem to be entitled, by all the rules of equity, to make clear to Spain where her best interests lie.

All of the writers who have treated the matter agree on this point. Consequently, we have had reason to hope that the civilized nations would hasten to our aid in order that we might achieve that which must prove to be advantageous to both hemispheres. How vain has been this hope! Not only the Europeans but even our brothers of the North have been apathetic bystanders in this struggle which, by its very essence, is the most just, and in its consequences the most noble and vital of any which have been raised in ancient or in modern times. Indeed, can the far-reaching effects of freedom for the hemisphere which Columbus discovered ever be calculated?

'The criminal action of Bonaparte,' you say, 'in seizing Charles IV and Ferdinand VII, the monarchs of that nation which three centuries ago treacherously imprisoned two rulers of South America, is a most evident sign of divine retribution, and, at the same time, positive proof that God espouses the just cause of the Americans and will grant them independence.'

It appears that you allude to Montezuma, the ruler of Mexico, who was imprisoned by Cortés, and, according to Herrera, was by him slain, although Solís states that it was the work of the people; and to Atahualpa, the Inca of Peru, destroyed by Francisco Pizarro and Diego Almagro. The fate of the monarchs of Spain and of America is too different to admit a comparison. The former were treated with dignity and were kept alive, and eventually they recovered their freedom and their throne; whereas the latter suffered unspeakable tortures and the vilest of treatment. Quauhtemotzin [Guatémoc], Montezuma's successor, was treated as an emperor and crowned, but in ridicule and not in honour, so that he might suffer this humiliation before being put to torture. A like treatment was accorded the ruler of Michoacán, Catzontzin; the *zipa* of Bogotá, and all the other *toquis, imas, zipas, ulmenes, caciques,* and other Indian dignitaries who succumbed before Spain's might.

The case of Ferdinand VII more nearly parallels what happened in Chile in 1535 to the *ulmen* of Copiapó, then ruler of that region. The Spaniard Almagro pretended, like Bonaparte, to espouse the cause of the legitimate sovereign; he therefore called the other a usurper, as did Ferdinand in Spain. Almagro appeared to re-establish the legitimate sovereign in his estates but ended by shackling the hapless *ulmen* and feeding him to the flames without so much as hearing his defence. This is similar to the case of Ferdinand VII and his usurper: Europe's monarchs, however, only suffer exile; the *ulmen* of Chile is barbarously put to death.

'These several months,' you add, 'I have given much thought to the situation in America and to her hopes for the future. I have a great interest in her development, but I lack adequate information respecting her present state and the aspirations of her people. I greatly desire to know about the politics of each province, also its peoples, and whether they desire a republic or a monarchy; or whether they seek to form one unified republic or a single monarchy? If you could supply me with this information or suggest the sources I might consult, I should deem it a very special favour.'

Generous souls always interest themselves in the fate of a people who strive to recover the rights to which the Creator and Nature have entitled them, and one must indeed be wedded to error and passion not to harbour this noble sentiment. You have given thought to my country and are concerned in its behalf, and for your kindness I am warmly grateful.

I have listed the population, which is based on more or less exact data, but which a thousand circumstances render deceiving. This inaccuracy cannot easily be remedied, because most of the inhabitants live in rural areas and are often nomadic; they are farmers, herders, and migrants, lost amidst thick giant forests, solitary plains, and isolated by lakes and mighty streams. Who is capable of compiling complete statistics of a land like this? Moreover, the tribute paid by the Indians, the punishments of the slaves, the first fruits of the harvest, tithes and taxes levied on farmers, and other impositions have driven the poor Americans from their homes. This is not to mention the war of extermination that has already taken a toll of nearly an eighth part of the population and frightened another large part away. All in all, the difficulties are insuperable, and the tally is likely to show only half the true count.

It is even most difficult to foresee the future fate of the New World, to set down its political principles, or to prophesy what manner of government it will adopt. Every conjecture relative to America's future is, I feel, pure speculation. When mankind was in its infancy, steeped in uncertainty, ignorance and error, was it possible to foresee what system it would adopt for its preservation? Who could venture to say that a certain nation would be a republic or a monarchy; this nation great, that nation small? To my way of thinking, such is our own situation. We are a small human race of our own. We inhabit a world apart, separated by broad seas. We are young in the ways of almost all the arts and sciences, although, in a certain manner, we are old in the ways of civilized society. I look upon the present state of America as similar to that of Rome after its fall. Each part of Rome adopted a political system conforming to its interest and situation or was led by the individual ambitions of certain chiefs, dynasties, or associations. But this important difference exists: those dispersed parts later re-established their ancient nations, subject to the changes imposed by circumstances or events. But we scarcely retain a vestige of what once was; we are, moreover, neither Indian nor European, but a species midway between the legitimate pro-prietors of this country and the Spanish usurpers. In short, though American by birth we derive our rights from Europe, and we have to assert these rights against the rights of the natives, and at the same time we must defend ourselves against the invaders. This places us in a most extraordinary and involved situation. Notwithstanding that it is a type of divination to predict the result of the political course which America is pursuing, I shall venture some conjectures which, of course, are coloured by my enthusiasm and dictated by rational desires rather than by reasoned calculations.

The role of the inhabitants of the American hemisphere has for centuries been purely passive. Politically they were non-existent. We are still in a position lower than slavery, and therefore it is more difficult for us to rise to the enjoyment of freedom. Permit me these transgressions in order to establish the issue. States are slaves because of either the nature or the misuse of their constitutions; a people is therefore enslaved when the government, by its nature or its vices, infringes on and usurps the rights of the citizen or subject. Applying these principles, we find that America was denied not only its free-dom but even an active and effective tyranny. Let me explain. Under absolutism there are no recognized limits to the exercise of govern-mental powers. The will of the great sultan, khan, bey and other despotic rulers is the supreme law, carried out more or less arbitrarily by the lesser pashas, khans, and satraps of Turkey and Persia, who have an organized system of oppression in which inferiors participate according to the authority vested in them. To them is entrusted the administration of civil, military, political, religious and tax matters. But, after all is said and done, the rulers of Ispahan are Persians; the viziers of the Grand Turk are Turks; and the sultans of Tartary are Tartars. China does not bring its military leaders and scholars from the land of Genghis Khan, her conqueror, notwithstanding that the Chinese of today are the lineal descendants of those who were reduced to subjection by the ancestors of the present-day Tartars.

How different is our situation! We have been harassed by a conduct which has not only deprived us of our rights but has kept us in a sort of permanent infancy with regard to public affairs. If we could at least have managed our domestic affairs and our internal administration, we could have acquainted ourselves with the processes and mechanics of public affairs. We should also have enjoyed a personal consideration, thereby commanding a certain unconscious respect from the people, which is so necessary to preserve amidst revolutions. That is why I say we have even been deprived of an active tyranny, since we have not been permitted to exercise its functions.

## The real colonial situation

Americans today, and perhaps to a greater extent than ever before, who live within the Spanish system, occupy a position in society no better than that of serfs destined for labour, or at best they have no more status than that of mere consumers. Yet even this status is surrounded with galling restrictions, such as being forbidden to grow European crops, or to store products which are royal monopolies, or to establish factories of a type the Peninsula itself does not possess. To this add the exclusive trading privileges, even in articles of prime necessity, and the barriers between American provinces, designed to prevent all exchange of trade, traffic and understanding. In short, do you wish to know what our future held? Simply the cultivation of the fields of indigo, grain, coffee, sugar-cane, cacao, and cotton; cattle raising on the broad plains; hunting wild game in the jungles; digging in the earth to mine its gold which can never sate that greedy nation.

So negative was our existence that I can find nothing comparable in any other civilized society, examine as I may the entire history of time and the politics of all nations. Is it not an outrage and a violation of human rights to expect a land so splendidly endowed, so vast, rich, and populous, to remain merely passive?

As I have just explained, we were cut off and, as it were, removed from the world in relation to the science of government and administration of the state. We were never viceroys or governors, save in the rarest of instances; seldom archbishops and bishops; diplomats never; as military men, only subordinates; as nobles, without royal privileges. In brief, we were neither magistrates nor financiers and seldom merchants—all in flagrant contradiction to our institutions.

Emperor Charles V made a pact with the discoverers, conquerors, and settlers of America, and this, as Guerra puts it, is our social contract. The monarchs of Spain made a solemn agreement with them, to be carried out on their own account and at their own risk, expressly prohibiting them from drawing on the royal treasury. In return, they were made the lords of the land, entitled to organize the public administration and act as the court of last appeal, together with many other exemptions and privileges that are too numerous to mention. The King committed himself never to alienate the American provinces, inasmuch as he had no jurisdiction but that of sovereign domain. Thus, for themselves and their descendants, the *conquistadores* possessed what were tantamount to feudal holdings. Yet there are explicit laws respecting employment in civil, ecclesiastical, and tax-raising establishments. These laws favour, almost exclusively, the natives of the country who are of Spanish extraction. Thus, by an outright violation of the laws and the existing agreements, those born in America have been despoiled of their constitutional rights as embodied in the code.

From what I have said it is easy to deduce that America was not prepared to secede from the mother country; this secession was suddenly brought about by the effect of the illegal concessions of Bayonne and the unrighteous war which the Regency unjustly and illegally declared on us. Concerning the nature of the Spanish governments, their stringent and hostile decrees, and their long record of desperate behaviour, you can find articles of real merit, by Mr Blanco, in the newspaper *El Español*. Since this aspect of our history is there very well treated, I shall do no more than refer to it.

The Americans have risen rapidly without previous knowledge of, and, what is more regrettable, without previous experience in public affairs, to enact upon the world stage the eminent roles of legislator, magistrate, minister of the treasury, diplomat, general, and every position of authority, supreme or subordinate, that comprises the hierarchy of a fully organized state.

When the French invasion, stopped only by the walls of Cadiz, routed the fragile governments of the Peninsula, we were left orphans. Prior to that invasion, we had been left to the mercy of a foreign usurper. Thereafter, the justice due us was dangled before our eyes, raising hopes that only came to nought. Finally, uncertain of our destiny, and facing anarchy for want of a legitimate, just, and liberal government, we threw ourselves headlong into the chaos of revolution. Attention was first given to obtaining domestic security against enemies within our midst, and then it was extended to the procuring of external security. Authorities were set up to replace those we had deposed, empowered to direct the course of our revolution and to take full advantage of the fortunate turn of events; thus we were able to found a constitutional government worthy of our century and adequate to our situation.

The first steps of all the new governments are marked by the establishment of juntas of the people. These juntas speedily draft rules for the calling of congresses, which produce great changes. Venezuela erected a democratic and federal government, after declaring for the rights of man. A system of checks and balances was established, and general laws were passed granting civil liberties, such as freedom of the press and others. In short, an independent government was created. New Granada uniformly followed the political institutions and reforms introduced by Venezuela, taking as the fundamental basis of her constitution the most elaborate federal system ever to be brought into existence. Recently the powers of the chief executive have been increased, and he has been given all the powers that are properly his. I understand that Buenos Aires and Chile have followed the same line of procedure, but, as the distance is so great and documents are so few and the news report so unreliable, I shall not attempt even briefly to sketch their progress.

Events in Mexico have been too varied, confused, swift and unhappy to follow clearly the course of that revolution. We lack, moreover, the necessary documentary information to enable us to form a judgement. The Independents of Mexico, according to our information, began their insurrection in September 1810, and a year later they erected a central government in Zitacuaro, where a national junta was installed under the auspices of Ferdinand VII in whose name the government was carried on. The events of the war caused this junta to move from place to place; and, having undergone such modifications as events have determined, it may still be in existence.

It is reported that a generalissimo or dictator has been appointed and that he is the illustrious General Morelos, though others mention the celebrated General Rayón. It is certain that one or both of these two great men exercise the supreme authority in that country. And recently a constitution has been created as a framework of government. In March 1812, the government, then residing in Zultepec, submitted a plan for peace and war to the Viceroy of Mexico that had been conceived with the utmost wisdom. It acclaimed the law of nations and established the principles that are true and beyond question. The junta proposed that the war be fought as between brothers and countrymen; that it need not be more cruel than a war between foreign nations; that the rules of nations and of war, held inviolable even by infidels and barbarians, must be more binding upon Christians, who are, moreover, subject to one sovereign and to the same laws; that prisoners not be treated as guilty of *lèse majesté*, nor those surrendering arms slain, but rather held as hostages for exchange; and that peaceful towns not be put to fire and sword. The junta concluded its proposal by warning that if this plan were not accepted rigorous reprisals would be taken. This proposal was received with scorn: no reply was made to the national junta. The original communications were publicly burned in the plaza in Mexico City by the executioner, and the Spaniards have continued the war of extermination with their accustomed fury; meanwhile, the Mexicans and the other American nations have refrained from instituting a war to the death respecting Spanish prisoners. Here it can be seen that as a matter of expediency an appearance of allegiance to the King and even to the Constitution of the monarchy has been maintained. The national junta, it appears, is absolute in the exercise of the legislative, executive and judicial powers, and its membership is very limited.

Events in Costa Firme have proved that institutions which are wholly representative are not suited to our character, customs and present knowledge. In Caracas party spirit arose in the societies, assemblies, and popular elections; these parties led us back into slavery. Thus, while Venezuela has been the American republic with the most advanced political institutions, she has also been the clearest example of the inefficacy of the democratic and federal system for our new-born states. In New Granada, the large number of excess powers held by the provincial governments and the lack of centralization in the general government have reduced that fair country to her present state. For this reason her foes, though weak, have been able to hold out against all odds. As long as our countrymen do not acquire the abilities and political virtues that distinguish our brothers of the north, wholly popular systems, far from working to our advantage, will, I greatly fear, bring about our downfall. Unfortunately, these traits, to the degree in which they are required, do not appear to be within our reach. On the contrary, we are dominated by the vices that one learns under the rule of a nation like Spain, which has only distinguished itself in ferocity, ambition, vindictiveness and greed.

It is harder, Montesquieu has written, to release a nation from servitude than to enslave a free nation. This truth is proved by the annals of all times, which reveal that most free nations have been put under the yoke, but very few enslaved nations have recovered their liberty. Despite the convictions of history, South Americans have made efforts to obtain liberal, even perfect, institutions, doubtless out of that instinct to aspire to the greatest possible happiness, which, common to all men, is bound to follow in civil societies founded on the principles of justice, liberty and equality. But are we capable of maintaining in proper balance the difficult charge of a republic? Is it conceivable that a newly emancipated people can soar to the heights of liberty, and, unlike Icarus, neither have its wings melt nor fall into an abyss? Such a marvel is inconceivable and without precedent. There is no reasonable probability to bolster our hopes.

## A prophetic view

More than anyone, I desire to see America fashioned into the greatest nation in the world, greatest not so much by virtue of her area and wealth as by her freedom and glory. Although I seek perfection for the government of my country, I cannot persuade myself that the New World can, at the moment, be organized as a great republic. Since it is impossible, I dare not desire it; yet much less do I desire to have all America a monarchy because this plan is not only impracticable but also impossible. Wrongs now existing could not be righted, and our emancipation would be fruitless. The American states need the care of paternal governments to heal the sores and wounds of despotism and war. The parent country, for example, might be Mexico, the only country fitted for the position by her intrinsic strength, and without such power there can be no parent country. Let us assume it were to be the Isthmus of Panama, the most central point of this vast continent. Would not all parts continue in their lethargy and even in their present disorder? For a single government to infuse life into the New World; to put into use all the resources for public prosperity; to improve, educate, and perfect the New World, that government would have to possess the authority of a god, much less the knowledge and virtues of mankind.

The party spirit that today keeps our states in constant agitation would assume still greater proportions were a central power established, for that power—the one force capable of checking this agitation—would not tolerate the preponderance of leaders at the metropolis, for they would regard these leaders as so many tyrants. Their resentments would attain such heights that they would compare the latter to the hated Spaniards. Any such monarchy would be a misshapen colossus that would collapse of its own weight at the slightest disturbance.

Mr de Pradt has wisely divided America into fifteen or seventeen mutually independent states, governed by as many monarchs. I am in agreement on the first suggestion, as America can well tolerate seventeen nations; as to the second, though it could easily be achieved, it could serve no purpose. Consequently, I do not favour American monarchies. My reasons are these. The well-understood interest of a republic is limited to the matter of its preservation, prosperity and glory. Republicans, because they do not desire powers which represent a directly contrary viewpoint, have no reason for expanding the boundaries of their nation to the detriment of their own resources, solely for the purpose of having their neighbours share a liberal constitution. They would not acquire rights or secure any advantage by conquering their neighbours, unless they were to make them colonies, conquered territory, or allies, after the example of Rome. But such thought and action are directly contrary to the principles of justice which characterize republican systems; and, what is more, they are in direct opposition to the interests of their citizens, because a state, too large of itself or together with its dependencies, ultimately falls into decay. Its free government becomes a tyranny. The principles that should preserve the government are disregarded, and finally it degenerates into despotism. The distinctive feature of small republics is permanence: that of large republics varies, but always with a tendency towards empire. Almost all small republics have had long lives. Among the larger republics, only Rome lasted for several centuries, for its capital was a republic. The rest of her dominions were governed by divers laws and institutions.

The policy of a king is very different. His constant desire is to increase his possessions, wealth, and authority; and with justification, for his power grows with every acquisition, both with respect to his neighbours and his own vassals, who fear him because his power is as formidable as his empire, which he maintains by war and conquest. For these reasons I think that the Americans, being anxious for peace, science, art, commerce and agriculture, would prefer republics to kingdoms. And, further, it seems to me that these desires conform with the aims of Europe.

We know little about the opinions prevailing in Buenos Aires, Chile and Peru. Judging by what seeps through and by conjecture, Buenos Aires will have a central government in which the military, as a result of its internal dissensions and external wars, will have the upper hand. Such a constitutional system will necessarily degenerate into an oligarchy or a monocracy, with a variety of restrictions the exact nature of which no one can now foresee. It would be unfortunate if this situation were to follow, because the people there deserve a more glorious destiny.

The Kingdom of Chile is destined, by the nature of its location, by the simple and virtuous character of its people, and by the example of its neighbours, the proud republicans of Arauco, to enjoy the blessings that flow from the just and gentle laws of a republic. If any American republic is to have a long life, I am inclined to believe it will be Chile. There the spirit of liberty has never been extinguished; the vices of Europe and Asia arrived too late or not at all to corrupt the customs of that distant corner of the world. Its area is limited; and, as it is remote from other peoples, it will always remain free from contamination. Chile will not alter her laws, ways and practices. She will preserve her uniform political and religious views. In a word, it is possible for Chile to be free.

Peru, on the contrary, contains two factors that clash with every just and liberal principle: gold and slaves. The former corrupts everything; the latter are themselves corrupt. The soul of a serf can seldom really appreciate true freedom. Either he loses his head in uprisings or his self-respect in chains. Although these remarks would be applicable to all America, I believe that they apply with greater justice to Lima, for the reasons I have given and because of the co-operation she rendered her masters against her own brothers, those illustrious sons of Quito, Chile and Buenos Aires. It is plain that he who aspires to obtain liberty will at least attempt to secure it. I imagine that in Lima the rich will not tolerate democracy, nor will the freed slaves and *pardos* accept aristocracy. The former will prefer the tyranny of a single man, to avoid the tumult of rebellion and to provide, at least, a peaceful system. If Peru intends to recover her independence, she has much to do.

*Confidence in the triumph of the cause*

From the foregoing, we can draw these conclusions: The American provinces are fighting for their freedom, and they will ultimately succeed. Some provinces as a matter of course will form federal and some central republics; the larger areas will inevitably establish monarchies, some of which will fare so badly that they will disintegrate in either present or future revolutions. To consolidate a great monarchy will be no easy task, but it will be utterly impossible to consolidate a great republic.

It is a grandiose idea to think of consolidating the New World into a single nation, united by pacts into a single bond. It is reasoned that, as these parts have a common origin, language, customs, and religion, they ought to have a single government to permit the newly formed states to unite in a confederation. But this is not possible. Actually, America is separated by climatic differences, geographic diversity, conflicting interests, and dissimilar characteristics. How beautiful it would be if the Isthmus of Panama could be for us what the Isthmus of Corinth was for the Greeks! Would to God that some day we may have the good fortune to convene there an august assembly of representatives of republics, kingdoms and empires to deliberate upon the high interests of peace and war with the nations of the other three-quarters of the globe. This type of organization may come to pass in some happier period of our regeneration. But any other plan, such as that of Abbé St Pierre, who in laudable delirium, conceived the idea of assembling a European congress to decide the fate and interests of those nations, would be meaningless.

Among the popular and representative systems, I do not favour the federal system. It is over-perfect, and it demands political virtues and talents far superior to our own. For the same reason I reject a monarchy that is part aristocracy and part democracy, although with such a government England has achieved much fortune and splendour. Since it is not possible for us to select the most perfect and complete form of government, let us avoid falling into demagogic anarchy or monocratic tyranny. These opposite extremes would only wreck us on similar reefs of misfortune and dishonour; hence, we must seek a mean between them. I say: Do not adopt the best system of government, but the one that is most likely to succeed.

By the nature of their geographic location, wealth, population and character, I expect that the Mexicans, at the outset, intend to establish a representative republic in which the executive will have great powers. These will be concentrated in one person, who, if he discharges his duties with wisdom and justice, should almost certainly maintain his authority for life. If through incompetence or violence he should excite a popular revolt and it should be successful, this same executive power would then, perhaps, be distributed among the members of an assembly. If the dominant party is military or aristocratic, it will probably demand a monarchy that would be limited and constitutional at the outset, and would later inevitably degenerate into an absolute monarchy; for it must be admitted that there is nothing more difficult in the political world than the maintenance of a limited monarchy. Moreover, it must also be agreed that only a people as patriotic as the English are capable of controlling the authority of a king and of sustaining the spirit of liberty under the rule of sceptre and crown.

The states of the Isthmus of Panama, as far as Guatemala, will perhaps form a confederation. Because of their magnificent position

between two mighty oceans, they may in time become the emporium of the world. Their canals will shorten the distances throughout
the world, strengthen commercial ties between Europe, America and
Asia, and bring to that happy area tribute from the four quarters of
the globe. There some day, perhaps, the capital of the world may be
located—reminiscent of the Emporer Constantine's claim that Byzantium was the capital of the ancient world.

New Granada will unite with Venezuela, if they can agree to
the establishment of a central republic. Their capital may be Maracaibo or a new city to be named Las Casas (in honour of that
humane hero) to be built on the borders of the two countries, in the
excellent port area of Bahía-Honda. This location, though little
known, is the most advantageous in all respects. It is readily accessi-
ble, and its situation is so strategic that it can be made impregnable.
It has a fine, healthful climate, a soil as suitable for agriculture as for
cattle raising, and a superabundance of good timber. The Indians
living there can be civilized, and our territorial possessions could be
increased with the acquisition of the Goajora Peninsula. This nation
should be called Colombia as a just and grateful tribute to the discoverer of our hemisphere. Its government might follow the English
pattern, except that in place of a king there will be an executive who
will be elected, at most, for life, but his office will never be hereditary, if a republic is desired. There will be a hereditary legislative
chamber or senate. This body can interpose itself between the violent
demands of the people and the great powers of the government
during periods of political unrest. The second representative body
will be a legislature with restrictions no greater than those of the
lower house in England. The Constitution will draw on all systems
of government, but I do not want it to partake of all their vices. As
Colombia is my country, I have an undeniable right to desire for her
that form of government which, in my opinion, is best. It is very
possible that New Granada may not care to recognize a central
government, because she is greatly addicted to federalism; in such
event, she will form a separate state which, if it endures, may prosper,
because of its great and varied resources.

'Great and beneficial changes', you say, 'can frequently be
brought about through the efforts of individuals.' The South Americans have a tradition to this effect: when Quetzalcoatl, the Hermes
or Buddha of South America, gave up his ministry and left his
people, he promised them he would return at an ordained time to
re-establish his government and revive their prosperity. Does not
this tradition foster a conviction that he may shortly reappear? Can
you imagine the result if an individual were to appear among these

people, bearing the features of Quetzalcoatl, their Buddha of the forest, or those of Mercury, of whom other nations have spoken? Do you suppose that this would affect all regions of America? Is it not unity alone that is needed to enable them to expel the Spaniards, their troops, and the supporters of corrupt Spain and to establish in these regions a powerful empire with a free government and benevolent laws?

Like you, I believe that the specific actions of individuals can produce general results, especially in revolutions. But is that hero, that great prophet or God of Anáhuac, Quetzalcoatl, capable of effecting the prodigious changes that you propose? This esteemed figure is not well known, if at all, by the Mexican people: such is the fate of the defeated, even if they be gods. Historians and writers, it is true, have undertaken a careful investigation of his origin, the truth or falsity of his doctrine, his prophesies, and the account of his departure from Mexico. Whether he was an apostle of Christ, or a pagan, is openly debated. Some would associate his name with St Thomas; others with the Feathered Serpent; while still others say he is the famous prophet of Yucatán, Chilan-Cambal. In a word, most Mexican authors, polemicists, and secular historians have discussed, at greater or lesser length, the question of the true character of Quetzalcoatl. The fact is, according to the historian, Father Acosta, that he established a religion which, in its rites, dogmas, and mysteries, bore a remarkable similarity to the religion of Jesus, the faith that it probably most resembles. Nevertheless, many Catholic writers have tried to dismiss the idea that he was a true prophet, and they refuse to associate him with St Thomas, as other celebrated writers have done. The general opinion is that Quetzalcoatl was a divine law-giver among the pagan peoples of Anáhuac; that their great Montezuma was his lieutenant, deriving his power from that divinity. Hence it may be inferred that our Mexicans would not follow the pagan Quetzalcoatl, however ingratiating the guise in which he might appear, for they profess the most intolerant and exclusive of all regions.

Happily, the leaders of the Mexican independence movement have made use of this fanaticism to excellent purpose by proclaiming the famous Virgin of Guadalupe the Queen of the Patriots, invoking her name in all difficult situations and placing her image on their banners. As a result, political enthusiasms have been commingled with religion, thus producing an intense devotion to the sacred cause of liberty. The veneration of this image in Mexico is greater than the exaltation that the most sagacious prophet could inspire.

Surely unity is what we need to complete our work of regeneration. The division among us, nevertheless, is nothing extraordinary, for it is characteristic of civil wars to form two parties, conservatives and reformers. The former are commonly the more numerous, because the weight of habit induces obedience to established powers; the latter are always fewer in number although more vocal and learned. Thus, the physical mass of the one is counterbalanced by the moral force of the other; the contest is prolonged, and the results are uncertain. Fortunately, in our case, the mass has followed the learned.

I shall tell you with what we must provide ourselves in order to expel the Spaniards and to found a free government. It is union, obviously; but such union will come about through sensible planning and well-directed actions rather than by divine magic. America stands together because it is abandoned by all other nations. It is isolated in the centre of the world. It has no diplomatic relations, nor does it receive any military assistance; instead, America is attacked by Spain, which has more military supplies than any we can possibly acquire through furtive means.

When success is not assured, when the state is weak, and when results are distantly seen, all men hesitate; opinion is divided, passions rage, and the enemy fans these passions in order to win an easy victory because of them. As soon as we are strong and under the guidance of a liberal nation which will lend us her protection, we will achieve accord in cultivating the virtues and talents that lead to glory. Then will we march majestically toward that great prosperity for which South America is destined. Then will those sciences and arts which, born in the East, have enlightened Europe, wing their way to a free Colombia, which will cordially bid them welcome.

Such, Sir, are the thoughts and observations that I have the honour to submit to you, so that you may accept or reject them according to their merit. I beg you to understand that I have expounded them because I do not wish to appear discourteous and not because I consider myself competent to enlighten you concerning these matters.

I am, Sir, etc., etc.

*Bolívar*

14

# On Latin American problems,
# and in criticism of the general indifference
# shown towards his efforts

*From reflections addressed to the publisher of* The Royal Gazette, *during his exile in Jamaica, where he was nearly assassinated. Kingston, 28 September 1815.*

I read in *The Courant* of the twenty-seventh of this month an article on New Granada which I found most interesting, both for its descriptions of the people and resources of that country, and its observations regarding the dissension which has been and is still current there.

The author of the article seems impartial and his opinions are correct, but I would have wished for more particulars and greater clarity regarding the real causes of the civil war which led General Morillo to land on those shores and attack Cartagena. The outcome of this operation will probably decide the fate of a large part of the continent.

I herein submit to you several observations which might help to justify the conduct of the inhabitants of New Granada and which will perhaps shed light on the possible outcome of the contest between the Spanish and Granadian forces. As a South American, I feel that I should draw attention to certain facts relevant to the nature of our domestic strife.

Virtually every republic that has inspired mankind's veneration has borne within it the seed of moral discord, whence it has even been said that disunity is often the thermometer of freedom, and that the enjoyment of a freely constituted government is generally in direct proportion to the effervescence of parties and the clash of political opinions. Freedom does not weigh heavy, but it is difficult to maintain in balance, even in the more educated and civilized countries.

Has any free nation, ancient or modern, not suffered from disunity? Was any history stormier than that of Athens? Have any factions been bloodier than those of Rome, or civil wars more violent than the English ones? Have any dissensions been more dangerous than those we have seen in the United States? And yet these four countries are those which have most greatly honoured the human race with their virtues, their freedom and their glory, and by citing the tragic and surprising examples of those nations I would also draw a veil over our own shameful divisions.

Our disagreements all spring from those two most abundant sources of public calamity: ignorance and weakness. Spain fostered the former through superstition, and perpetuated the latter through tyranny. In the previous state of affairs we lived in an almost total void, removed from everything that was going on outside, estranged from any vision of political life and kept apart from anything which might in any way exercise our minds or enhance our resources or our strength. South Americans have strayed through the centuries like blind men in a world of colours; they were present in the theatre of action, but they were blindfolded and they saw nothing, heard nothing. Why? Because they could not see justice, much less hear the truth.

Moreover, we were abandoned by the whole world; no foreign nation guided us with its wisdom and experience, nor defended us with its arms, nor protected us with its resources. This was not the case of the United States during its struggle for freedom: though possessing all kinds of advantages over us, the three most powerful European nations, all owners of colonies, helped it to attain independence; and yet Great Britain did not retaliate against that very same Spain which waged war against her to deprive her of her colonies. All the military and political resources which have been denied to us have been given in profusion to our enemies: to mention only one example, *The Courant* of Jamaica and *La Gaçeta de Santiago de la Vega*, taking its information from the former, have published the list of arms, ammunition and uniforms they have received. Even the victories of the great and immortal Wellington have been indirectly harmful to us, since the Spaniards, ignorant in the art of warfare, learnt it from the heroic British commanded by the illustrious captain who, at one time, was to liberate South America. These are the singular facts which will go down in history along with others too numerous to mention. The United States which by its trade could have supplied us with the necessities of war, deprived us thereof because of its dispute with Great Britain. Otherwise Venezuela would have triumphed alone and South America would have been spared the devastation of Spanish cruelty and the destruction of revolutionary anarchy. We have no weapons with which to confront the enemy but our arms, our breasts, our horses and our lances. The weak need a long battle to triumph; the strong, as at Waterloo, need to wage a single battle and an empire disappears.

When parties are deficient in authority, either for lack of power or because of the triumph of their opponents, stirrings of discontentment weaken them. The cause is subdivided into as many parts as there are leaders; this occurs, particularly, when no agreement exists with a foreign power, compelling them to carry on the system that they have both recognized and committed one another to maintaining. Since no nation has entered into formal dealings with us, nor into official communications, we consequently have no political relationships binding us to any country.

## 15

# Racial harmony in the mixed society of the New World, and other thoughts in Jamaica

*From a draft prepared for the editor or publisher of the* Royal Gazette *in Kingston, probably also in September 1815.*

Most European and American politicians who have foreseen the independence of the New World have held the opinion that the main obstacle to its attainment lies in the difference between the races that make up the people of this immense country. I shall venture to examine this question in the light of various criteria deduced from the positive knowledge and experience we have acquired in the course of our revolution.

Between 15 and 20 million people are scattered throughout this vast continent, of American Indian, African and Spanish origin, as well as those of mixed blood; and of these, whites are certainly in the minority. But it is also certain that the latter possess intellectual qualities which confer on them relative equality and an influence which may seem excessive to those who have not been able to judge for themselves of the moral situation and material circumstances in South America. Understanding of these could not fail to foster a desire for unity and harmony among all the inhabitants, regardless of the numerical disproportion between one colour and another.

It is significant that, when the Spaniards appeared in the New World, the Indians thought them to be a race of mortals superior to ordinary men; and to some extent this idea lingers on, owing to the strong influence of superstition, fear of brute force, displays of disproportionate wealth, the wielding of authority, intellectual superiority and any number of circumstantial advantages. They have, in fact, always looked on white people with great reverence, as beings specially favoured by heaven.

'The Spanish American', says M. de Pons, 'has made his slave his companion in indolence'. In some respects, this fact has had fortunate results. The Spanish settler does not overburden his servant with work: rather, he treats him as a fellow being, instructing him in the moral and human principles prescribed by the Christian religion. Being gentle by nature, he treats his servant with kindness and communicates with him on a familiar basis. He is rarely driven by greed or necessity, which produce that ferocity of character and rigidity of principle that are so contrary to human values. The South American lives at ease in his native land, satisfying his needs and inclinations at little expense; quantities of gold and silver are a source of ready wealth with which to procure European goods. Fertile fields, plains swarming with wildlife and lakes and rivers brimming with fish provide him with more than enough food to eat; the climate allows him to dispense with clothing and all but the simplest housing—in short, he can live alone, self-reliant and independent of others. Nowhere else in the world is such a situation to be found: the earth is crowded with men, while America alone is virtually untouched.

It therefore seems reasonable to infer that, given the kind of individual independence that is possible in these immense countries, it is unlikely that factions representing various races will form in such a way that one of them manages to overwhelm the others. The spaciousness, abundance and variety of colours themselves tend to neutralize such pretensions, to the point of virtually extinguishing them.

The Indian is so peace-loving by nature that he desires only rest and to be left alone; he has no ambition even to become the chief of his own tribe, let alone prevail over outsiders. Fortunately, this type of people is the one that least strives for supremacy, even though it is greater in numbers than all the other peoples combined. This section of the American population is a sort of barrier keeping the others in their place; it does not aspire to power because it feels no desire for it, nor does it feel capable of exercising it. The Indian is quite content with peace, land and his family. He is friendly towards all, since he has full rights before the law and since, in order to win the favours of wealth and rank that government confer, he need only resort to rendering services and acquiring knowledge; but his distaste for such aspirations outweighs any desire for such favours.

It seems, then, that this spirit of gentleness extends to much more than half the people, since Indians and whites make up three-fifths of the total population; and if we add those of mixed race, who are a blend of both, the fraction is increased and, consequently, the threat of hostility between races decreases.

The slave in Spanish America vegetates in complacent inertia on his master's estate, enjoying all the benefits that accrue from being part of such an establishment, as well as a considerable degree of freedom. Since religion has taught him that to serve is a sacred duty, and since all his life he has lived in this state of domestic dependence, he feels that he is leading a natural life, as a member of his master's family, whom he loves and respects.

Experience has shown us that the Spanish serf, even when goaded by the most provocative incitements, has not rebelled against his owner; on the contrary, he has often chosen peaceful servitude in preference to rebellion. The Spanish leaders of Venezuela—Boves, Morales, Rosete, Calzada and others—following the example of Santo Domingo (but without understanding the real causes of that revolution) attempted to foment an uprising of all the coloured people, slaves included, against the white Creoles, so as to have them lay waste the country under the banners of Ferdinand VII; they were urged to rob and murder the whites; they were offered employment and property, and mesmerized by superstitious doctrines in favour of the Spanish side. Yet, despite such powerful incentives, the war-mongers were compelled to resort to force, and to announce that *those who did not serve the king were traitors or deserters.* Consequently, all those who did not enlist in their murderous gangs were put to death, they, their wives and children and even whole communities, since all were obliged to fight on the side of the king. After so much cruelty, as well as so many enticements, it seems incredible that the slaves should have refused to abandon their haciendas, and that, when they were forced to do so, and had no alternative, they deserted at the earliest opportunity. We have proof that these, and even more extraordinary occurrences, actually took place.

After repeated terrible setbacks in Venezuela, the Spaniards finally managed to reconquer the country. General Morillo's army came to reinforce them and complete the country's subjugation; it would seem that the independents' side was in despair, as indeed it was. But, by a strange twist of fate, those very same freed soldiers and slaves who contributed so greatly—though under duress—to the royalists' victory have gone over to the revolutionary side, even though the latter had not offered them absolute freedom as the Spanish partisans had done. The present defenders of the cause for independence are the selfsame supporters of Boves, now united with the white Creoles, who have never abandoned this noble cause.

Accordingly, we feel justified in believing that all the sons of Spanish America, of whatever colour or condition, hold one another in a reciprocal brotherly affection which no amount of scheming can ever alter. Some will claim that the civil wars prove the contrary. No, sir, America's domestic disputes have never stemmed from differences of race: rather, they were born of divergent political opinions, and the personal ambition of a few men, like all those that afflict other nations. There have hitherto been no outcries against a particular colour, state or condition: only against the European Spaniards, who so richly deserve our opprobrium. Until now, the most perfect harmony has reigned among those who were born on this soil; and there is no reason to fear that it may be otherwise in the future, since by then order will have been established, and governments strengthened by arms, public opinion, foreign relations and European and Asian emigration, which will inevitably increase the population.

Considering the satisfactory balance that the people of America enjoy, in numbers, material circumstances and unlimited spiritual resources, why should new governments not come to be established in this part of the world? In Athens, did not the slaves outnumber the citizens by four to one? Were not the fields of Sparta worked by the Helots? Throughout the Orient, Africa and parts of Europe, have there not always been fewer free men than serfs? Furthermore, a great difference is apparent between the captives of antiquity and the wretched drudges of America: the former were prisoners of war, accustomed to handling weapons, wealthy traders and navigators, highly learned philosophers who knew their rights: and all endured their custody unwillingly. Their modern counterparts are of a savage race, kept in their primitive condition by the work to which they are put, and degraded to the level of beasts.

What is truly shocking, in my opinion, is the indifference with which Europe, until now, has regarded the struggle of justice against oppression, for fear of causing greater disorder. That indifference is itself conducive to disorder, and militates against the prosperity and the shining future for which America hopes. The neglect we have been shown may one day drive the supporters of independence, in despair, to demagogic propaganda in an attempt to win the people's sympathy; it is, I repeat, a potential direct cause of subversion—and as such will undoubtedly force the weaker side to take highly pernicious but highly necessary measures to save the Americans, those Americans who are currently engaged in the defence of their fatherland against persecution on a scale unknown anywhere outside of Spanish America. When men are desperate, they are not fastidious in choosing the means to extricate themselves from danger.

*The American*

## 16

## Tribute to the noble President Petion, and the defence of the home country

*Letter from the Liberator to the President of Haiti, Alexandre Pétion, written in French. Taken from the book* Letters from the Liberator *by Vicente Lecuna, Vol. I, 1799–1817, Caracas, 1829.*

TO HIS EXCELLENCY
THE PRESIDENT OF HAITI

Mr President:

I am overwhelmed by your many kindnesses. Mr Villaret has returned with glowing reports of Your Excellency's welcome. You have been most generous and indulgent in every way.

Our preparations are almost completed; we shall undoubtedly be ready to leave in a fortnight. All that is lacking is the last of your favours; and if it is possible for me to do so, I will come in person to express my full gratitude to you.

Through Mr Injinac, your worthy secretary, I have taken the liberty of putting several new requests to you.

In my proclamation to the people of Venezuela, and in the decrees which I shall issue for the freedom of the slaves, I do not know if I am at liberty to express my innermost feelings towards Your Excellency, and so leave to posterity an unimpeachable monument to your philanthropy.

As I say, I do not know if it is appropriate for me to announce that you are the author of our liberty. I beg Your Excellency to advise me of your wishes in this matter.

Lieutenant-Colonel Valdés is sending you a petition which I have ventured to recommend to your generosity.

Please accept my most respectful homage and highest consideration, and be assured that I remain Your Excellency's most humble and obedient servant.

*Bolívar*

## 17
## 'Absolute freedom for the slaves'

*Decree issued in Carúpano on 2 June 1816, in which the Revolution was extended to the social foundations of Venezuela. Bolívar was to say: 'In a revolution for freedom, it would be sheer madness to attempt to keep slavery'. The decree was also a tribute to the President of the hospitable Haitian people.*

### SIMÓN BOLÍVAR
Supreme Leader and Field Marshal of the Armies
of Venezuela and New Granada, etc., etc.

#### TO THE PEOPLE OF RÍO CARIBE,
#### CARÚPANO AND CARIACO

Greetings,

Our country's policy of justice for all imperatively demands that each citizen have the rights that nature bequeathed to him; therefore I hereby decree absolute freedom for the slaves, who have suffered under the Spanish yoke for the past three centuries. Since the Republic needs all her sons to serve her, it is our duty to impose the following conditions on these new citizens:

*Article 1.* Every able-bodied man between 14 and 60 years of age shall report in the parish of his district for enlistment under the banners of Venezuela, within twenty-four hours of the publication of this decree.

*Article 2.* Elderly people, women, children and invalids shall be exempt from the present time onward from military service; and likewise from domestic and field work, in which they were employed previously for the profit of their masters.

*Article 3.* Any new citizen who refuses to take up arms to perform the sacred duty of defending his freedom shall remain in servitude, and not only he but also his children, even if under the age of 14, his wife, and his parents, even if elderly.

*Article 4*. The relatives of soldiers enlisted in the ranks of the liberation army shall enjoy the rights of citizens and the absolute freedom that this decree bestows on them in the name of the Republic of Venezuela.

The present regulations shall have the full force of law and shall be faithfully implemented by the Republican Authorities of Río Caribe, Carúpano and Cariaco.

Done at the General Headquarters of Carúpano, on 2 June 1816.

*Bolívar*

## 18

# Full confidence in the campaign against tyranny

*Message written on 1 January 1817, in Barcelona, to Pedro Briceño Méndez and to 'the bravest of the brave of Venezuela', summoning them to join the fight for freedom.*

My dear friends,

How happy I was to learn of the safety of people who are so dear to me! I was filled with tender feelings on hearing that my brave, faithful comrades in arms were out of danger! Nothing in my life could ever equal the sorrows and the pain I suffered when I was unsure of your fate. Only the idea that my country might succumb for ever could rank with my sufferings on your behalf. But fortunately your dear lives have been heroically saved.

All that is lacking for my happiness is to embrace you all. That day will be a memorable one for me; and all the more so if, to all the laurels you have already won, you should by then have added those of conquerors and liberators of Guayana. This sublime and crucial undertaking will anchor the Republic securely, should further storms assail it. You will fulfil the hopes of all citizens if you succeed in overpowering the Guayanese region, which has done us so much harm and which can be so useful to us. But, this accomplished, will you not then fly to rescue your brothers from the prisons of the enemy's tyranny? Yes, yes, you will, you will fly with me to the rich lands of Peru. Our destinies beckon us to the farthest reaches of the American continent. For such brave, faithful and loyal men, nothing is impossible. May the world gaze in wonderment, whether they end in victory or defeat! Fortune will ever smile on him who fears not death; and life itself is of little worth if it be not filled with glory.

Farewell, my dear comrades. Accept the deep affection of one who is honoured to be called, not the leader, but the brother of the *bravest of the brave* of Venezuela.

Health, glory and constancy.

*Bolívar*

19

## 'The printing press is as useful as stores and ammunition'

*In a letter to Don Fernando Peñalver, from Guayana, on 1 September 1817, the Liberator includes a printing press among the material indispensable for winning the freedom and independence of the home country and founding a sovereign and constitutional republic.*

For the time being we need only the articles which I requested before, since without them much precious time is being wasted. I should be most willing to send mules and cattle to Trinidad to enable you to buy all the necessary munitions, but, my friend, a labyrinth of difficulties prevents the government from carrying on trade at present. First, we lack ships suitable for such traffic; second, great care is needed to keep such animals from perishing, and in unskilled hands they might as well be thrown overboard; third, they could be seized as payment of some debt if it is learned that they belong to the government; and, finally, it would only increase the already extraordinary amount of troubles with which I must contend and which could not be greater if I were a king responsible for a whole kingdom, such is the reign of disorder and disorganization in which we now find ourselves. Everything remains to be done; as yet, we have done nothing; and unless we have men capable of helping the government, we never shall.

I need scarcely repeat that no effort should be spared to supply us with these articles, since I am sure of being constantly in your thoughts, especially as I am serving my country.

Above all, send me by some means or other the printing press, which is as useful as stores and ammunition. Regarding everything else you tell me in your letters, I acknowledge and approve all that they contain. I am today more than ever certain of something I have always known: that you are one of those who can do most to serve our country, by virtue of your sound judgement, zeal and patriotism. Therefore, my friend, come as soon as you have carried out all the tasks for which you are responsible. But do not delay so long that I am already far from here, for by then, perhaps, the chance will have been missed to make use of you as you deserve.

20

# Distribution of national property among the soldiers of the people's revolution

*Law on Land Distribution, the first legal step toward agrarian reform to incorporate the Revolution in the economic order. Bolívar unerringly includes it among 'the most worthy acts' of his rule. Promulgated in the Angostura area on 10 October 1817.*

## SIMÓN BOLÍVAR
Head of the Republic of Venezuela, etc.

Considering that the first duty of the government is to reward the services of the virtuous defenders of the Republic, who have unselfishly sacrificed their lives and property for the freedom and happiness of their country, have unflinchingly waged, and are still waging, the calamitous war of independence, although they and their families have no means of subsistence; and considering that, in the territory occupied by the troops of the Republic and in those territories, held by the enemy, which we shall soon occupy, there are many estates belonging to Spaniards and Royalist Americans, which, in compliance with the decree and regulations published on 3 September this year, should be seized and confiscated, I hereby decree the following:

*Article 1.* All landed property and buildings which, according to the said decree and regulations, have been seized and confiscated, or will be seized and confiscated, and which have not been, nor can be, disposed of to benefit the public treasury, shall be divided and distributed among the generals, commanders, officers and soldiers of the Republic, on the terms set out below.

*Article 2.* In view of the fact that the ranks won in the campaign are indisputable proof of the different services performed by each of the individuals belonging to the army, the division and distribution of property described in the preceding article shall be carried out in accordance with those ranks, as follows:

Commander-in-chief . . . . . . . . . . . . . . . . . . . . . . $25,000
Major-general . . . . . . . . . . . . . . . . . . . . . . . . . .  20,000
Brigadier-general . . . . . . . . . . . . . . . . . . . . . . .  15,000
Colonel. . . . . . . . . . . . . . . . . . . . . . . . . . . . . .  10,000
Lieutenant-colonel . . . . . . . . . . . . . . . . . . . . . . .   9,000
Major . . . . . . . . . . . . . . . . . . . . . . . . . . . . . . .   8,000
Captain. . . . . . . . . . . . . . . . . . . . . . . . . . . . . .   6,000
Lieutenant . . . . . . . . . . . . . . . . . . . . . . . . . . . .   4,000
Sub-lieutenant . . . . . . . . . . . . . . . . . . . . . . . . .   3,000
First and second sergeant . . . . . . . . . . . . . . . . . .   1,000
First and second corporal . . . . . . . . . . . . . . . . . .     700
Private soldier . . . . . . . . . . . . . . . . . . . . . . . . .     500

*Article 3.* Officers, sergeants, corporals and private soldiers who are promoted after the distribution shall have the right to claim any difference that may exist between the amount they received when occupying their previous posts and the amount due to them for those to which they have subsequently been promoted and still occupy at the time of the next distribution.

*Article 4.* If, when the value of the divisible property has been calculated, it proves insufficient to provide shares for all, the government shall offer to make good the lack by donating any other national property, and especially by granting ownership of uncultivated land.

*Article 5.* If, before or after the distribution of property, the government should see fit to reward the distinguished valour, service or deeds of a soldier, it shall be free to do so by transferring to him any of the said property, without necessarily taking into account the beneficiary's rank or the amount of property granted.

*Article 6.* In the event of a soldier having merited and been awarded the favour mentioned in the preceding article, he shall not have the right to claim the share assigned to him under the terms of Article 2, should the value of the property granted to him be greater than that corresponding to his rank.

*Article 7.* When the properties to be shared are of greater value than the amounts assigned to the different ranks, the government shall ensure that the distribution is conducted in the best interests of all, for which purpose soldiers may associate or combine and so collectively request a specific estate.

*Article 8.* The distribution shall be carried out by a special commission to be appointed in due course, which shall comply with the regulations to be published for this purpose.

*Article 9.* The government shall have sole direct authority over this commission.

May this document be published and communicated to all whom it may concern, and a copy forwarded to staff to be included in the agenda, which shall be circulated among all the divisions and brigades of the Republican army for implementation.

Written and signed by my hand, sealed with the provisional seal of the Republic, and countersigned by the Secretary of the Supreme Government, at the headquarters of Santo Tomás de la Nueva Guayana, on 10 October 1817.

*Bolívar*

*J. G. Pérez*
Secretary

21

# Welcome to our brothers from democratic Spain

*A long and enthusiastic letter to His Excellency Don Mariano Renovales, Lieutenant-General, from San Fernando de Apure, 20 May 1818.*

Honoured Sir:

It is my pleasure to answer the official document, dated 13 December last year, which Your Excellency was good enough to send me through our representative in London. Unfortunately, this communication has been delayed until now, for reasons which are both unknown and regrettable.

Words cannot express how gratifying it has been for the Government of Venezuela to receive Your Excellency's generous offer of your inestimable services, for the continuation of a struggle that we cannot fail to renew, strong in the support of the military qualities and abilities of so distinguished a general. Your Excellency's name has been gloriously associated with the just war that Spain waged against its invaders, in which Your Excellency revealed those eminent virtues characteristic of a man of greatness: valour in the face of danger, intelligence in overcoming it, love of one's country and hatred of tyranny. You, Your Excellency, with singular virtues, have dissociated yourself from all the inclinations of human desire and have been strong enough to disdain the advantages of fortune, preferring to seek out the honour, the glory and the freedom that always shun such a country of slaves as present-day Spain has become. I cannot, without the deepest feeling of disgust, remind Your Excellency of the atrocious plight in which the wretched King Ferdinand has left Your Excellency's country, not to mention my own. But my heart is filled with great joy when I think that not all Spaniards are our enemies, and that Spain has the merit of giving birth to generous and high-minded souls who come like guardian angels to support the sacred cause of freedom in this country; this country which once was laid waste and today is under armed attack by your nation. Since Your Excellency is one of these well-wishers, I hope that you will accept the tributes of gratitude which my country pays to you through me, its spokesman.

Your Excellency is doing us a great service by offering your active co-operation in restoring the independence of America; and this will be even greater if you succeed in winning to our cause the largest possible number of Spanish soldiers, who wish to adopt a free country in the American hemisphere. Nothing can be as precious to us as the acquisition of skilled and experienced soldiers, accustomed to our way of life and akin to us in language and religion. Your Excellency and the brave men who have the magnanimity to accompany you will be received with all the honour due to ben-efactors of the Republic, and will be granted ranks corresponding to their merits and services. Your Excellency may rest assured on this matter.

Señor Luís Lopez Méndez will be able to draw up with Your Excellency and other leaders and officials any stipulations that you may deem necessary, before undertaking the voyage to Venezuela.

May God protect and keep Your Excellency many years.

22

# 'All Americans should have only one home country'

*Message to the Honourable Señor Juan Martín Pueyrredón—Governor of the United Provinces of the River Plate—from Angostura, dated 12 June 1818, in which relations of warmth and solidarity are established between the farthest reaches of the South American continent. The message was published in the* Correo del Orinoco *on 27 June 1818.*

Honourable Sir:

It is my privilege to answer the letter dated 19 November 1816 that Your Excellency was kind enough to send me. Its slowness to arrive, although considerable, could not lessen my inexpressible joy at the initiation of relations which we have for so long desired to establish. Overcoming the obstacles of distance, isolation and the lack of direct channels of communication, you have taken a step forward which infuses fresh life into both governments by enabling us to know one another better.

Your Excellency does my country the honour of regarding it as a lone monument destined to remind America of the price of freedom and to keep alive the memory of a great-hearted and incorruptible people. Without a doubt, Venezuela, wholly devoted as she is to the sacred cause of freedom, sees her sacrifices as triumphs. Rivers of her blood, the burning of her towns, the total destruction of all things made by man and even those made by nature have been offered up on the altar of the fatherland.

You are far too kind in heaping such undeserved praise upon me. I have done no more than follow, with hesitant step, the long path traced out for me by my country. I have been no more than a fragile tool in the service of the great movement of my fellow citizens. I offer to Your Excellency the most heartfelt thanks for the honour that both my country and I myself have received from Your Excellency and from the other independent people of South America; from the people who are the glory of the hemisphere of Columbus, the tomb of tyrants and conquerors and the bastion of American independence. Accept, Your Excellency, my most profound admiration for the civic virtues, the political skills and the military prowess of the people of Buenos Aires and their illustrious leader.

The proclamation that Your Excellency has seen fit to make to us is shining proof of the brotherly and generous feelings of our comrades in the south. It gives me great satisfaction to deliver to Your Excellency the cordial reply that, through me, my fellow citizens wish to communicate to the sons of the River Plate. It speaks eloquently of the feelings of tender solicitude that all Venezuelans feel for their worthy compatriots of the south.

Your Excellency may assure your noble countrymen that they will be treated and welcomed not only as members of a friendly republic, but as members of our Venezuelan society. All Americans should belong to a single country, since we are already perfectly united in every other way.

Most Honoured Sir: when the victory of the Venezuelan forces has secured its independence, or when more favourable circumstances allow us to communicate more frequently and maintain closer relations, we will hasten, on our part, to draw up an American pact which, by forming a single political body of all of our republics, will show America to the world in a light of majesty and grandeur unrivalled by the nations of antiquity. Thus united—if heaven should grant this fervent wish—America could truly call herself the Queen of Nations and the Mother of Republics.

I hope that the River Plate, with its powerful influence, will co-operate effectively in completing the political structure whose corner-stone we laid on the first day of our new life.

May God watch over you for many years.

*Bolívar*

*Pedro B. Méndez*
Secretary

23

# Thanks to those who bring science, art, industry, talent and virtue

*Letter written in Angostura on 17 September 1818 to General John D'Evereux, regarding the immigrants awaited by Latin America.*

Sir:

Great is my appreciation of the efforts you have made in the service of my country; I have already had the satisfaction of learning, from your important letter of 4 July last year, that Venezuela was honoured by your favour and by your intention to lend it your services.

In my reply of 30 June last, of which I am herewith sending you a copy, although I imagine you received the letter, I accepted your generous offer.

Having absolute trust in the sincerity of your advice, and convinced that it is of great advantage to my country to be able to count you among our adopted sons, I wish to express, with all my heart, the gratitude of Venezuela, my own personal respect for you and the high esteem in which America holds those virtuous and magnanimous foreigners who prefer freedom to slavery and, abandoning their own country, come to America bringing science, art, industry, talent and virtue. Consequently, General, you may rest fully assured of military rank equivalent to that which you might, in other circumstances, obtain in your own country; I cannot say more, or make you further concrete and specific promises, but I can guarantee that your regiments or legion will receive at least the same privileges and protection as those enjoyed by us all under the pact that unites us. On my own responsibility, I will venture to add that the importance of your services will be greater in proportion to the number of troops in your legion; the greater their number, the more the government will avail itself of every opportunity to show you its gratitude.

I repeat, General, the sincerest assurances of friendship, esteem and respect on the part of your humble and obedient servant.

*Bolívar*

24

# Solemn and official creation of the Republic on the basis of freedom and law. Reasons for the Constitution. Account of his principal measures

*The 'Angostura Speech', unanimously considered by historical critics to be one of Bolívar's principal writings. Read before the Congress of Venezuela at its inauguration ceremony, in the city of Angostura, 15 February 1819.*

Fortunate the citizen whose privilege it is to convene, under the coat of arms of his own leadership, the sovereign body of the nation, so that it may exercise its absolute will! Indeed, Divine Providence smiles upon me today in giving me the great honour of bringing together the Representatives of the People of Venezuela in this august Congress, the source of the nation's legitimate authority and sovereign will, and the arbiter of its destiny.

By transferring the supreme power which was conferred upon me to the Representatives of the People, I am fulfilling my own heartfelt wishes as well as those of my fellow-citizens and of generations to come; they expect the utmost of your wisdom, rectitude and prudence. By carrying out this most pleasurable duty, I am freeing myself of the burden of immense authority and infinite responsibility which weighed so heavily upon my shoulders. Only urgent necessity and the imperious will of the people could ever have imposed on me the awesome and perilous responsibilities of Dictator and Supreme Head of the Republic. But now, on returning this authority to you—which I succeeded in maintaining despite great dangers, difficulties and hardships, in the midst of the most frightful tribulations that can be afflicted upon a people and a nation—I breathe more easily once more.

This period of the Republic over which I have presided has been much more than a mere political upheaval, bloody war or popular rebellion; rather it has been the onslaught of every kind of disruptive force, an infernal, uncontainable flood that has swept over the land of Venezuela. What could a mere mortal such as I do; what barriers construct against such devastating waves? On this sea of troubles I was like a straw swept along by the hurricane of revolution, a mere plaything of the elements. I was able to do neither good nor evil: irresistible forces directed the sequence of events, and to attribute them to me would be unjust and assign me an importance I do not deserve. If one truly wishes to discover the authors of the past events and the present order, consult the annals of Spain, America, Venezuela; examine the laws of the Indies, the rule of the old governors, the influence of religion and foreign domination; observe the first measures of the republican government, the ferocity of our enemies and the national character. Do not question me as to the effects of these lamentable upheavals—I can only be thought of as a simple instrument of these great forces that have been brought to bear on Venezuela; nevertheless, my life, my conduct and all my public and private actions are submitted to the judgement of the people. Representatives! it is your duty to pass judgement. I submit the history of my leadership to your impartial decision; I shall add nothing further to defend it, for all that I could say has now been said. If I should deserve your approval, I shall have gained the supreme title of good citizen, more precious to me than that of liberator, which Venezuela gave me, or peace-maker as I was named in Cundinamarca, or any others that might be bestowed upon me the world over.

Legislators! I place in your hands the supreme command of Venezuela. It is now your lofty duty to devote yourselves to the well-being of the Republic; our fate and the measure of our glory is in your hands, those very hands which will sign the decrees establishing our Freedom. At this moment the Supreme Head of the Republic is no more than a simple citizen, and this he desires to remain until his dying day. Nevertheless, I shall serve the military cause as long as there are enemies in Venezuela. The homeland has many worthy sons able to lead it; many of those present here as Representatives of the People have a wealth of talent, virtue, experience and all that is required to lead free men, and outside this sovereign body there are many citizens who have constantly demonstrated courage in facing danger, prudence in averting it and, finally, the art of governing themselves and others. These worthy gentlemen will undoubtedly deserve the support of Congress, and they will be placed in charge of the government, which I hereby renounce for ever, in all sincerity and goodwill.

The continuation of authority in a single individual has frequently been the downfall of democratic governments. Repeated elections are essential in popular systems, because nothing is more dangerous than allowing the same citizen to remain in power over a long period of time. The people become accustomed to obeying him, and he becomes accustomed to commanding them; this is how power is usurped and tyranny takes root. The freedom of the Republic must be jealously safeguarded, and our citizens should justly fear that the same magistrate who has governed them for many years might come to rule them for ever.

Through this act, then, that bears witness to my allegiance to Venezuela's freedom, I may hope to be numbered among those who are the most faithful to its cause; allow me to express, with the frankness of a true republican, my respectful opinion in this draft constitution which I am taking the liberty of offering you in testimony of the sincerity and candour of my feelings. Since the well-being of all is at stake, I am venturing to assume that I have the right to be heard by the Representatives of the People. I am well aware that your wisdom has no need of advice, and I fear that my draft may seem faulty and impracticable to you. But, gentlemen, I ask you to accept this work indulgently, for it is rather the tribute of my sincere submission to the Congress than the result of any frivolous presumption. Moreover, since the task that lies before you involves not only the creation of a political body but also, one might say, the creation of an entire society, surrounded by all the difficulties arising from a situation of such great complexity, perhaps the cry of a citizen will help point out the presence of a concealed and unknown danger.

Glancing back at the past, let us examine the basis of the Republic of Venezuela.

When America was separated from the Spanish monarchy, it found itself in a similar situation to the Roman Empire, when that enormous mass broke up in the midst of the Ancient World. The fragments that were left then formed independent nations in conformity with their situations or interests; but with the difference that each one re-established its original system. We do not even retain the vestiges of what went before: we are not Europeans, or Indians, but rather a species mid-way between the original inhabitants and the Spaniards. Americans by birth and Europeans in our rights, we find ourselves in the predicament of fighting with the Indians for the ownership of the land and contending with the opposition of invaders for the privilege of remaining in the country of our birth; thus, our case can be seen to be fraught with difficulties. What is more, our condition has always been a passive one, our political existence null; and our difficulty in attaining freedom is all the more painful because, before, we stagnated in the most wretched servitude; not only were we stripped of freedom, but even of a role of domination in our domestic affairs. Let me explain this paradox. Under the regime of absolute power, all authority goes unchallenged. The will of the despot is the supreme law arbitrarily executed by inferiors who participate in organized repression as a consequence of the authority they wield. They are in charge of civil, political, military and religious functions. But whereas the satraps of Persia were Persians, the pashas of the Great Sultan were Turks, the sultans of Tartary, Tartars; and whereas China had its own mandarins even when it had fallen under the rule of Genghis Khan, America, on the contrary, received everything from Spain and we were in fact deprived of any role of domination in our domestic affairs and internal government. This denial made it impossible for us to understand the course of public affairs; neither did we enjoy the personal esteem which the show of authority commands in the eyes of the people, and which is of such importance in great revolutions. In short, gentlemen, we were excluded and kept apart from the world's affairs in all that concerned the science of government.

Bound as we were by the triple yoke of ignorance, tyranny and corruption, we were unable to acquire learning, power or virtue. And since we were schooled by such evil tutors, the lessons we received and the examples we studied were of a most ruinous nature. We were enthralled by deception even more than by force; and corruption degraded us even more than superstition. Slavery is the daughter of darkness; an ignorant people is the blind instrument of its own destruction; ambition and intrigue take advantage of the credulity and inexperience of men who have no political, economic or civil understanding: they take to be realities what are in fact only illusions; they confuse licence with liberty, treason with patriotism, vengeance with justice. Such a people resembles an able-bodied blind man who, encouraged by his feeling of strength, strides forward with the assurance of the most clear-sighted and, stumbling into every pitfall, is no longer able to find his way. If such a degraded people should ever attain their freedom, they will not delay in losing it, for there will be no way of persuading them that happiness consists in the practice of virtue, that lawful government is more powerful than the rule of tyrants because it is more inflexible and requires that all obey its beneficent discipline, that morality and not force is the basis of the law, and that the exercise of justice is the exercise of freedom. Thus, legislators, your task is all the more difficult because the men you must form have been perverted by misleading illusions and destructive motives. Freedom, says Rousseau, is a most succulent dish, but one that is difficult to digest. Our frail fellow-citizens will have to build up their strength long before they are able to digest the life-giving nutrient of freedom. Will they, with their limbs stiffened from such long enchainment, their sight enfeebled by the darkness of their dungeons, and their spirit crushed by pernicious servitude, be able to stride firmly toward the august temple of freedom? Will they be able to gaze unblinkingly into its splendid rays, and inhale the pure air which surrounds it?

Consider your choice carefully, legislators. Do not forget that you are about to lay the foundations of a new people, and that they will rise to the greatness for which nature has equipped them if you so shape this foundation to match the eminent status that awaits them. If your choice is not governed by the guiding spirit of Venezuela, which should inspire you in choosing the right form and nature of the government you are to adopt for the happiness of the people, if, I repeat, you should fail to choose rightly, all our new beginnings will end in slavery.

### The freedom movement

The annals of the past provide thousands of governments for your contemplation; consider the nations whose brilliance has dazzled the world and you will see, in dismay, that virtually the whole universe has been, and is still, the victim of its governments.

You will see many different systems for guiding man, but all oppress him; and if we were not so accustomed to seeing the human race thus driven by the herdsmen of peoples, we should be horrified at the shocking spectacle of our docile species grazing on the surface of the earth like dumb flocks destined to feed their cruel leaders. In truth, nature equips us at birth with the desire for freedom; but whether due to sloth, or an inherent propensity of men, the fact remains that it reposes undisturbed within us, although bound with the shackles it is forced to wear. On contemplating this wretched state of prostitution, it would seem that we are right in thinking that most men believe the truth of the humiliating maxim that contends that it is harder to maintain the balance of freedom than to bear the burden of tyranny. Would that this maxim, so abhorrent to the morality of nature, prove false! Would that the truth of this maxim were not proved by the apathy of man towards his most sacred rights!

Many are the ancient and modern nations which have shaken off oppression; but far too few of them have been able to enjoy more than a fleeting moment of precious freedom, and very quickly they have relapsed into their former political vices, for it is the people, rather than the governments, who drag tyranny in their wake. So inured are they to domination that they have become imperceptive of the delights of national honour and prosperity;

and they are indifferent to the glory of being a living part of the movement for freedom, under the protection of laws enacted by their own will. The annals of history proclaim this disgraceful truth.

Only democracy, in my view, is capable of absolute freedom; but which democratic government has brought together power, prosperity and stability at one and the same time? On the other hand, we have seen the aristocracy, the monarchy, hold huge and powerful empires together for centuries and centuries; we have seen governments as long-lived as that of China, republics as enduring as Sparta and Venice, empires as far-flung as that of Rome. Did not France live under the monarchy for fourteen centuries? And which nation is greater than England? All these nations, however, have been or are aristocracies or monarchies.

Notwithstanding such painful reflections, I am overwhelmed with joy at the great steps which our republic has taken in embarking on its noble course. Imbued with purpose, inspired by love of justice, aspiring toward perfection, it has, with the separation of Venezuela from the Spanish nation, recovered its independence, its freedom, its equality and its national sovereignty. By constituting itself as a democratic republic, it has proscribed the monarchy, distinctions, nobility, exemptions, privileges; it has proclaimed human rights and endorsed freedom to act, think, speak and write. These eminently liberal measures can never be praised enough for the purity which inspired them. The first Congress of Venezuela has inscribed in the annals of our legislation, in ineradicable letters, the majesty of the people expressed in all its dignity, with the ratification of a social act such as will ensure the happiness of a nation. I need to summon up all my strength in order to express the force of my feelings with regard to the supreme good contained in this immortal code of our rights and laws. And yet, what words can I find to speak my thoughts! Dare I criticize the sacred tables of our laws? There are certain feelings which cannot be stifled in the breast of a true patriot; they flow out from the vehemence of his love for his country and, although he may try to conceal them, they make themselves felt with irresistible force. I am deeply convinced that the Government of Venezuela needs to be reformed; and although many worthy citizens feel as I do, not all of them have the heart publicly to profess the adoption of new principles. This has spurred me to take the initiative in a matter of the utmost gravity, since it constitutes a daring attempt to give advice to the counsellors of the people.

For all that I admire the excellence of the Federal Constitution of Venezuela, I am more and more persuaded of the impossibility of its application to our state. And in my opinion it is a miracle that its model in North America has survived so prosperously rather than collapsing at the first difficulty or threat of danger. Notwithstanding the fact that the North American people are such a singular model of political virtue and moral worth, and that freedom was their cradle, their school and their daily sustenance, and that in many respects they are a people unique in the history of the human race, it is, even so, a miracle, I repeat, that the weak and complicated federal system has been able to govern it in such difficult and delicate circumstances as those we have seen. But whatever this government's case may be with respect to the American nation, it has never remotely occurred to me to liken the situation and nature of states so disparate as the English American and the Spanish American. Would it not be extremely difficult to apply England's code of political, civil and religious freedom to Spain? How much more difficult would it be, then, to adapt the Laws of North America to Venezuela. Does not the *Spirit of Laws* state that these should be suited to the people making them, that only by a pure coincidence may those of one nation meet the requirements of another, that the laws should be suited to the country's physical condition, its climate, the quality of its soil, its situation, its extent and its people's way of life; that they should conform to the degree of freedom that the Constitution can tolerate, to the religion of the inhabitants, their interests, commerce, customs and traditions? This is the code which we should consult, and not that of Washington!

The Constitution of Venezuela, although its basis was a most excellent one, having regard to the validity of its principles and the beneficial effects of its administration, differed widely from the American in an essential, and undoubtedly the most important point. The Congress of Venezuela, like the American Congress, participates in some of the functions of the executive power. We, moreover, subdivided this power by entrusting it to a collective body, and this has the drawback of making the government's existence a periodical one, of suspending and dissolving it whenever its members separate. Our triumvirate lacks, so to speak, unity, continuity and individual responsibility: it is stripped of the power of immediate action, continuous life, true uniformity and direct responsibility; and a government which does not possess all that combines to form a moral presence might as well not exist.

Although the powers of the President of the United States are limited by numerous restrictions, he exercises alone all the functions of government which the Constitution assigns him, as a result of

139

which his administration is inevitably more uniform, constant and truly his own than that of a power distributed among several individuals, the combination of which can be nothing short of monstrous.

The Judicial Power in Venezuela is similar to the American—indefinite in duration, temporary and not perpetual; it enjoys a degree of independence appropriate to its needs.

The first Congress, in its Federal Constitution, consulted the wishes of the different provinces rather than basing itself on any firm idea of forming an indivisible and centralized republic. Here our legislators gave in to a number of provincial citizens who were unwisely carried away by the dazzling brilliance of the happiness of the American people, imagining that the blessings they enjoy they owe exclusively to their form of government rather than to the character and customs of its citizens. And in fact, the example of the United States with its extraordinary prosperity was too tempting not to be followed. Who could resist the attraction of the full and absolute enjoyment of sovereignty, independence and freedom? Who could resist the devotion inspired by an intelligent government able to link, at the same time, individual to general rights, transforming the common will into the supreme law of the individual will? Who could resist the rule of a beneficent government which, with a sure, quick and powerful hand brings every expedient everywhere into constant play in the interests of social improvement, which is the sole purpose of all human institutions?

However promising this magnificent Federal system might seem, and in fact be, the Venezuelans were not destined to enjoy it as soon as they threw off their chains. We were not ready for so much good; good, like evil, can be fatal when it is sudden and excessive. Our moral constitution did not yet have the consistency necessary to receive the benefit of a completely representative government, so sublime if it could be applied to a republic of saints.

Representatives of the People! You are called upon to confirm—or annul—all that in your view should be maintained or reformed—or discarded—in our social pact. It falls to you to correct the work of our first legislators; I might say that it is your task to conceal some of the beauty contained in our political code; for not all hearts are made to love all beauty; nor are all eyes capable of gazing at the heavenly light of perfection. The Book of the Apostles, the doctrine of Jesus, the divine writings sent to us by Providence for man's improvement, so sublime and so holy, would kindle an ocean of flame in Constantinople and fire the whole of Asia were they to be suddenly imposed as the Code of Religion, Laws and Customs.

*The mixing of the races and equality*

Allow me to draw the attention of Congress to a matter which may be of vital importance. Let us remember that our people are neither European nor North American; they are a compound of African and American elements, rather than an emanation of Europe, as even Spain itself is no longer entirely European because of its African blood, its institutions and character. It is impossible to determine precisely to which human family we belong. The greater part of the indigenous population have been annihilated, Europeans have interbred with Americans and Africans, and the latter have interbred with Indians and Europeans. We are all born of the same mother, but our fathers, being of different origin and extraction, are all visibly different in the colour of their skin; this dissimilarity brings with it an obligation of the greatest importance.

The citizens of Venezuela all enjoy, by virtue of the Constitution, the interpreter of nature, perfect political equality. Whereas the equality may not have been a guiding principle in Athens, France and America, we ourselves should affirm it in order to remedy the distinction which apparently exists. My opinion, legislators, is that the fundamental principle of our system depends directly and exclusively on equality being established and practised in Venezuela. It has been upheld by wise men throughout the ages that all men are born with equal rights to the benefits of society; it has also been affirmed that all men are not born equally equipped to attain every rank. For all men should practise virtue, and yet many do not; all should be brave, and yet many are not; all should possess talents, and yet all do not. Hence the effective distinctions which may be observed between individuals in the most liberally established of societies. The principle of physical and moral inequality is no less generally recognized than that of political equality. Nature creates men unequal in disposition, temperament, force and character. The laws correct this difference because they place the individual in society in such a way that education, industry, the arts, services and virtues may give him a fictitious equality, properly called political and social. It is eminently felicitous inspiration to have gathered all the classes in one state, the diversity of which has grown with the propagation of the species. By this step alone, cruel discord has been torn up by its roots. How many jealousies, rivalries and hatreds have been thus avoided!

Having thus dealt with justice, with humanity, let us now turn to politics and society and seek to remove the difficulties facing such a simple and natural system, which is nevertheless so fragile that the slightest mishap can upset and ruin it. Our diversity of origin requires an unfailingly steady hand, an infinitely delicate tact in managing our heterogeneous society, for its complicated structure can be dislocated, fragmented and dissolved at the slightest disturbance.

The most perfect system of government is that which produces the greatest possible amount of happiness, social security and political stability. The laws enacted by the first Congress give us reason to believe that good fortune will be the lot of Venezuela; by means of your laws, we entertain the hope that security and stability will perpetuate this happy destiny. It falls to you to solve the problem. What can we do, having broken the shackles of our old oppression, to prevent the remnants of our harsh irons from being hammered into liberty-destroying weapons? The relics of Spanish domination will endure for many years before we succeed in annihilating them: the contamination of despotism has fouled our atmosphere, for neither the flames of war nor the remedy of our salutary laws have been able to purify the air we breathe. Although our hands are now free, our hearts still suffer from the afflictions of servitude. As Homer said, when man loses his freedom he loses half his spirit.

Venezuela's government is a republican one, as it has been and must be; its foundation should be the sovereignty of the people: the division of powers, civil liberty, the abolition of slavery, monarchy and privilege. We must have equality in order to reshape, so to speak, the human species, with its political opinions and public customs, into one single whole. Then, fixing our gaze on the long road that lies before us, we must devote our attention to the dangers to be avoided. History should be our guide on this journey. Athens, first of all, gives us the most brilliant example of an absolute democracy, and at the same time Athens gives us the saddest example of the extreme fragility of this kind of government. The wisest legislator of Greece was not able to see his republic endure ten years, and suffered the humiliation of having to acknowledge the insufficiency of absolute democracy for governing even the most cultured, moderate and orderly societies, for its rays of freedom are no more than lightning flashes. Let us admit then that Solon was right when he taught that it is most difficult to lead men with laws alone.

The Republic of Sparta, which seemed to be a chimerical invention, produced more real effects than the ingenious design of Solon. The legislation of Lycurgus brought about glory, virtue, morality and consequently national happiness. Although two kings in one state would seem like two monsters ready to devour it, Sparta suffered little from that double royalty, and Athens enjoyed the most splendid fortune with absolute sovereignty, free and frequently renewed elections of its magistrates, and gentle, wise and politic laws. Pisistratus, a usurper and a despot, did more good to Athens than her laws; and Pericles, although also a usurper, was her most useful citizen. The Republic of Thebes did not live longer than Pelopidas and Epaminondas, for it is sometimes men, and not principles, that form governments. The wisest codes, systems and statutes in the world are lifeless things that influence but little the progress of societies—and can never replace the virtuous, patriotic men who are the backbone of all republics!

The Roman Constitution gave the greatest measure of power and fortune to any people on earth, and yet there was no precise distribution of power. The consuls, the senate, the people were at once all legislators, magistrates and judges; they all took part in every division of power. The executive body, consisting of two consuls, had the same drawback as that of Sparta, yet notwithstanding this shortcoming the republic did not suffer the disastrous contentions that every forecast would have judged inevitable in a leadership composed of two individuals equally endowed with the powers of monarchs. A government whose only inclination was war and conquest did not appear likely to forge the happiness of the people; and yet a government that was monstrous in its hunger for war elevated Rome to the highest splendour of virtue and glory, and made the world a Roman province, to prove to mankind the force of political virtues, and to show how immaterial institutions generally are.

And moving from antiquity to modern times we find England and France, the cynosure of all the nations and providing eloquent lessons of every kind in the realm of government. The Revolution of these great peoples, like a radiant meteor, flooded the world with such a profusion of political brilliance that every thinking creature has been made aware of what man's rights and duties are and what constitute the vices and virtues of governments. Everyone today can appreciate the intrinsic value of the speculative theories of modern philosophers and legislators. And finally, this star in its brilliant course inflames even the apathetic Spaniards who also flung themselves into the political whirlwind; they had their ephemeral taste of freedom, recognized their inability to live under the gentle dominion of the laws and once more buried themselves in their immemorial prisons and persecution.

Legislators, it is fitting to recall what the eloquent Volney says in his preface to *The Ruins of Palmyra*: 'To the nascent people of the

Spanish Indies, to the generous leaders who guide them to freedom: may the errors and misfortunes of the ancient world teach wisdom and happiness to the new world.' The lessons of experience, therefore, should not be lost; the consequences of Greece, Rome, France, England and America should instruct us in the difficult science of creating and conserving our nations with their own just, legitimate and, above all, fitting laws. We should never forget that the excellence of a government does not lie in its theories, in its form or in its mechanisms, but rather in its appropriateness to the nature and character of the nation for which it is devised.

Rome and Great Britain are the two most outstanding nations of ancient and modern times. Both of them were born to command and be free, and yet neither was founded on meretricious notions of freedom, but rather on solid foundations. Thus, representatives, I recommend that you study the British Constitution, which appears to be the one most likely to bring the greatest good to the peoples that adopt it; however, as perfect as it may be, I am far from advocating its slavish imitation. When I speak of the British Government I am referring only to its elements of republicanism—for, in truth, can a system in which there is recognition of the sovereign will of the people, the division and balance of powers, civil liberty, freedom of conscience, the press and all that is highest in politics be called a pure monarchy? Could any republic ever have a higher degree of freedom? And could more ever be hoped for in terms of social order? Therefore I recommend to you this popular Constitution, with its division and balance of powers and civil liberty, as the most worthy model for those who aspire to the enjoyment of human rights and all the political well-being that is compatible with our fragile nature.

We would in no way be altering our fundamental laws by adopting a legislative power similar to that of the British Parliament. Like the Americans, we have divided our national representation into two Houses, those of the Representatives and the Senate. The first is most judiciously composed, since it enjoys all the necessary power, and it is not required to undergo essential reform, the Constitution having provided it with the foundation, form and authority required for the people's will to be legitimately and competently represented.

*Powers and institutions*

If the Senate, instead of being elected, were hereditary, in my opinion it would be the foundation, the binding force and the soul of our

Republic. In political storms, this body would stay the thunderbolts of the government's anger and roll back the waves of popular feeling. Supporting the government in the legitimate interests of its own preservation, it would always oppose any encroachment by the people on the jurisdiction and authority of its magistrates. For, it must be confessed: most men do not realize where their true interests lie and constantly try to assail those in the hands of their depositaries: the individual fights against the crowd, and the crowd against authority. In all governments, therefore, there should be a neutral body which will always take the side of the wronged party and can disarm the offender. In order to be truly neutral, this body should not owe its creation to the choice either of government or the people; in this way it will be fully independent and have nothing to fear nor expect from these two sources of authority. A hereditary senate, as part of the people, would share its concerns, its feelings and its spirit. For this reason, it should not be presumed that a hereditary senate would become estranged from the interests of the people or forget its legislative duties. The senators of Rome and the House of Lords in London have been mighty foundations supporting the edifice of political and civil freedom.

The senators will be elected in the first instance by Congress. The successors to the Senate should be the object of special attention by the government, which should educate them in a college especially created for instructing the future guardians and legislators of the country. They would study the arts, sciences and letters which enhance the mind of a public man; from their infancy they would be aware of the career for which they were destined, and from an early age would be morally and spiritually prepared for the dignity awaiting them.

The creation of a hereditary senate would in no way be a violation of political equality; I have no intention of establishing a nobility which, in the words of a famous republican, would be both to destroy equality and freedom. Rather, it is an office for which the candidates must receive preparation, one which requires great knowledge, and for which the means of instruction should be provided. Not everything can be left to fate or the hazard of elections, for the people are all the more easily deceived when nature is perfected by art, and while admittedly these senators would not necessarily reflect all the virtues, they would be the product of an enlightened education.

Furthermore, the liberators of Venezuela are entitled to occupy a high and permanent rank in the Republic which owes them its existence. I believe that posterity would be impoverished by the extinction of the illustrious names of its first benefactors: I will go further and say that is in the public interest, and a natural expression of Venezuela's gratitude and the national honour, to conserve for the rest of time the glory of a breed of virtuous, prudent and industrious men who have overcome all the obstacles in their way to found the Republic at the cost of the most heroic sacrifices. And if the people of Venezuela do not applaud the elevation of their benefactors, they are unworthy of being free and never will be truly so.

A hereditary senate, I repeat, will be the fundamental basis of the legislative power and therefore the basis of all government. Likewise, it would act as a counterweight to the government and the people: it would be an intermediary, cushioning the blows exchanged between these two eternal rivals. In all human conflict the composure of a third party is needed to act as the agent of reconciliation, and thus the Senate of Venezuela will serve as a restraining influence on this complex structure so liable to be shaken by violence. It will be the conciliator capable of calming tempests and maintaining harmony between the members and the head of this political body.

Nothing could corrupt a legislative body invested with such high honours, so self-sufficient and with nothing to fear from the people or expect from the government: one which has no other purpose than to stamp out all tendencies to evil and encourage every attempt to do good, and which is passionately interested in the existence of a society with which it shares both adversity and prosperity. It has been most justly remarked that the British House of Lords is so precious to the nation because it serves as a bulwark of freedom; and I would add that the Senate of Venezuela would not only be a bulwark of freedom, but also a buttress to ensure the abiding nature of the Republic.

The British executive power is invested with all the sovereign authority that is his right, but he is also ringed by a triple system of dykes, barriers and palisades. He is the Head of State, indeed; but his ministers and officials depend more on the laws than on his authority because they can be held personally responsible—a responsibility from which not even royal authority can exempt them. He is Commander-in-Chief of the Army and Navy, he makes peace and declares war; but it is Parliament that decrees the annual sums to be paid out for the military forces. Even though the courts and judges come under him, the laws emanate from the Parliament which has approved them. For the purpose of neutralizing his power, the person of the King is made inviolable and sacred; for just as his head is left free, his hands are bound. The Sovereign of England has three formidable rivals: his Cabinet, which is responsible to the people and the Parliament; the Peers, who defend the interests of the people as representatives of the nobility of which they are part; and the House of Commons, which is the organ and tribune of the British people. Moreover, since the judges are responsible for the enforcement of the laws, they do not stray from them; and the administrators of the exchequer, being accountable not only for their own infractions but also for those of the government itself, take good care not to misuse public funds. As closely as we may examine the nature of the executive power in England, nothing can be found to disincline us from judging it to be the most splendid model for either a monarchy, an aristocracy or a democracy. By applying this concept of executive power to Venezuela in the person of a President, appointed by the people or by its representatives, we shall have taken a great step toward the country's happiness.

Whichever citizen comes to fill this post will be assisted by the Constitution: having the authority to do good, he cannot do evil, for, as long as he obeys the laws, his ministers will co-operate with him; but if, on the contrary, he attempts to infringe them, his own ministers will leave him isolated in the midst of the Republic, and even accuse him before the Senate. Since responsibility for any transgressions committed falls upon the ministers and they must pay the penalty for this, it is they who will carry out the business of governing. Not one of the least advantages of this system is the obligation under which it places the officials closest to the executive power to take a vital and active part in the deliberations of government, and to regard this department as their own. It may happen that the President himself is not a man of great talents or virtues but, notwithstanding the absence of these essential qualities, the President will perform his duties in a satisfactory way; for in such cases the ministry, doing everything on its own, will bear the burden of state.

However excessive the degree of authority of England's executive power may appear, it is perhaps not so in the case of the Republic of Venezuela. Here, Congress has tied the hands and even the heads of the country's magistrates. This legislative body has taken over part of the executive powers, contrary to the maxim of Montesquieu which says that a representative body should not take any active decisions: it should make laws, and see that they are enforced. Nothing is more disruptive of the harmony between the powers than their mingling, and nothing is more dangerous for the people than the weakness of the executive. If it has been deemed necessary to endow it with so many powers in a monarchy, these become infinitely more indispensable in a republic.

Let us concentrate on this difference, and we will find that the balance of powers should be determined in two ways. In republics, the executive should be the stronger, for everything conspires against it; whereas in monarchies it should be the legislative power, because everything conspires in favour of the monarch. The veneration peoples hold for royalty is a source of prestige which has a powerful influence in increasing the superstitious respect paid to this authority. The splendour of the throne, the crown and the purple; the formidable support provided by the nobility; the vast wealth which whole generations have accumulated within a single dynasty, and the fraternal protection that all kings offer one another are very considerable advantages which act in favour of royal authority and give it almost unlimited sway. These very advantages are consequently what makes it necessary to grant a republican magistrate a greater degree of authority than that possessed by a constitutional prince.

A republican magistrate is an individual isolated in the midst of a society; his task is to restrain the people's inclination to licence, and the judges' and administrators' propensity to abuse the laws. He is directly subject to the legislative body, the senate and the people; he is one man alone, resisting the combined attack of the opinions, interests and passions of society, which, as Carnot says, is continually struggling between the desire to dominate and the desire to remove itself from domination. In short, he is one athlete who must compete against an entire field of athletes.

The only remedy for such weakness is a firmly established and balanced form of power able to contend with the resistance which the executive authority inevitably meets from the legislature, the judicial body and the people of a republic. If the executive does not have access to all the means to which it is entitled, it inevitably falls into incapacity or misuse of its authority; in other words, in the death of government, whose successors are anarchy, usurpation and tyranny. It is argued that the executive authority should be surrounded by restrictions and safeguards, and nothing is more just; but it should be made clear that the ties that it is sought to preserve will become stronger, but no closer.

Let the whole system of government, therefore, be strengthened, and the balance established in such a way that it cannot be lost or, because of its fragility, become the cause of decline. Precisely because no form of government is more vulnerable than the democratic system, its structure should be as solid as possible, and its institutions should collaborate with a view to preserving this stability. Otherwise, what we shall have will be a tentative government and not a permanent system, and an uncontrollable, rebellious and anarchic society rather than a social establishment where happiness, peace and justice reign.

## Moderation and realism

Let us not be presumptuous, legislators; let us be moderate in our ambitions. We are not likely to achieve more than mankind has already done; neither shall we exceed the accomplishments of the greatest and wisest nations. Unlimited freedom and absolute democracy are the rocky shores on which all republican hopes have foundered. We have only to consider the republics of antiquity and in modern times, and those being born today; almost all of them have seen the frustration of their just aspirations. Those who yearn for legitimate institutions and social perfection are most certainly praiseworthy, but who has told those men who call so imperiously for the union of power with justice that they already possess all the necessary wisdom and practise all the virtues that are required? Angels, not men, are the only creatures who can exist in freedom, peace and good fortune in the exercise of such sovereign power!

The Venezuelan people are already enjoying legitimate rights which are easily within their reach; let us, therefore, restrain the flood of excessive ambitions which might lead to the adoption of a form of government unsuitable to the people's needs. Let us surrender that federal system which is inappropriate for us, as well as the triumvirate of executive power; and, concentrating such power in a president, let us vest in him the authority he needs in order to continue to combat the problems arising from our recent situation, from the state of war we have endured and from the host of external and domestic enemies with whom we shall have to contend for a long time to come. The legislative power should surrender those functions belonging to the executive; and yet, it should acquire new consistency and new influence in the balance of these powers. The courts should be strengthened by the stability and independence of the judges; by the setting up of juries, and of civil and criminal codes which are neither dictated by antiquity nor by victorious kings, but rather by the voice of nature, by the appeal of justice and by the light of wisdom.

My desire is that all the parts of the government and the administration should acquire no more than the degree of power necessary to maintain the balance, not only between the members that make up the government, but between the different sectors of our society. It would not matter if the springs of a political system ran down, were it not for the fact that this would bring about the dissolution of the social body and the ruin of all concerned. The voice of mankind, from the field of battle or the scene of internal revolt, cries in anguish to the heavens against the thoughtless and purblind legislators who believed it was possible to experiment with chimerical institutions with impunity. All the peoples of the world have aspired to freedom, some by arms and others by laws, alternately moving from anarchy to despotism or despotism to anarchy; but few are those who have been content with moderate ambitions and adopted constitutions suited to their capacities, their character and their situation.

Let us not aspire to the impossible, for by flying too close to the burning orb of absolute freedom, man is always precipitated into the abyss of absolute power and tyranny; the only middle way between these two extremes is that of supreme social freedom. Abstract theories are always at the root of the pernicious idea of boundless freedom. Let us ensure that state power is kept within the limits that reason and our own interests ordain; that the national will is contained within the bounds prescribed by a just power; and that our judicial system is strictly governed by a civil and criminal legislation analogous to our present Constitution. Then true balance will be achieved, and the state will be able to advance unhindered, without the complications which obstruct societies in their progress.

Stable governments can only be formed on the basis of a common national endeavour that seeks the achievement of two essential goals: the moderation of the general will and the curbing of state authority. The theoretical terms that express these two propositions are not easy to establish, but it may be assumed that they should be guided by a rule of mutual constraint and concentration so that there may be the least friction possible between the people's will and the legitimate power. This is an art which is gradually learned through practice and study. It is the process of enlightenment that opens the way for practical accomplishments, and enlightenment cannot progress without integrity of spirit.

The feelings of a republican should be entirely absorbed in love of country, laws and the country's magistrates. The Venezuelans love their country, but they do not love their laws, for these have been harmful and a source of evil; neither do they love their magistrates, because in the past they were wicked and at the present time they are hardly known in the career they have recently taken up. But without reverence for the country, the laws and the authorities, society falls into a state of chaos and is doomed to end abysmally in a hand-to-hand combat of man against man.

All our moral powers will not suffice to rescue our infant Republic from this fate, unless we bring the mass of the people together into a single whole, and the government into a single body, and likewise consolidate the laws and the national spirit. Unity, unity, unity should be our slogan. Different blood flows in the veins of our fellow citizens—let us mix it to make it one; our Constitution has divided the political powers—let us bind them together to give them unity of purpose; our laws are loathsome relics of all the despotisms of antiquity and modernity—let us tear down this monstrous edifice and on its ruins raise a temple to justice, and, under the auspices of its divine inspiration, enact a code of Venezuelan laws. Should we wish to consult great monuments and models of legislation, Great Britain, France and North America can offer us admirable ones.

The education of the people should be the primary concern of a truly patriotic Congress. Morality and enlightenment are the two guiding principles of a republic, and these are our prime needs. From Athens, let us take the Areopagus and the guardians of customs and laws; from Rome, the censors and tribunals; and forming a holy alliance of these moral institutions, let us renew in the world's history the idea of a people not content merely to be free and strong, but aspiring also to be virtuous. From Sparta, let us take the austerity of her establishments—and from these three springs form a fountain of virtue, a fourth power within our Republic, the domain of which will be youth and the hearts of men, public spirit, upright behaviour and republican morality. Let us constitute this Areopagus in such a way that it may watch over the instruction of children and the education of the nation; purify all that has become corrupt in the Republic; denounce the ingratitude, selfishness and indifference in men's hearts towards their homeland, and the sloth and negligence of the citizens; and pass judgement on every sign of corruption and pernicious behaviour, reprimanding such conduct with moral sanctions just as the laws inflict punishment for crimes. This should apply not only to anything that clashes with the laws, but to any attempt to bring them into disrepute; not only to attacks upon them, but to anything that weakens them; not only to violations of the Constitution, but to anything that violates public respect. The jurisdiction of this truly noble tribunal should be effective as regards education and instruction: on matters of penalties and punishments it should simply perform an advisory function. But the minutes or records setting out both the court's proceedings and deliberations and the moral principles and actions of the citizens will become the registers of virtue and vice, which will be consulted by the people for their elections, by magistrates for their decisions and by judges for their verdicts. As fanciful as such an institution may seem, it is infinitely more attainable than others which both ancient and modern legislators have established, and which have proved to be of far less value to mankind.

Legislators! The constitutional draft which I respectfully submit to your wisdom will reveal to you the spirit which inspired it. By proposing the division of the citizens into active and passive elements, I have sought to promote national prosperity by means of the two great levers of industry: labour and knowledge. Through the activation of these two driving forces of society, men may attain those two most difficult goals: honour and happiness. By imposing just and prudent restrictions on the primary and electoral assemblies we will be erecting the first barrier to contain any tendency by the people to licence, thus avoiding the unreasoning and disorderly contest which has always stamped elections with error and which, consequently, has surrounded the magistrates themselves and the workings of government with error also; for from this act of election springs either the freedom or the slavery of a people.

By increasing the influence of Congress in the balance of powers, by the number of legislators, and the nature of the Senate, I have attempted to provide a firm base for this first body of the nation and to invest it with considerable importance, for the successful discharge of its sovereign duties.

By separating, within well-defined limits, the executive jurisdiction from the legislative jurisdiction, I did not set out to divide but to bind together, by means of a harmonious relationship which is born of independence, those supreme powers whose prolonged clashes have never failed to destroy one of the contenders. By assigning to the executive greater powers than it has previously enjoyed, I do not intend to give rein to despots wishing to dominate the Republic, but simply prevent the despotism of decision-making bodies from paving the way for a cycle of tyrannical changes in which anarchy is alternately replaced by oligarchy and undivided rule. By asking for the permanence of judges and for the creation of juries and a new code, I am calling upon Congress to guarantee civil liberty, which is so precious, just and necessary—in a word, freedom itself, without which the other guarantees are as nothing. I have called for redress of the lamentable abuses that afflict our judicature, which derive their wretched origin from the overwhelming flood of Spanish legislation into which have flowed indiscriminately and down through the ages the product of folly and wisdom alike, good sense and extravagance, genius and caprice. This judicial encyclopedia, a many-headed monster which until now has been the scourge of the Spanish peoples, is the most refined torture devised by Heaven's wrath yet to be visited on that unfortunate empire.

In my meditation on the most effective way of regenerating the character and habits which tyranny and war have bequeathed us, I have dared to suggest a moral power, drawn from the depths of dark antiquity and from those forgotten laws which for a time kept virtue alive among the Greeks and Romans. It might well be considered as the raving of a fool, but it is far from being impossible, and I flatter myself that you will not entirely ignore a notion which, with the benefit of experience and wisdom, may prove to be most effective.

Horrified as I am by the discord that reigns—and which is bound to reign—amongst us as a result of the subtleties which characterize the spirit of the federal government, I have been driven to beg you to adopt centralism and the uniting of all the states of Venezuela into a single and indivisible republic. This urgent and vital step is, in my opinion, of such importance that without it our drive towards regeneration will end in death and destruction.

It is my duty, legislators, to present you with an accurate and faithful picture of my political, civil and military administration, but to do so would be to strain your valuable attention and take up your precious time. Consequently, the secretaries of state will give an account to the Congress of their different departments, presenting documents and records to make you thoroughly acquainted with the real and positive state of the Republic.

## Abolition of slavery and distribution of land

I would not draw your attention to the most outstanding measures introduced during my leadership if they did not concern most Venezuelans. I am speaking here of the most important decisions of the recent period.

The disgraceful and ungodly institution of slavery covered the land of Venezuela with its sombre shadow, and our sky was heavy with stormy clouds which threatened us with a rain of fire. I implored the protection of the God of humanity, and redemption dispersed the storm. Slavery broke its chains, and Venezuela found itself surrounded by new sons, who, in their gratitude, have transformed the instruments of their bondage into the arms of freedom. Yes, those who were once slaves are now free: those who were once the enemies of an unloving mother are now defenders of a homeland. It is unnecessary to applaud the necessity and benefits of justice when you are all aware of the history of the Helots, of Spartacus and Haiti: when you all know that one cannot be a slave and free man at one and the same time, except by violating every natural, political and civil law. I leave to your sovereign authority the reform or repeal of all my statutes and decrees; but I implore you to confirm the absolute freedom of the slaves as if I were begging for my own, and the Republic's, life.

To recount the military history of Venezuela would be to recall the history of republican heroism among the ancients; for Venezuela has taken its place among those who have made the greatest sacrifices on the altar of freedom. And as they fought, the noble breasts of our generous warriors craved no more than the sublime honours which the benefactors of mankind deserve. Their greatest rewards were not power, or fortune, or even glory, but only freedom and the noble title of Liberators of the Republic. Therefore, in founding a sacred society with these illustrious gentlemen, I have instituted the Order of the Liberators of Venezuela. Legislators! it now falls to you to confer honours and award decorations, and to carry out this noble act of national gratitude.

These men, who gave up all the privileges and properties which their virtue and talents had produced, who experienced the cruelties of horrible warfare, undergoing the worst privations and sufferings, these worthy sons of the Republic have merited the government's attention. Therefore, I have ordered them to be rewarded with national estates. If I am deserving of any kind of favour from the people, I ask its representatives to respond to my petition in recognition of my humble services. May Congress ordain the distribution of national estates, according to the law which, in the name of the Republic, I have decreed in favour of the Venezuelan military.

After we had destroyed the Spanish armies in a series of resounding victories, the Court of Madrid, in despair, vainly attempted to agitate the feelings of the magnanimous sovereigns who had just recently driven usurpation and tyranny out of Europe, and who should be the protectors of the legitimacy and the justice of the American cause. Incapable of achieving our submission through force of arms, Spain has resorted to its insidious policy of manipulation. Ferdinand has humiliated himself by going so far as to confess that he needs foreign protection to bring us back under his ignominious yoke—a yoke which no power on earth could ever impose on us again! The Venezuelan nation, convinced that it is in possession of sufficient strength to repel its oppressors, has made it known through the government that it intends to fight to the death to defend its political life—not only against Spain, but also against the world itself, should the world stoop to assuming the defence of a rapacious government such as Spain's, that wants only extermination by the sword or in the flames of the Inquisition; that seeks not lands, but deserts, not cities but ruins, and not subjects but their sepulchres. The declaration of the Republic of Venezuela is the glorious, heroic and noble document of a free people; and it is with the greatest satisfaction that I have the honour of laying it before this Congress, endorsed as it is by the unanimous support of the people of Venezuela.

During the second period of the Republic our army lacked military equipment; it was constantly short of arms and without munitions and supplies. But today the defenders of the Republic bear not only the arms of justice but also those of force. Our troops can hold their own against the finest in Europe, for we now possess equal means of destruction. These great advantages we owe to the boundless generosity of a few benevolent foreigners who, on seeing mankind in chains and the cause of justice perishing, determined not to look on with indifference but rather to fly to our aid with their protection and assistance; and they have lent the Republic all it needed so that their philanthropical principles might triumph. These friends of humanity are the guardian angels of America, and we are bound by a debt of eternal gratitude towards them and by the sacred duty of fulfilling the obligations which were established between us. The national debt, legislators, is the repository of Venezuela's faith, honour and gratitude. Respect it like the Holy Ark, for it embraces not only the rights of our benefactors but the glory of our fidelity. It would be better that we perish rather than sully by default the endeavour that has saved our country and the lives of our children.

The union of New Granada and Venezuela into one great state is the universal desire of the peoples and governments of these republics. This bond, so longed for by all the inhabitants of Great Colombia, was forged in the furnace of the war, and our union is already a reality. These sister peoples are now entrusting you with the care of their interests, their rights and their destinies. In contemplating the unification of this vast region, my soul soars aloft to look down on the colossal perspective of such an extraordinary spectacle; my imagination flies forward in time to behold the centuries to come, and gazes with wonder on the prosperity, splendour and vitality which this vast area has inherited. I stand enthralled before this vision, in which this region seems to be at the very centre of the world, spread between its extensive coasts, and between those oceans that nature has separated but which our homeland unites with long, broad canals. I see it as the bond, the centre and the great marketplace of the human family; I see it sending, to the furthest corners of the earth, the treasures extracted from its mountains of silver and gold, I see it bringing health and life, with its magnificent plants, to the sick and ailing of the Old World. I see it yielding up its precious secrets to the scientists who are unaware that its wisdom exceeds even the riches which nature has showered upon it. I see it seated on the throne of freedom, grasping the sceptre of justice, crowned with glory, displaying the majesty of the New World to the Old.

Legislators, be so gracious as to hear with indulgence the voice of my political conscience, the deepest wishes of my heart and the fervent entreaties which, in the name of the people, I have taken the liberty of addressing to you. Give Venezuela a truly popular, just and moral government which can stand firm against oppression, anarchy and wickedness. A government which will usher in a reign of innocence, humanity and peace. A government which, under the rule of inexorable laws, will cause equality and freedom to prevail.

Gentlemen: begin your labours; I have finished mine.

25

# A plan for a fourth branch of government: a moral and educational power

*Proposal contained in the constitutional text submitted for consideration by the Congress of Angostura, and commented on in the speech made on 15 February 1819. It was not approved by the Congress, which agreed, however, that it should be published as an appendix to the Constitution.*

The Moral Power provided for in the draft constitution presented by General Bolívar, as supreme chief of the Republic, was considered by some deputies to be a most beneficial and suitable instrument for promoting the improvement of social institutions. Others regarded it as a moral inquisition, as undesirable and dreadful as religion. Everyone felt that it would be very difficult to establish, and would be quite impracticable at the present time. After lengthy debates it was agreed that, since we were still in the early stages of our political life, we should not, in dealing with matters of such great concern both to the state and to mankind, implicitly trust our theories and opinions in favour of or against the draft. Rather, we should study printed works on the matter by learned men throughout the world. We should undertake some partial experiments and gather information on the advantages and disadvantages of this institution, so that in the light of this information, we could then proceed to adopt such an institution or reject it. It was decreed, therefore, that the section on the Moral Power should be published as an *Appendix to the Constitution*, and that all men of learning, who as such should consider themselves as citizens of the world, should be invited to communicate their reflections on this subject to this fair land.

## The Moral Power

### SECTION I

*Composition, election, term of office, prerogatives and duties of this power*

*Article 1.* The Moral Power of the Republic shall reside in a body consisting of a president and forty members which, under the name of the Areopagus, shall exercise full and independent authority over public morality and primary education.

*Article 2.* The Areopagus shall consist of two Chambers as follows: first: the Morality Chamber; second: the Education Chamber.

*Article 3.* The Congress shall by majority vote elect the first members of the Areopagus, choosing them from among fathers of families who have achieved the highest distinction in the education of their children, and particularly in the exercise of public virtues. Once the Areopagus has been constituted, it shall itself fill the seats that become vacant.

*Article 4.* The President of the Areopagus shall always be appointed by the Senate from two lists, each containing the names of twelve candidates selected from among the most virtuous citizens of the Republic, one list to be presented by the House of Representatives and the other by the President of the Republic. A majority of two-thirds of the members present in the Senate shall be required for this election.

*Article 5.* Candidates for membership of the Areopagus must have attained the age of thirty-five years, in addition to possessing the requisite public virtues.

*Article 6.* When a member of the Areopagus has exercised his functions for twenty-five years, he shall be accorded the title of Father Emeritus of the Fatherland, and shall until the day of his death retain the right, without the obligation, to attend the meetings of the Areopagus and to vote.

*Article 7.* The members of the Areopagus shall be called Fathers of the Fatherland, their persons shall be sacrosanct and all the authorities of the Republic and the courts and corporations shall pay them filial respect.

*Article 8.* The first session of the Areopagus shall be opened with special solemnity and ceremonies and manifestations designed to create the most exalted and most respectful impression of its establishment; and its opening shall be marked by celebrations throughout the Republic.

*Article 9.* The Congress shall determine, in a special enactment, the rules governing the honours to be paid to the Areopagus, the precedence to be accorded to it in festivals and public ceremonies, the costumes and insignia which its members are to wear and all other matters concerning the splendour which this Moral Power should possess.

*Article 10.* Tenure of the office of the president or member of the Areopagus shall be terminated only by dismissal.

*Article 11.* No member of the Areopagus may be dismissed except by the Areopagus itself.

*Article 12.* Since the Areopagus must be venerable and above reproach, every good citizen shall inform it of any shortcomings he may notice in its members, and the Areopagus shall dismiss such members if they fail in any way to deserve public respect and veneration.

*Article 13.* When a member of the Areopagus has committed a reprehensible act and the Areopagus has failed to dismiss him, the government shall invite it a second time to do so; and, should it then still fail to do so, the government shall inform the Senate. If the Senate finds that the accused does not possess the virtues necessary in a Father of the Fatherland it shall rule that the Areopagus must dismiss him.

*Article 14.* When the Areopagus has dismissed one of its members, it shall wear mourning for three days, and the seat occupied by the member who has been dismissed shall remain covered for fifty years with a black cloth bearing the member's name written in large white letters.

*Article 15.* If, within a period of twelve years, the Areopagus acts in such a manner that the Senate is obliged three times to rule that a member must be dismissed, the Congress shall automatically proceed, once again, to elect the membership as it did when the Areopagus was first established, and the entire Republic shall wear mourning for one month. But in this case, the Congress shall examine the records and shall be bound to re-elect those members who, on each of the three occasions, were opposed to the reprehensible conduct.

*Article 16.* The Areopagus, with its two Chambers meeting in joint session, shall:

1. Appoint the twenty members of each Chamber and determine

which of them is to preside over each Chamber, when the Chairmen of the Chambers are not appointed by the President of the Areopagus, who has the right to attend and vote in either of the Chambers.

2. Decide on the dismissal of any of its members, according to established practice, and appoint new members to seats vacated by death or dismissal.

3. Appoint from among its members the secretary or secretaries it considers it requires for its proceedings and for those of each Chamber.

4. Address applications to the Congress for the funds it needs each year for its expenditures and functions, demand accounts from its agents or employees concerning the use of these funds, and present them to the Congress.

5. Distribute civic prizes or awards each year to citizens who have most distinguished themselves by outstanding displays of virtue and patriotism, and withdraw these awards from persons who, after obtaining them, have shown themselves to be unworthy of them. Distribution and withdrawal of awards shall be effected at a public meeting, with the greatest possible solemnity.

6. Declare to be eminently virtuous, or to be heroes or great men, persons who have proved themselves worthy of such honours. Unless such a declaration has been previously made, the Congress will not be able to erect or authorize the erection of statues or other public monuments in memory of any person.

7. Proclaim and honour, in the sessions which have been mentioned above, the names of virtuous citizens and the greatest achievements in morality and education; proclaim with opprobrium and ignominy the names of wrongdoers and acts of corruption and indecency; and invite public admiration of teachers who have made the greatest progress in their schools.

## SECTION II

*The special powers of the Morality Chamber*

*Article 1.* The Morality Chamber shall guide moral opinion throughout the entire Republic, shall punish wrongdoing with opprobrium and infamy, and shall reward public virtues with honour and glory. Its decisions shall be published in the press.

*Article 2.* Isolated acts shall not be subject to consideration by it unless they are so extraordinary that they may influence public morality for better or for worse. Repeated acts, which constitute habits or customs, shall come directly within its competence.

*Article 3.* Its authority shall be independent and absolute. There shall be no appeal from its decisions, except by opinion and posterity; it shall take into account in its judgements no accuser other than outrage and no attorney other than truth itself.

*Article 4.* Its jurisdiction shall extend not only to individuals but also to families, departments, provinces, corporations, courts, all authorities and even the Republic as an entity. If these engage in wrongdoing, they must be denounced to the whole world. Even the government shall be subject to this Chamber which shall brand it with a mark of infamy and declare it unworthy of the Republic if it violates its treaties or distorts their meaning, or violates a pact or fails to perform some duty or honour some promise.

*Article 5.* All moral and political works, periodicals and all other writings shall be subject to its censorship, which shall be undertaken after publication. Politics shall be of no concern to it, except in relation to morality. In its judgement it shall determine whether the works examined merit approval or contempt; and it may go so far as to determine whether the author is a good citizen and a lover or an enemy of morality and whether as such he is worthy or unworthy of belonging to a virtuous Republic.

*Article 6.* Its jurisdiction shall cover not only what is written about morality or in relation to it, but also everything that is spoken, recited or sung in public; and its function shall always be to censor the spoken word and if necessary impose moral penalties, but never to restrain it.

*Article 7.* Its censure and its admonishments shall be addressed always to the public, and it shall be concerned with the public only. It shall not address itself or reply to individuals or corporations.

*Article 8.* Public gratitude, the national debt, treaties, pacts, and good faith in business, not only in business relations but also with regard to the quality and authenticity of merchandise, are areas in which the Chamber shall exercise the most active and scrupulous vigilance. In these areas, every mistake and omission shall be rigorously and inexorably punished.

*Article 9.* Ingratitude, disrespect for parents, husbands, old people, teachers, judges and all citizens acknowledged and declared to be virtuous, failure to honour any sort of commitment and indifference to public calamity or to the misfortunes of friends and close relatives shall be especially recommended to the vigilance of the Chamber, which may punish them even if only a single act is involved.

*Article 10.* The Chamber shall organize moral supervision, appointing for this purpose as many censors as it sees fit. As a reward for zeal and effort, the honorary title of Cato will be attributed to every censor who, by his services and virtues, has proved himself worthy of it.

*Article 11.* Every year the Chamber shall publish statistical tables of virtuous and wrongful acts, for which the higher and lower courts will present it with precise and detailed accounts of all law suits and criminal cases. It shall also publish every year comparative lists of men who have been outstanding in the exercise of public virtues, or in the practice of public wrongdoing.

*Article 12.* The people, the electoral colleges, the municipalities, the provincial governments, the President of the Republic and the Congress shall consult these lists in making their elections and appointments, and in distributing honours and rewards. A citizen whose name is entered on the list of wrongdoers shall not be employed in any branch of the public service, or elsewhere; and no national award, special honour or even decoration shall be given to persons whose names are not included on the lists of the virtuous, although they may be employed by the Government.

*Article 13.* Women, like men, shall be subject to the jurisdiction of the Chamber, and shall receive awards or punishments from it, according to their merit.

### SECTION III

*Powers of the Education Chamber*

*Article 1.* The Education Chamber shall be responsible for the physical and moral education of children, from their birth until the end of their twelfth year.

*Article 2.* Since the co-operation of mothers in the education of their children is indispensable, in their first years, and since these are the most precious years for installing their first ideas into them, and also the most dangerous years for the state of their health, the Chamber shall take special care to publish and circulate throughout the Republic brief and simple instructions, suited to the intelligence of all mothers of families, on a variety of subjects. Priests and departmental officials shall disseminate these instructions, so that each and every mother will be familiar with them. Every mother shall present the instructions she has received, and shall demonstrate that she is familiar with them, on the day when her child is baptized or its birth is registered.

*Article 3.* In addition to these instructions, the Chamber shall publish in our language the foreign works most appropriate for enlightening the nation on this matter, and shall express its views on them and make the necessary observations or correlations.

*Article 4.* It shall encourage scientists and others to write and publish original works on this subject, in conformity with our traditions, customs and principles.

*Article 5.* Since the Chamber will itself soon be amassing, on a larger scale than anyone else, all the facts and the knowledge needed for such works, it shall compile and publish its own works which will serve to encourage others to engage in this activity, and will provide enlightenment to everyone.

*Article 6.* It shall use every possible means and shall not spare any expense or sacrifice to obtain this knowledge. For this purpose it shall commission zealous and educated persons without any other commitments to travel throughout the world, make inquiries and collect every kind of knowledge on this subject.

*Article 7.* It shall be the exclusive responsibility of the Chamber to establish, organize and direct primary schools, both for boys and for girls, and to ensure that they are taught to speak, read and write correctly, that they learn the most basic rules of arithmetic and the principles of grammar, and that they are inspired by the ideas of honour and probity, love of country, law and work, respect for their parents, for the elderly and for judges, and support for the Government.

*Article 8.* Since our existing schools are inadequate for a major educational plan, the Chamber shall give special attention to the planning and building of the schools needed throughout the Republic, both for boys and girls, who should be separated at least from the time they begin to grow up. The form, design and location of these establishments shall in each case be that which is best suited to their purpose; and, in their construction, attention shall be given not only to their solidity and dimensions, but also to the elegance, cleanliness, comfort and recreational possibilities for young people.

*Article 9.* The Chamber shall determine the number of schools to be established; it shall indicate the province and, if possible, the precise location in which each one of them is to be built; and it shall for this purpose assess the advantages of the place, in terms of its accessibility for children, the salubriousness of the site, the abundance and quality of food supplies, etc.

*Article 10.* Each school shall be under the direct control of a teacher who shall be appointed by the Chamber, which shall choose him from among the most virtuous and learned men, irrespective of their place of birth. The teacher's wife shall be the headmistress of the girls' department, under the direction of her husband. These posts shall be very highly esteemed, and those who occupy them shall be honoured, respected and loved as the first and most valuable citizens of the Republic.

*Article 11.* The Chamber shall establish rules for the general organization and administration of these establishments, and shall specify the type of schooling which children need to enable them to acquire in infancy useful and sound ideas and basic notions suited to their condition and fortune, and also noble and moral ideals and the principles of sociability and patriotism. This plan shall be presented to the Congress so that, after being examined and approved, it shall then become the Law of the Republic.

*Article 12.* The Chamber shall each year publish precise and detailed reports on births and deaths of children, their physical condition, their health and illnesses, their school promotions and their particular inclinations, qualities and talents. In compiling these reports, it shall consult teachers, priests, doctors, departmental officials, enlightened citizens and all the authorities, since, from the President himself downwards, everyone is subject to its authority in the matter of education.

*Article 13.* In addition to these powers, the Education Chamber shall direct public opinion on literary matters, until the Philosophy Institute is established. It shall examine, or have examined, works published on every subject, and shall express its judgements on them in the *Bulletin* of the Areopagus.

26

# A school for orphans, foundlings and poor children at Santa Fe

*Decree issued on 17 September 1819, at Bogotá, in the month following the Battle of Boyacá, which was won after the 'Crossing of the Andes', a much-praised military feat. This school was one of the first practical benefits for the people of New Granada.*

## SIMÓN BOLÍVAR
### President of the Republic, etc., etc.

Considering that education and public instruction are of primary importance for general well-being and constitute the soundest basis for the freedom of peoples, and considering also that in New Granada there are large numbers of unfortunate children who, because their parents were sacrificed on the altars of the fatherland by the cruelty of the Spaniards, have no home and no hope of subsistence or education from sources other than the Republic, I have decided to decree and do so decree as follows:

*Article 1.* The monastery abandoned by the Capuchin Fathers in this capital shall henceforward be a school for orphans, foundlings or poor children whom the Republic has a duty to support and educate.

*Article 2.* For the moment the only children shall be the orphans of parents who were killed for the fatherland by the Spaniards on gallows and scaffolds or on the fields of battle.

*Article 3.* The school shall be placed under the care and responsibility of a headmaster, who shall be entrusted with its direction, financial management and internal supervision. He shall be the first head of the school, and shall have the duty of providing the children with the most virtuous education, in conformity with the liberal principles of the Republic.

*Article 4.* The headmaster and the other teachers shall be elected and appointed by the government.

*Article 5.* Until the government has sufficient funds to establish teaching posts in all subjects, the children shall be taught reading and writing, the grammatical principles of the language, the principles of our religion and morality, drawing, logic, mathematics, physics, geography and surveying.

*Article 6.* The funds for the school shall comprise the 24,200 pesos which were bequeathed to the cause of public education by Doctor Juan Ignacio Gutiérrez, and all monies previously belonging to the monastery and community of the Capuchins. State revenue shall be used only to cover expenditures for which the above-mentioned funds are insufficient.

*Article 7.* All other matters concerning the education to be provided and the administration, servicing and financial management of the school shall be set forth in detail in a special regulation.

The present decree shall be published, printed and distributed to all those responsible for its execution.

Done, signed by my hand, sealed with the provisional seal of the Republic and countersigned by the Secretary of Government in the General Headquarters at Santafé, on 17 September 1819.

*Simón Bolívar*

*Alejandro Osorio,*
Secretary a.i.

27

# Concern for the drilling of troops and the training of officers

*Bolívar here reveals his constant concern for the revolutionary army. In instructions transmitted to General Santander from the General Headquarters at Barichara on 10 October 1819, the Liberator advances some important military concepts, such as the use of 'training officers' and 'recruitment centres' for discipline and training, and also the use of provincial 'academies' for the same purpose.*

Sir,

You will send, to each of the provinces of Tunja, Socorro and Neiva, two or three training officers who will give instruction in the use of weapons at the large recruitment centres which I wish to see established in all provinces. These officers will constantly visit the various centres in turn, so that—with wooden rifles, since there are at present no real ones—recruits may receive instruction in weapon-handling and drill. I repeat my instructions that 1,000 recruits are to be enlisted in each free province of New Granada and are to be billeted in the manner most suitable for their provisioning and discipline, concerning which you will issue detailed orders adapted to the circumstances in each province. In New Granada there is no shortage of elderly veteran officers who are no longer fit for service but could be of the greatest value in training recruits. Pardo and Ley should come here, and you should send others of the same quality to the other provinces, even if they do not wish to go.

In the capital town of each province, an academy will be established for twenty-four young officer cadets, possessing skills in reading and writing, as well as the necessary talents and character, etc., for the purpose of instructing them in all duties relating to the service. They will be freed from all other responsibilities and given the option of becoming officers as soon as they have acquired the necessary training. In this connection, you will go into all the necessary details when you give instructions for the creation of these academies.

28

## 'The unanimous determination to die free rather than to live as slaves'

*On his return from the feats and sacrifices of the Battle of Boyacá, which resulted in the independence of New Granada, the Liberator gave a report on his victories to the Congress of Angostura on 14 December 1819, and proposed the creation of the Republic of Colombia, formed by Venezuela, New Granada, Panama, Quito and Guayaquil.*

Gentlemen of the Legislature:

My first sentiment as I enter this august precinct is one of gratitude for the immense honour the Congress has deigned to bestow upon me by allowing me once more to occupy this chair, which less than a year ago I yielded to the President of the Representatives of the People.

When, at the beginning of this year, I was undeservingly, and against my deepest convictions, entrusted with the responsibility of executive power, I protested to the sovereign body that my profession, my character and my talents were incompatible with the functions of that supreme office. Having thus been relieved of those duties, I left it to the Vice-President to perform them, and I assumed the sole responsibility for directing the war. I then marched to the Western Army, which was confronted by General Morillo with a superior force. Nothing would have been more hazardous than to give battle in circumstances in which the capital city of Caracas was liable to be occupied by the expeditionary forces lately despatched from Europe, and when we ourselves were awaiting further reinforcements. General Morillo abandoned the plainlands of the Apure at the onset of winter, and I deemed it more advantageous for the Republic to secure the freedom of New Granada than to complete that of Venezuela.

It would take far too long to describe in detail to the Congress all the efforts that were required of the troops of the army of liberation in order to achieve success in the undertaking we had set ourselves. Wintertime in plainlands subject to sudden flooding, the frozen summits of the Andes, abrupt changes in climate, an experienced army with the strength of three holding all the major military strongholds in southern America, and many other obstacles—all these we had to overcome at Paya, Gámeza, Vargas, Boyacá and Popayán, in order to liberate, in less than three months, twelve provinces of New Granada.

I commend to the supreme assembly of the nation the merits of these great services that have been rendered by my valiant companions-in-arms who, with unparalleled endurance, have suffered mortal privations and, with a valour unprecedented in the annals of Venezuela, have vanquished and seized the army of the King. However, we are not indebted for these victories to the army of liberation alone. The people of New Granada have shown themselves worthy to be free. Their efficient co-operation made good our losses and increased our forces. The delirium caused by a passion unleashed is less ardent than that experienced by New Granada when it regained its freedom.

These generous people offered up all their possessions and lives on the altar of the motherland, a gesture of sacrifice which is all the more meritorious because of its spontaneity! I say to you that the unanimous determination to die free rather than to live as slaves has given New Granada a right to our admiration and respect. Its desire for the reunion of its provinces with those of Venezuela is also unanimous. The people of New Granada are firmly persuaded of the immense advantage that would result for both peoples from the creation of a new Republic composed of these two nations. The reunion of New Granada and Venezuela has been my sole aim ever since I first took up arms: it is the declared wish of the citizens of both countries, and it is the guarantee of freedom in South America.

Legislators, the time has come to give our Republic solid and enduring foundations. It is for your wisdom to decree this great social act, and to establish the principles of the pact on which this vast Republic is to be founded. Once it is proclaimed to the world, my services will be rewarded.

29

# The creation of Colombia:
## 'Power, prosperity, grandeur, stability'

*On 20 December 1819, the 'Fundamental Law of the Republic of Colombia' as approved three days earlier by the Congress, was sent from Angostura to the Vice-President of Cundinamarca. Thus, the ideas of Miranda began to take shape, and the accompanying letter would appear to reflect Bolívar's well-defined ideas on Latin American solidarity.*

Sir,

It is with satisfaction that I hereby remit to you the Fundamental Law of the Republic of Colombia, approved by decree of the Supreme Congress. The law itself mentions the powerful motives which led the Congress to realize at last the wishes of the citizens of both nations and unite the two into a single republic. The prospects opened up by this memorable act are vast and magnificent. Power, prosperity, grandeur and stability will result from this felicitous union.

The unanimous vote of the deputies of Venezuela and New Granada has laid the foundations for a sound and lasting edifice, and has determined the name, rank and status by which our nascent republic is to be known to the world and in accordance with which its political relationships are to be established.

Although this provisional act is not invested with all the necessary formalities, and the free provinces of Cundinamarca have had no part in its making, the incalculable advantages to be derived from it and, above all, the absolute necessity of availing ourselves of the favourable disposition of foreign powers moved the representatives of Venezuela and New Granada to take a first step which would in their view promote the stability, durability and prosperity of Colombia.

In ten years of indescribable struggle and labour, in ten years of suffering almost beyond human endurance, we met with indifference from all Europe and even from our brothers in the north, as they remained unmoved spectators of our extermination. This may primarily be due *inter alia* to the profusion of sovereign nations that have now been established.

The lack of unity and cohesion, the absence of agreement and concord, and particularly the lack of resources which inevitably resulted from the fragmentation of the republics are, I repeat, the true reason for the total lack of interest in our fate which was displayed by our neighbours and by the Europeans. Sections and fragments of territory which, albeit of considerable size, have neither population nor resources can never inspire either interest or confidence in those who may wish to establish relations with them.

The Republic of Colombia has the means and resources that are necessary to maintain it in the rank and status to which it has been elevated and to convince foreigners that it is able to maintain its position. This makes it easier to obtain allies and to procure the assistance it needs to consolidate its independence.

The riches of Cundinamarca and Venezuela, the population of both nations, and the advantageous situation of the latter with its innumerable Atlantic ports will ensure for Colombia an importance which neither Venezuela nor New Granada would have enjoyed if they had remained separate.

The lovers of the true well-being and splendour of Colombia are those who have made the greatest contribution to union. Convinced of the mutual advantages, they have made every effort and applied all their wisdom and powers of persuasion to achieve union. The Vice-President, Mr Francisco Antonio Zea, holds the distinction of having been the prime mover in this covenant, which promises so many considerable advantages.

Mr Zea has, in fact, been appointed emissary extraordinary of Colombia to the Cabinet in Washington, and he will later travel to France, where he is very well known and enjoys a very high reputation. His mission will be to secure friends for us there, to incline the government in our favour and to obtain for us war material and whatever else he believes that Colombia might need. The government places great store on the suitability of this emissary, and is confident that he will be successful in view of the trust and confidence that the resources and achievements of the Republic of Colombia are bound to inspire.

Our agents in London, Messrs Peñalver and Vergara, inform the government that the British people are very favourably disposed towards us, as is their government too. They are still hopeful of securing the loan of 3 million duros which they were sent there to negotiate—and this despite the imprisonment of Mr Real, agent of New Granada at the British Court, who was arrested for debts of 150,000 pesos and released after the above-named gentlemen had stood bail for him. Great Britain's attitude causes them to urge the union of the two republics; and they believe that our credit and our reputation will be enhanced considerably by such an act.

That is another of the major reasons why the Congress favoured a union of the two nations—i.e. a doubling of our resources and a consequent doubling of our credit. There can be little doubt that we shall eventually obtain that loan, in view of the importance of the Republic of Colombia and the guarantees it offers.

The fundamental law of the Republic of Colombia must be solemnly proclaimed in all villages and army centres; it must be posted up in all localities, and enforced in the department of Cundinamarca, as provided for by the Congress.

To you falls the honour of giving effect to the decree, which elevates your country to a position of grandeur and dignity which even the most vivid imagination can hardly envisage, and to ensure its execution and implementation by all villages, army centres, corporations and municipalities.

As soon as the Congress has adopted regulations for convening the representatives of Colombia in the town of Cúcuta, I shall give effect to them. There, the present document will be invested with all the solemnity, legality and formality which governments, through their legitimate representatives, demand.

May God be with you, etc.

*Bolívar*

30

# Recognition of the heroism of women

*A moving speech made by the Liberator to the courageous women of Socorro, the historic town of New Granada, on 14 February 1820.*

Ladies of Socorro,

No earthly power could ever be strong enough to subjugate a people that has produced women of such great valour. Daughters of Socorro, you are destined to be the reef on which your oppressors will founder—they who in their fury have defiled the most sacred, most innocent and most gracious members of our species by humiliating you. And your answer has been to enhance your dignity by steeling your tender hearts beneath the blows of your cruel oppressors.

Heroic womenfolk of Socorro, you will remember that the mothers of Sparta did not ask for the lives of their sons but for the victory of their fatherland; the mothers of Rome beheld with contentment the glorious wounds of their relatives and urged them on to achieve the supreme honour of giving up their lives on the battlefield. But I say that yours has been an even more noble and selfless patriotism—you have taken up the sword, joined the ranks and sought to die for your country. Mothers, wives, sisters, who will be great enough to follow in the traces of such heroic acts? Will any man be worthy of you? No, I say, and again, no! But you have earned the admiration of the universe and the adoration of the liberators of Colombia.

Headquarters, Socorro, 24 February 1820

*Simón Bolívar*

## 31

## On the reasons for abolishing slavery

*In the Archives of the Liberator, there are two copies of this memorandum, dated San Cristóbal, 20 April 1820, containing the philosophical reasoning behind this political act, which had been rejected by General F. de P. Santander to whom the letter is addressed.*

Sir,

I have the honour to reply to your letter of 2 April in which you refer to the leasing of salt mines and to the instructions from General Valdés in which, you say, there is some reference to declaring the emanicipation of slaves in the province of El Cauca.

The relevant article states as follows: 'All slaves who may be of use for military service shall be assigned to the army.' If I am not mistaken, this is not tantamount to declaring the emancipation of slaves, but it does involve my using the powers invested in me by the law, which reads as follows: '*Article 3*. Nevertheless, those who are called to arms by the President of the Republic or who perform some meritorious service, shall forthwith enter into possession of their freedom.'

I am therefore acting fully within the law, which itself gives an answer to all the comments you have raised. However, as is my custom, I shall explain my orders.

I have ordered that all useful slaves shall be called to arms. This must be construed as relating only to those whom the forces need, since too many such recruits would do more harm than good.

The military and political grounds for my ordering the enlistment of slaves are obvious. We need tough, able-bodied men who are accustomed to hardship and fatigue, men who can embrace the cause and take up the struggle with eagerness, who can identify their cause with the public cause and for whom the value of death is a little less than that which they attach to their lives.

The political reasons are still more compelling. The freedom of slaves has been proclaimed both *de jure* and *de facto*. The Congress has borne in mind Montesquieu's statement that:

In moderate governments political liberty makes civil liberty precious; whoever is deprived of the latter is also deprived of the former; he beholds a contented society of which he is not the slightest part; he finds security bestowed upon others but not upon himself. Nothing is closer to the state of animals than to see other men free without being free oneself. Such people are the enemies of society, and, if there were many of them, they would be dangerous. One should not take pride in the fact that moderate governments have seen their nations troubled by the rebellion of slaves, whereas this has occurred so seldom in despotic states.

It is, therefore, proved by the maxims of politics, taken from the examples of history, that any free government which commits the absurdity of maintaining slavery is punished by rebellion, and at times by extermination, as in the case of Haiti.

There can be no doubt that the law of the Congress is wise in all respects. What better and more legitimate way is there of earning one's freedom than by fighting for it? Would it be right that free men only should die in order that slaves might be free? Is it not proper that slaves should acquire their rights on the battlefield, and that their dangerously large numbers should be reduced by means so compelling and legitimate?

In Venezuela we have seen free people die and captives live on! I do not know if that is politic, but I do know that, if we do not use our slaves in Cundinamarca, the same events will recur.

I am therefore exercising the powers vested in me by the law on the emancipation of slaves, and I repeat my previous orders, i.e. that the Southern Army shall enlist as many slaves as its forces may require, and that 3,000 young, single men shall join the Northern Army. On these last points I most strongly insist.

32

# The service of education:
# teachers and schools for the Indians

*Extract from the Decree on the Indians, their freedom and their property, issued in El Rosario de Cúcuta on 20 May 1820.*

*Article 6.* The revenue from the land leased in accordance with Article 4 shall be destined in part for the payment of taxes and in part for the payment of the salaries of teachers in the schools to be established in each locality. Each schoolmaster shall receive an annual salary of 120 pesos when the revenue from the land reaches or exceeds this amount; if it is less, then the schoolmaster shall receive the full amount available.

*Article 7.* The magistrate, with the agreement of the priest in each locality, shall appoint the aforementioned teachers and shall notify the governors of the province of such appointments, so that the provincial governors may in turn advise the governor of the department.

*Article 8.* The provincial governors shall determine the regulations to be observed in the schools in their respective provinces, and shall specify the methods of teaching and learning.

*Article 9.* All children between the ages of 4 and 14 shall attend school, where they shall be taught reading and writing, arithmetic, the principles of religion and the rights and duties of citizens in Colombia, in accordance with the law.

*Article 10.* After the teachers' salaries have been deducted, all revenue remaining from the leasing of land shall be applied for the payment of taxes. The total tax payable by the village concerned shall then be reduced by an amount equal to the amount so applied, and the taxes payable by individuals shall be reduced proportionately.

33

# 'A properly trained legislator needs to be brought up in a school of righteousness, justice and law'

*Expanding upon his Angostura Address, the Liberator writes this letter to his intellectual friend, Guillermo White, from San Cristóbal, on 26 May 1820.*

My dear friend,

I am taking this opportunity to forward to you my address to the Congress, which has been re-printed in Bogotá, and which I beg you to examine with greater indulgence than before. I understand that you have criticized me for establishing a hereditary senate and a system for educating future senators. The first of these acts is in conformity with the practice of every democratic republic, and the second with the demands of reason. Education forms men of virtue, and it is clear that a properly trained legislator needs to be brought up in a school of righteousness, justice and law. You quote the example of England as being contrary to my ordinance; and yet, in England, is there not much good still remaining to be done? As regards my senate, I would stress that it constitutes neither an aristocracy nor a nobility, the former being based on the right to rule the republic, and the second relying on detestable privileges. The function of my senate is to temper absolute democracy and to combine an absolute form of government with a moderate in-stitution, since it is now an established principle in politics that absolute democratic government is as tyrannical as the rule of a despot; consequently, only a moderate government can be free. How do you propose that I should temper a democracy other than with an aristocratic institution? Since we may not combine monar-chic structures with the popular form we have adopted for ourselves, we must at least ensure that there is within the republic an im-mutable body capable of ensuring its stability since, without stability, every political principle becomes corrupt and eventually destroys itself.

Please be so kind as to read my address carefully, paying atten-tion not so much to the parts as to the whole. The complete text demonstrates how little faith I have in the morality of our fellow citizens; and, without republican morality, there can be no free government. In order to build up such morality, I have conceived of a fourth power that might nurture men in virtue and oblige them to abide by it always. That fourth power may also appear imperfect to you; but, my friend, if you want a republic in Colombia, you must also wish for political virtue. The institutions of the ancient world prove to us that men can be governed by the severest of precepts. The whole course of history demonstrates that men will submit to anything which a clever legislator requires of them and to anything which a strong authority imposes on them. Dracon gave Athens laws of blood, and Athens bowed to them, and even abided by them until Solon sought to reform them. Lycurgus enacted in Sparta what Plato would never have dared even to dream of in his *Republic*, were it not for the example given by the Spartan lawmaker. Is there anything to which men have not submitted, or to which they will not submit in the future? If there is a just violence, it is the violence which sets itself the task of making men good and therefore happy; and there is no legitimate freedom other than freedom which aims to enhance the dignity of mankind and improve its lot. Everything else is pure illusion, and perhaps dangerous illusion at that.

Please forgive this lengthy digression on my address. You deserved to receive it long ago, but I had spared you it, more by neglect than by intent.

Your friend, as always.

*Bolívar*

## 34

## The prospects for peace

*A wide-ranging, spontaneous and optimistic review of the complex political situation, for his friend General Carlos Soublette, written from Rosario on 19 June 1820.*

My dear General and friend,

I received yesterday a highly interesting communication that was intercepted by Colonel Carmona in Chiriguana. It was dated Cartagena, 20 May, and has brought us good news from Spain up to the month of April. On 7 March, Ferdinand VII accepted the Constitution and the Cortes in a decree forced upon him by pressure from the people and at the insistence of General Ballesteros. It would seem that the entire country was in rebellion, and the King had no other resort than to accept the Constitution. His situation is, therefore, most critical and he will need to comply with the wishes of the people and the army, who are calling for peace, so that the sacrifices and the loss of life can be ended. Even the liberals will have to solicit the support of the army with the promise of peace, because the question is simply that there should be no further expeditions to America. The best way of allaying even the faintest suspicion that more expeditions will be sent is to end the war, a measure on which the entire Peninsula now seems to be agreed.

Also, Spain has been unable to subjugate us with her expeditions, and will now achieve even less without them. Her only other concern is exclusive trade with America: and, as we have countless privateers whose numbers will increase in inverse proportion to our military reverses—or, in other words, the less territory we have, the more privateers there will be—her trade will consequently be wiped out. As the liberals are anxious to propagate liberal principles which are bound to encounter considerable opposition in Spain and the rest of Europe, it is essential that the Cortes should come out in our favour, partly because the issue now is not merely one of political economy but rather of the internal balance of power in general, and partly because, with the free governments which exist in America, they will always find points of agreement with us and even means of joint action against the faint-hearted spirits, since affinity of principles always produces mutual regard in politics. What is more, these faint-hearted spirits, especially Ferdinand, greatly need peace in order to put an end to discontent in the army, which is now demanding peace, and nothing but peace, and will not be satisfied by anything less. Men are not content with treatment for the disease from which they suffer; they demand that the disease itself be eradicated, because of the fear it creates and the constant threat that it may afflict them again. Thus, the Spanish troops will not be satisfied until hostilities with us have ceased, since they know full well that every type of system that has governed Spain has sent them off to America. If there is anything which is likely to delay our negotiations with Spain, it will certainly not be lack of will on the part of Spain or any internal obstacle to such a decision. I believe, however, that, in view of the imminent dangers which both parties will face, and because of their constant preoccupation with their immediate interests, they will not for the moment be thinking of negotiating. For this very reason we must provide the enemy with the means and opportunities to treat with us. Such means could be initiated by our envoys in London and in the United States directly with the respective Spanish envoys, and indirectly with all other foreign envoys who are most interested in our cause. These steps could be taken in a hundred different ways, some perhaps being more effective than others, some direct and some unofficial, through public or private channels, through the press, in private talks, through friends and even through enemies. It will never be humiliating to offer peace on the terms set forth in the *Declaration of the Republic of Venezuela*, which should serve as the basis for any negotiations, first, because the law of the Republic so requires, and secondly, because the nature and the salvation of Colombia so demand. To offer peace to the Spaniards in this way is, for us, to claim the victory since, as there is no other subject of contention, to obtain independence is to win. As for the Spaniards, who are now convinced that they have no power over us, and who have suffered in this war all the calamities that could be inflicted upon them, to offer them peace is to award them a victory, too, which is no less important and desirable. They are in the predicament of Plato's rich man; they have everything to lose and nothing to gain, whereas we have nothing to lose—but stand to gain everything they have. The war has left us with nothing else but life, which for desperate men is beyond price. This question if properly expounded is vast in scope and embraces all the considerations which are likely to influence our enemies and indeed ourselves. We must, therefore, offer nothing more than peace in exchange for independence. For us, independence will bring us all the blessings of heaven; and for the Spaniards, peace is a source of immense future prosperity.

Such are my ideas, and I would like you, the Vice-President of Colombia and the Secretary of State, to give deep thought to them and put them to good use at the appropriate time. By this, I do not mean that you should await such an opportunity, but that you should rather seek it, or even create it by every possible means, because at present time is of the essence and Seneca was not the only man to appreciate the value of time.

If perchance anything is known or any reports are received of diplomatic negotiations, I should be informed post-haste; and rich rewards will be offered for getting the news to me promptly. In this matter, nothing is to be done without my knowledge. Nothing is easier than to procrastinate, say that my arrival is imminent and then wait for me. Personal experience is important in all matters, particularly in diplomacy. In the business of peace as in war, it is most important to be a veteran.

35

# Superintendence,
## administration and control of educational institutions are the responsibility of the state

*Decree promulgated in El Rosario on 21 June 1820, in which Bolívar declares that the state is to assume overall responsibility for the guidance and direction of education.*

## SIMÓN BOLÍVAR
### Liberator President

Considering: (1) that the civic and literary education of the young is one of the government's primary and most cherished aims; (2) that, since it is at present impossible to reform the literary education imparted in the few establishments set up by the Spanish Government, such establishments should be supervised and their advancement and improvement ensured; (3) that the difference in the educational methods and systems applied in the various institutions is undesirable and harmful; (4) that this undesirable state of affairs is inevitable until the schools are governed by a single authority and, above all, by the government; (5) that the administration or superintendence exercised by the ecclesiastical authorities in the seminaries was delegated to them by the King of Spain; and (6) that the canonical provisions concerning the seminaries are in no way to be modified on condition that the ecclesiastical authorities continue to exercise their rights of inspection and allocation of seminary scholarships without interfering in the general administration of the establishment, I have decided to decree and do so decree as follows:

*Article 1.* The superintendence, administration and control of schools and educational institutions established in the Republic shall be the responsibility of the government, regardless of the manner in which such institutions came into being.

*Article 2.* The seminary colleges that exist throughout the Republic, whose principals, rectors, teachers and other staff shall come under the authority of, and shall be appointed by the government, are expressly included under the terms of the above article.

*Article 3.* The right reverend archbishops, bishops and their chapters and vicars-general in vacant sees shall retain their rights and privileges with respect to the provision and supervision of seminary scholarships and shall fulfil and exercise all their responsibilities with regard to the aforementioned scholarships.

*Article 4*. The vice-presidents of departments, acting as the direct agents of the government in their respective departments, shall be the superintendents of schools and educational institutions.

*Article 5*. The Minister of the Interior and of Justice shall be entrusted with the execution of this decree, which shall be published and communicated to all whom it may concern.

Done at El Rosario, on the 21st day of June 1820—Year Ten.

*Simón Bolívar*

## 36

# North-south co-operation for independence

*Message from Bogotá dated 10 January 1821, and addressed to Don José de San Martín, Captain-General of the Liberation Army of Peru, etc., etc.; it provides evidence of the close ties of friendship between the two heroes, which helped to crown Bolívar's efforts to complete the liberation of the continent.*

Sir,

I have the honour to acknowledge receipt of your dispatch of 12 October last year from Pisco. I had been hoping and wishing for this moment all my life, and only the opportunity of embracing you and seeing our two flags united could mean more to me. The victor of Chacabuco and of Maipó, and first son of La Plata, has overlooked his own glories in paying such exaggerated tributes to me; and yet they do honour to him, since they are striking evidence of his generosity and selflessness. As soon as I knew that you had set foot on the shores of Peru, I believed already that they were free; and I hasten to congratulate you on this third fatherland which owes its existence to you.

I am at present marching to fulfil my promise to reunite the Empire of the Incas and the Empire of Liberty; it is doubtless easier to march into Quito than into Lima, but I am sure that you will accomplish what is difficult with greater ease than I achieve what is simple. Soon, Divine Providence, which has hitherto protected the banners of Law and Freedom, will bring us together in some corner of Peru, once we have trampled under our feet the trophies of the tyrants of the American world.

You will note from the enclosed papers the events that have recently been taking place in these parts. Amongst other things, there is an armistice and a treaty for the regularization of the war, which is worthy of your attention.

Please accept the assurance of my highest consideration and respect.

Your obedient servant,

*Bolívar*

## 37

# On the difficulties facing a new republic

*Letter to the illustrious and valiant Colombian leader, General Antonio Nariño, dated Barinas, 21 April 1821.*

I shall be very glad when I know that you have reached Cúcuta without mishap. The sudden passing of your predecessors must surely sadden you somewhat, and I pray to God that you do not follow them on their journey to the land of the dead. Here, it has been said that our mutual and worthy friend Azuola must have passed away; I shall be most grievously sorry if such a misfortune has indeed befallen the Republic and his family.

I lay great store on your ability to smooth away all the difficulties that are preventing the convening of the Congress which I now most fervently desire. Without exaggeration, I wish to see the legislature meet so that it can lay the last bricks on the building of the Republic, which is yet to be completed. Up to now, all we have done is clear the lands of twenty-two provinces and write a book which addresses itself to no one, a book called the Constitution. However, you will see for yourself that there is as yet nothing else: the change of government, the sending of a few envoys to foreign countries, the death of two vice-presidents, the absence of ministers, the difficulties involved in convening Congress, the non-existence of a central revenue department, the disorganization in all branches, my absence from the capital and the fact that I stay so long with the army—all these things and many more are, so to speak, making an orphan of the Republic. Colombia is being ruled by the swords of her defenders and, instead of being a society, it is a military camp. Hence, the abuses, the neglect and the lack of any basic organization which are the inevitable result of principles which I have been unable to correct, for many reasons: first, because in a short time and with only scant resources of general knowledge, no one man can do everything, whether good or bad; secondly, because I have devoted all my time to the expulsion of our enemies; and thirdly, because there are an infinite number of considerations to be borne in mind in this amazing confusion of patriots, Spaniards, egoists, whites, half-breeds, Venezuelans, Cundinamarcans, federalists, centralists, republicans, aristocrats, good men and bad, and the host of hierarchies within all these many groups; that is why, my friend, I have often had to be unjust for political reasons and I have never been able to be just with impunity.

I am deeply convinced that the government should be headed by someone else who is not a soldier such as I am, and not constantly away at the front; and I also believe that the supreme office of the Republic and the command of the army should be kept separate. I therefore tender my resignation, trusting that you and all other good citizens will pledge yourselves to accept it. If not, you may expect that the government will be orphaned forever, and that I shall desert on the very day the enemy has been defeated. Believe me, dear friend, I have given deep thought to this matter over the eight years I have governed the Republic. I do not know how to govern; I am not able and I do not wish to govern. In order to carry out a task successfully, one must have some liking or even a driving passion for it.

For my part, this office fills me with growing aversion each day that passes; and if I am to remain now and in the future at the head of the army, it is because from the very first day of my public life I have been spurred on by a compelling desire to contribute to the expulsion of our former oppressors. Consequently, I perform this service out of passion rather than merit. I trust that you will use all your influence to ensure that I am not compelled to commit an act which would be more contrary even to my inner convictions than to the credit of the Republic, and one from which we would both suffer to an inconceivable degree. Imagine what foreigners would make of the desertion of the Head of State, and what anarchy would ensue amongst the people of Colombia!

If you do not wish to become President, please suggest some other person who could discharge that function as worthily as you would. General Santander is an excellent possibility; if not, then there are Urdaneta, Montilla, Restrepo, Peñalver, Zea and many others of greater or lesser value than these. My opinion on this matter is that the President should be an army officer from Cundinamarca and the vice-president a civilian from Venezuela so as to avoid jealousy and dispute—that is, if disputes can be avoided in the tumult of blind passions.

Goodbye, dear friend.

*Bolívar*

## 38

# The social complexities of America

*The recurring topic of the problems created by a situation of crisis is discussed in a letter to General F. de P. Santander, written from San Carlos on 13 June 1821, eleven days before the Battle of Carabobo—which was to be decisive for the independence of Venezuela.*

My dear General,

In the midst of my military preoccupations, I think of you constantly, although not for the same reasons as before (i.e. not because of the silver you used to send us, since I have given up all hope of receiving it, now that the barrier has been set up at Cúcuta). Today, I think of you only out of friendship. I imagine you are very busy, both with raising a reserve army and with appeasing the complaints of the Congress against the military. Both are equally important in order to avoid the ravages of war or civil strife. You must procure rifles and ammunition in sufficient quantities to prevent Bogotá from being taken by a third military expedition. The truth is that the enemy is losing land, support and troops everywhere; and despite our disadvantages, our forces are equal to theirs. The enemy is now confined to Carabobo, but if we lose a major battle, Colombia is a large country and they would gain much territory.

We receive here little news of the Congress and Cúcuta. They say there is considerable support for the idea of federation in Cundinamarca. I am comforted, however, by the knowledge that neither you, nor Nariño, nor Zea, nor myself, nor Páez, nor any of the respected authorities of the Army of Liberation will be party to such nonsense. The men of letters are surely at the root of it all, and they may well eventually be banned from the Republic of Colombia, as Plato banned his poets. These gentlemen think that public opinion is behind them, little knowing that in Colombia the people are the army, not only because that is the truth, but also because the army saved the people from the hands of the tyrants. In addition, it is the people who have an objective, are working for it, and are capable of achieving it; all the others are but sluggards. Whether they be ill-intentioned or not, patriots or not, none of them have any right to be other than passive citizens. Such a policy, which is certainly not derived from Rousseau, will surely one day have to be developed, so that such gentlemen can no longer be our undoing. They claim, like us, to be performing the second act of Buenos Aires, whereas in fact they will be playing the second part of El Guarico. These gentlemen believe that Colombia is full of uncouth boors packed together around the hearths of Bogotá, Tunja and Pamplona. They have not cast a glance at the Caribs of the Orinoco, the shepherds of the Apure, the mariners of Maracaibo, the oarsmen of the Magdalena, the bandits of Patia, the uncontrollable citizens of Pasto, the *guajibos* of Casanare and all the wild hordes from Africa and America who like deer untamed, roam the wilds of Colombia.

Would you not agree, my dear Santander, that these lawmakers, more ignorant than ill-disposed, more brash than ambitious, will eventually lead us to anarchy, then tyranny, and most certainly in any case to ruin?

This is, anyway, my belief and conviction. Consequently, if our final extermination is not achieved by the *llaneros* [lowlanders], then it will be the soft-spoken philosophers of officialdom in Colombia—those who see themselves as latter-day reincarnations of Lycurgus, Numa, Franklin, Camilo, Torres, Roscio, Uztaris or Robira, and other characters sent down to earth from Heaven to hasten mankind's progress towards eternity, not to give men republics such as those of Greece, Rome or America, but to pile up rubble from hideous constructions and to build on Gothic foundations a Grecian edifice placed on the brink of a crater.

I take leave of you, my dear Santander, and wish you luck in your undertakings. Have faith in our victory at Carabobo; build up your reserve army, be kind to the Congress, and keep for me the esteem I feel for you.

Your friend,

*Bolívar*

P.S. Urdaneta's division will be arriving in two or three days. The General has stayed in Carora because of his old ailments. General

Páez has been with me since the day before yesterday. We shall soon be going into battle.

## 39

# A further appeal for the emancipation of slaves

*A message from Valencia, dated 14 July 1821 and addressed to the President of the second Congress of Colombia, convened in Cúcuta. It reaffirms Bolívar's insistence on the fundamental idea of the absolute freedom of slaves.*

The wisdom of the General Congress of Colombia is totally in conformity with prevailing laws regarding the emancipation of the slaves; the Congress could, however, have extended the scope of its beneficence to future Colombians who, born in a cradle of cruelty and savagery, arrive in this world to bow their head to the yoke of slavery. Henceforth, children of slaves to be born in Colombia should be free, since these beings belong to no one but God and their parents, and neither God nor their parents would have them be unhappy. The General Congress, empowered by its own laws and even more so by the laws of nature, can decree the absolute freedom of all Colombians at birth within the territory of the Republic. In this way, rights of ownership, political rights and natural rights would be reconciled.

I ask you to submit this request of mine to the General Congress of Colombia, so that it may deign to grant it to me as a reward for the battle of Carabobo, that was won by the army of liberation whose blood was shed for liberty alone.

40

# 'I prefer the title of Citizen to that of Liberator'

*Speech made to the Congress of the Republic in El Rosario de Cúcuta on 3 October 1821. Bolívar again refers to his idea of 'good citizenship', as he did before the Congress of Angostura.*

Sir,

The sacred oath of office I have just taken as President of Colombia is for me a moral covenant which multiplies my obligations to submit to the law and to the fatherland. Only a profound respect for the nation's will compels me to take on the formidable burden of the supreme magistracy. The gratitude I owe to the representatives of the people imposes on me, too, the agreeable obligation to continue my services to defend with my property, my blood, and even my honour, this Constitution which enshrines the rights of two brother nations, united through the bonds of liberty, righteousness and glory. The Constitution of Colombia, together with independence, shall be the sacred altar on which I shall make my sacrifice. For that I shall march to the furthest corners of Colombia to break the chains of the sons of Ecuador and to invite them, once I have set them free, to unite with Colombia.

Sir, I trust that you will authorize me to unite, through the bonds of mutual benefit, those peoples which nature and Heaven have created to be brothers. Once this task, the objective of your wisdom and of my desires, has been completed, we shall then need only peace to give Colombia all she desires—fortune, tranquillity and glory. I therefore entreat you, sir, not to remain deaf to the call of my conscience and honour, which both cry out that I should be but a citizen of this country. I feel the need to relinquish the first office of the Republic, to which the people appoints a leader out of its heart's desire. I am the offspring of war, the man who has been elevated to the presidency by combat: good fortune has sustained me in that position and victory has confirmed it. Yet these are not the attributes hallowed by justice, well-being and the national will. The sword that has governed Colombia is not like the scales of Astrea, it is a scourge of the spirit of evil which Heaven at times sends down to Earth as a punishment to tyrants and a warning to mortals. This sword will be of no use whatever on the day of peace, which day should be the last of my term of power, because I have so sworn to myself and have so promised to Colombia, and because there can be no republic where the people are not assured of the exercise of their own prerogatives. A man such as I is a dangerous citizen in a people's government and an immediate threat to national sovereignty. I wish to be a citizen, in order to be free and that all may be free. I prefer the title of Citizen to that of Liberator, for the latter derives from war, and the former from law. Sir, take from me all my titles of honour in exchange for that of 'good citizen'.

41

# A tribute of gratitude, affection and consideration to an immortal scientist

*Letter to the learned naturalist, Alexander von Humboldt, dated 10 November 1821, Bogotá. Humboldt was later to say that he loved Colombia like 'a second homeland'.*

### TO BARON ALEXANDER VON HUMBOLDT

Dear Sir and respected friend,

Mr Bollmann, who leaves tomorrow for Europe, has agreed with pleasure to be entrusted with these letters which will bring you the expression of my gratitude, affection and consideration. The Baron von Humboldt will for ever be remembered in the hearts of those who justly appreciate a great man, a man who with his eyes has wrested America from ignorance, and with his pen has depicted our continent as beautiful as it is in nature. Yet these are not the only merits for which you deserve the recognition of Americans. The traits of your moral character and the eminent qualities of your generous personality seem to be alive in our very midst; and we regard them always with delight. I, for one, am moved by the deepest of feelings when I contemplate the tokens which record your journeys in Colombia. I therefore ask you, worthy friend, to accept the most cordial regards of a man who had the honour to respect your name before he knew you, and to hold you in great affection once he had met you in Paris and Rome.

With my highest consideration and respect, I am, Sir, your obedient servant,

*Bolívar*

42

# A thorough and modern
# approach to teaching

*An exposition of methods and instructions for the education of his nephew Fernando, addressed by Bolívar to the principal of the school where he was being educated in North America.*

The education of children should always be suited to their age, inclinations, disposition and temperament.

As my nephew is now more than 12 years of age, he should be applying himself to the learning of modern languages, without neglecting his own. Dead languages should be studied only when one has mastered the living ones.

Geography and cosmography should be among the first subjects a young person should study.

History, like languages, should begin with the learning of contemporary events and should then go gradually backward in time to the obscure ages of mythology. It is never too early to acquire knowledge of the exact sciences, since these teach us to analyse all things, moving from what is known to what is unknown, and thus teaching us to think and to reason logically. It is however essential to bear in mind the pupil's ability to calculate, since children are not all equally competent in mathematics.

In general, all children can learn geometry and understand it, but the same does not apply to algebra or integral and differential calculus.

A rapid ability to memorize is always a brilliant faculty, but it is detrimental to understanding; children who show considerable facility in memorizing their lessons by heart should be taught things which force them to think, such as solving problems or equations. On the other hand, those who memorize slowly should be taught to learn by heart and recite compositions selected from the great poets; memory, like mental arithmetic, is likely to improve through practice.

The memory should be exercised whenever possible, but never worked so heavily that it weakens.

Statistics is an important subject in the time in which we are living, and I wish my nephew to be instructed in it.

It would be preferable for him to be taught mechanics and civil engineering but not against his will, if he is not inclined towards such studies. It is not essential for him to study music, unless he should show a passion for this art; however, he does need to possess knowledge, albeit rudimentary, of draughtsmanship, astronomy, chemistry and botany, and his studies should be pursued further in any of these subjects for which he should show more particular inclination or interest.

Education in good manners and social customs is as essential as instruction; for this reason, special care should be taken in seeing that he learns from the letters of Lord Chesterfield to his son the principles and manners of a gentleman.

Morality in religious teachings and in the care for health and life is a part of education no teacher should neglect.

He should study Roman law, as the basis of universal legislation. Since it is difficult to appreciate where art ends and science begins, if he should be inclined to decide to learn a craft or trade I should be delighted, since we have plenty of doctors and lawyers but lack good mechanics and farmers who are the keys to the country's progress, prosperity and well-being.

Dancing, which is the poetry of movement and which gives grace and nimbleness to the person, and is at the same time a healthy exercise in temperate climes, should be practised by him if such is his pleasure. Above all, I commend you to instil in him the taste for cultured society, where the fair sex exerts its beneficial influence, as well as respect for men of greater age and experience and higher social standing who inspire enchantment in youth by sharing with them their hopes for the future.

43

# Solidarity with San Martín in the attainment of full independence

*Bolívar writes to His Excellency the Protector of Peru, General José de San Martín, from Quito on 17 June 1822, reaffirming the substantive unity between them.*

### TO HIS EXCELLENCY THE PROTECTOR OF PERU

Sir,

Having reached this capital city, after the triumphs achieved by the forces of Peru and Colombia on the battlefields of Bombóna and Pichincha, I have great satisfaction in writing to you to express the feelings of deepest gratitude with which the people and Government of Colombia welcomed the distinguished liberators of Peru, who came with their victorious forces to lend their powerful aid in the campaign which freed three provinces of southern Colombia together with this most attractive city, so worthy of the protection of all America, since it was here that one of the first heroic examples of liberty was given. However, our tribute of gratitude is not a mere homage paid to the army and Government of Peru, but reflects our most fervent desire to lend the same, if not more powerful aid to the Government of Peru if, by the time this dispatch reaches you, the liberating armies of the south have not already gloriously terminated the campaign which was to be undertaken this season.

It is with immense satisfaction that I announce to you that the war in Colombia is now over, and that its army is now ready to march wherever its brothers require it to go, and particularly to the land of our neighbours to the south who, for so many reasons, deserve preference as our closest friends and brothers-in-arms.

Accept, Sir, the assurance of my highest consideration.

Your humble and obedient servant,

*Bolívar*

## 44

# 'First friend of my heart and of my fatherland'

*Letter addressed to His Excellency, General José de San Martín, Protector of Peru, from Guayaquil on 25 July 1822, and anticipating the understanding reached between them at the meeting which took place on 26 July at that Pacific port.*

TO HIS EXCELLENCY GENERAL DON JOSÉ DE SAN MARTÍN, PROTECTOR OF PERU

My most worthy friend, it is with great pleasure that I give you for the first time the title which my heart has long since bestowed on you. I call you friend, and this is the only name we should use between us for the rest of our lives, since friendship is the only tie which binds brothers-in-arms, in action and in opinion. I therefore rejoice, since you have honoured me with the expression of your affection.

If you were not to come to this city, I would be as distressed as if we had lost a dozen battles; but, no, you would not wish to frustrate my desire to embrace, on this soil of Colombia, the first friend of my heart and of my fatherland. How could you possibly come so far and yet leave us, here in Guayaquil, without the physical presence of so distinguished a man whom all of us long to know and, if possible, touch?

It would not be possible, my respected friend. I am expecting you, and I too shall go to meet you wherever you may be so good as to await me; but I shall not abandon my request that you honour us with your visit to this city. As you say, a few hours are sufficient for talks between military men, but a few hours will not be enough, to appease the demands of friendship when I start to enjoy the good fortune of getting to know personally a friend who was previously admired only because of the repute and the fame he enjoyed.

I assure you again of my sincerest regards,

Your most affectionate friend and servant,

*Bolívar*

45

# Union and association in performing the common task

*Report to Santander on the Guayaquil Meeting, only three days after that momentous event. Bolívar states that the great Liberator of the South 'desires that everything should be done under the watch-word of union, for he realizes that without it there can be no peace and tranquillity'. Guayaquil, 29 July 1822.*

My dear General,

The day before yesterday General San Martín left in the evening after a visit of some thirty-six to forty hours. It may be said to have been a visit in the true sense of the term, for we did no more than greet each other, talk together and take our leave. I believe he came to assure himself of our friendship, in order to use it to counter his enemies, at home and abroad. With him went 1,800 Colombians as reinforcements since he had suffered a second bout of heavy casualties, which cost us more than 600 men: thus, Peru will receive reinforcements of 3,000 men, at least.

The Protector pledged his eternal friendship for Colombia; he is to intervene in favour of the settlement of the boundaries; he will not seek any involvement in the affairs of Guayaquil; he has offered total and absolute federation, even if only with Colombia, and the Congress should meet in Guayaquil. He agreed to send an envoy from Peru to conduct, in conjunction with ourselves, negotiations with Spain's emissaries; he has also recommended that Mosquera should go to Chile and Buenos Aires to persuade them to agree to federation; he would also like to arrange exchanges of garrisons between the two states. In short, he desires that everything be done under the watchword of union, for he realizes that without it there can be no peace and tranquillity. He says that he does not wish to become king, but neither does he wish to set up a democracy; he would prefer to see a European prince come to reign in Peru. I believe, however, that this last comment was for form's sake. He says he will retire to Mendoza, since he is tired of command and of being attacked by his enemies.

He spoke to me of no specific plan and demanded nothing of Colombia: the troops that went with him had already been prepared for that purpose. He simply laid great emphasis on the negotiation of garrison exchanges; and, from his side, there was no kind of friendship or support which he did not offer me.

He seemed to me to be a very soldierly character, energetic, quick to react, and far from stupid. He has ideas of the sort you would like; but he gave me the impression of being insufficiently subtle in the grandeur of his ideas and undertakings. You will come to understand his character once you have received the minutes of our conversations, which I am sending with Captain Gómez, though you will miss the spice of the criticisms I should make of every word of his.

The members of the electoral college of this province are at present deliberating on union with Colombia; I think this will come about, but they are probably holding out for many advantages and privileges. As for me, since I am entrusted with the executive power in these parts, I shall take charge of the province, leaving the sovereign Congress free to act according to its sovereign will and resolve its difficulties with its sovereign power. Here the separation of powers will be of some use to me, as will the scholastic distinctions of yielding to the majority and rejecting the minority. We have now succeeded in uniting opinion. The visit of San Martín also made a considerable contribution to this, since he spoke of the independents with the utmost contempt. This is what is called profiting from every occasion. The foregoing remark is not self-congratulatory, but is rather addressed to those who know how to flatter at the right moment, whether or not the people they flatter are aware of it. The *Prueba* and the *Venganza* would not exist in Peru today, were it not for the policy of San Martín: but now there is nothing more to expect from those fools, and he lays all the blame upon them.

Thanks be to God, my dear General, I have done great things with much good fortune and much glory: first, the liberation of the south; secondly, the incorporation of Guayaquil, Quito and the other provinces into Colombia; third, the friendship of San Martín and of Peru for Colombia, and lastly, the departure of the allied army, which is sure to give us glory and gratitude in Peru. Everybody is grateful, for I have served them all, and everybody respects us, since I have yielded to no one. Even the Spaniards are filled with respect and gratitude towards the Government of Colombia. I aspire to nothing else, dear friend, but to place this treasure hoard of my success in safety, to hide it in a secluded spot, so that no one may steal it from me; in other words, I wish for nothing else but to retire and die. By God, I swear I want nothing else; it is the first time I have had no desire and have been content with my lot.

Colonel Lara is commanding these forces, and General Valdés is to follow him. For the moment, I have no other news to tell, and remain, as always,

Yours affectionately,

## 46

## Congratulations and praise to O'Higgins for restoring the rights of the people of Chile

*This message to General Bernardo O'Higgins, Director of the Republic of Chile, dated Guayaquil, 29 August 1822, provides evidence of the friendship between the two men and the agreement on objectives.*

Sir,

I have pleasure in writing to you personally to express my most cordial and sincere admiration and esteem for you. I have for long wished to congratulate you on the successes and accomplishments with which fortune, courage and prudence have crowned the actions of the government over which you preside so worthily. There could be no better or more propitious occasion for me to follow the dictates of my heart than the present occasion, now that you have put the seal on your great career by restoring to your people the full exercise of their rights. The proclamation which you have issued to the citizens of Chile is most liberal in content, and is particularly suited to a people who aspire to maximum freedom. You do not restrict national representation in any manner or form; from the outset, this will set in motion a form of independence which will undoubtedly be strongly approved even by the enemies of our cause and of our leaders. The people of Chile are a good, patriotic and courageous people; and for these noble reasons, they have a right to the most justifiable aspirations for well-being and national glory. These people are to be the last to set out on the road to constitutional government, and as such it is fortunate to have the immense advantage of being able to see in advance the pitfalls which must be avoided and the examples which must be followed. The history of America's misfortunes and mistakes is eloquent, indeed, for those who care to study it. You will doubtless be submitting to the Chilean people an account of all our vicissitudes, so that they can avoid the precipices over which all our legislative experiments have fallen to their fate.

Chile would do well to form a government that is strong in structure and liberal in principle. You will forgive me if I proceed no further with my ideas on this matter, but I stated them officially at the Congress of Venezuela and I understand that they are well known in your city.

The convening of your representatives has never been more important than it is now. From the enclosed paper you will see that the agents of the Spanish Government are in league against us in an attempt to delay recognition of our independence. All the pictures painted by the Spanish Minister of the situation in America are, of course, slanderous; but we can draw satisfaction from our ability to refute this slander by pointing to outstanding events such as that which has prompted my congratulations to you today. I should like us to exchange letters as often as possible, and I would like these letters to be written with the sincerity and candour that are appropriate for bringing together two companions-at-arms who were born to be friends. For my part, I offer you true friendship and admiration of all your outstanding qualities.

I am delighted that our envoy, Mr Mosquera, has had the honour to submit to you our plans for American unity, and also that you yourself, moved by the same sentiments as the Protector of

Peru and Colombia, will be glad to agree to the pact of salvation that has already begun to take shape between Peru and ourselves.

Accept, sir, the sincere assurances of my highest consideration, Your obedient servant,

*Simón Bolívar*

47

## 'We are at the centre of the Universe, in contact with all nations. Who else can say as much?'

*Thoughts of the politician looking to the future, in a letter addressed to General F. de P. Santander from Ibarra on 23 December 1822.*

By the time this letter reaches you, the Congress will be on the point of convening. The Pasto incident has delayed the progress of the deputies from the south, and I doubt whether many will go via the Dagua in view of the dangerous and terrifying difficulties this journey involves for the inhabitants of that area. I insisted somewhat that they should go that way, but not so strongly as to turn the Congress into something detestable for them because of the danger involved in reaching it. You know how difficult it was to travel to Cúcuta; so you can imagine what it will be like for these people to cross the sea or travel through torrid, isolated and insalubrious stretches of enemy territory. National representation in Colombia, although the country is far smaller than the United States, presents considerable difficulties, because the peasants here have no sense of national pride; they are poor, and even less endowed with intelligence, and therefore consider themselves to be of no value to the Congress and consequently under no obligation to attend. If we divide up the legislature, then we divide up our countrymen, our interests and our weapons, and we bring together only the armies to fight brother against brother. I believe the question of our present difficulties can be stated in the following terms. Will it be easier to remedy the problems which confront a large country in convening its national parliament, or will it be easier to face up to all the contingencies of the war which is bound to break out in this very nation? Last night I was reading Rousseau, where he says of the small Republic of Geneva that 'the size of a large state is self-preserving. It operates under its own momentum, whereas the slightest shortcoming in a small nation ruins it.' I immediately turned my thoughts to history and I saw that great empires have indeed remained indestructible, despite numerous wars and upheavals, and that small nations, such as Caracas, have been reduced to nothing by a single conqueror, an ill-intentioned citizen or an earthquake. I believe the primary quality of things is their existence—all else is secondary. Let us, then, ensure that we exist, albeit with our faults and difficulties, since in the end *being* is always better than *not being*. When I look at America, I see it surrounded by Europe's naval forces, i.e. encircled by the floating fortresses of foreigners and consequently enemies. I then see at the head of America's great continent a mighty nation, endowed with great wealth, warlike and capable of anything; that country is the enemy of Europe and an opponent of the powerful English, who will wish to have their way with us and who inevitably will. I then look at the huge and mighty Mexican empire which, with its riches and the unity of its blood, would be able to attack Colombia from a position of considerable advantage. I then turn my eyes to the long coastline of Colombia, harassed by mariners from every land, by Europeans from all the colonies which surround us and by the Africans of Haiti whose power is greater than primeval fire. Facing us across the waters we have the fine, rich, Spanish-held islands, which will always be our enemies. At our backs, there is ambitious Portugal with its immense Brazilian colony; to the south, Peru, with its many millions of pesos, its rivalry with Colombia and its relations with Chile and Buenos Aires. In the first dispute we have with the Peruvian navy, which must of necessity be its strongest force since its coastline is so long, they would have the advantage, and we would see our shores seized in their powerful grip. Colombia will never be able to compete with Peru in the seas of the Pacific, because her first concern must be with the Atlantic, and Peru has only one seaboard.

This picture is not inaccurate, and yet we see that we have the means to defend ourselves against so many adversaries. We are inferior to our brothers in the south, to the Mexicans, to the Americans, to the English, and, lastly, to all the Europeans who are our neighbours in their respective possessions in the Antilles. We are at the centre of the Universe, in contact with all nations. Who else can say as much? We have two and a half million inhabitants scattered over a broad expanse of desolate landscape. Some are wild, some are slaves, most are each other's enemies and all are corrupted by superstition and despotism. What a wonderful contrast with all the other nations of this world! Such is our situation, such is Colombia, and, in addition, they wish to divide her.

Oh, my friend, how much have I thought of the wretched child of our efforts; and I wish some good man would take the trouble to present this portrait to the public in all its vivid colours.

---

## 48

## 'My policy has always been to seek to create stability, strength and true freedom'

*Message addressed to the Vice-President of the Republic from Tulcán (Ecuador) on 31 December 1822.*

I have the honour to address to you my congratulations to the General Congress, feeling bound to convey them at a time when I assume it to be meeting. The nation is expecting the greatest benefits from the Congress, which must necessarily enact the improvements desired by the people for greater prosperity. At the same time, however, I remain convinced that the legislators will not be distracted from the spirit of innovation which has done so much for the city. You and all Colombia know that I have devoted my life to Colombia's integrity, freedom and welfare. My policy has always been to seek to create stability, strength and true freedom. The Congress of Guayana heard my opinions on government and has partially heeded them; the Congress of Cúcuta also. You also know that, out of a sense of submission and obedience, I took an oath to abide by the Constitution and stood as its guarantor. This Constitution may not be amended for ten years: and, like the 'social contract' of the world's first republican, it could be unalterable for a generation, since a generation is sufficient time for a country to organize itself according to its own experiences.

The sovereignty of the people is not unlimited, since it derives from basic justice, and it ends when its usefulness is complete. This is the constitutional gospel of today. On what grounds can the representatives of the people claim to be authorized constantly to change the organization of society? What would then become of citizens' basic rights, their property, honour and lives? It would be preferable to be ruled by the most savage of despots, since at least in such a case men's protection would be secured by the very power which oppresses them. I therefore consider myself authorized, sir, to urge the executive to do all in its power to ensure that the present legislature alters nothing in Colombia's fundamental laws. For my part, I declare that, being bound by oath to the provisions of the Constitution, I can obey none other that might weaken or violate them; I am resolved to leave Colombia rather than give my assent to laws which destroy the magnificent work of the liberation army.

For the above considerations, and many others, I beg you to submit to the General Congress, at the opportune moment and when overriding circumstances so require, my solemn vow that during my term of office I shall not countenance any congressional act which might repeal, alter or otherwise change the fundamental laws of the Republic of Colombia.

With my highest regards, I am, sir, your humble servant,

## 49

# 'He who opposes freedom must expect the chains of misfortune and universal condemnation'

*Dramatic thoughts on his public action, expressed in a letter addressed to General F. de P. Santander on 29 April 1823 from Guayaquil.*

Each new day brings us further news of Emperor Iturbide and of his reverses at Veracruz. The *Gaceta de Guayaquil* will give you an idea of the insurrectional activities of Iturbide's generals. I believe such events will be decisive for the future of that empire. As Bonaparte said of himself, 'He sinned against liberal principles and thus succumbed.' What a lesson, my friend, to those in power today! He who opposes freedom must expect the chains of misfortune and universal condemnation. The Abbé De Pradt rightly observes that in the past command was a comfortable position, whereas nowadays there is no better occupation than that of a citizen; the offices of kings, ministers, priests and the like are of no interest, since inflexible reason is the order of the day, not warring despotism.

Every day I make my general confession, I examine my conscience; and in truth I live in fear of my sins, committed against my own will, in support of the cause, and through the fault of the reactionaries. Who knows? One day I may be punished with some severe penance for my ill-understood patriotism. My friend, things are difficult; the only way to command nowadays is by loving one's neighbour and showing profound humility. The citizens are most easily offended, and will have nothing of Gothic architecture, considerations of state or attentuating circumstances. What they demand is constitutional architecture, legal geometry, and meticulously precise symmetry; nothing to offend the eyes, ears or any other sense. To protect ourselves, ask Its Holiness the Congress for authorization to sin against liberal ideas, with remission of sins and absolution from punishment. Otherwise we shall have achieved nothing after saving our country, as Iturbide, O'Higgins and San Martín did, since self-righteous citizens refuse to fight or provide for the payment of fighters, for fear of committing an offence against the holy commandments and the saintly laws of philanthropy; but, once the fighting is over and won, they appear again to share in the spoils though they constantly condemn all those who shed blood, since it is very good and sound practice to condemn and at the same time to collect.

50

# Establishment of a nautical school in Guayaquil

*This letter, providing evidence of an initiative taken by Bolívar, was written in Babahoyo on 12 June 1823.*

TO THE ACTING ADMINISTRATOR OF THE
DEPARTMENT OF GUAYAQUIL

His Excellency the Liberator has consented to the establishment in Guayaquil of a nautical school, and has appointed Citizen Domingo Gómez as its teacher with an annual endowment of 1,800 pesos, to be paid out of city funds. The aforementioned citizen has been given leave to travel to Chile for family reasons but will be returning for the full month of July to make arrangements for the establishment of the school. His Excellency has also given instructions that the school be opened temporarily in one of the classrooms of the College of Guayaquil. He now orders you, in agreement with the Rector, to select and indicate the classroom to be used, to withdraw from the funds of Guayaquil the sums needed for the construction of desks and benches or seats for the students, and to provide pens, paper and inkwells for immediate requirements.

## 51

# 'A court to condemn
# what laws cannot prevent'

*Illustrating his well-known attitude to public opinion, as expressed in the Press, Bolívar set out, on 15 June 1823, his arguments in favour of the Moral Power, which he had proposed to the Congress of Angostura. He asks his friend José Rafael Arboleda, from Guayaquil, to support his initiative.*

I have been meaning to write to you for some time but, much to my regret, I have not done so before now. I saw an article in *El Fósforo* on the Moral Power which prompted me to send you these few lines in order to thank you, if you are the author of the article, and if not, to beg you to forward thanks to the person who did write it. I assume, however, that it was you who supported the idea of the Moral Power with such skill and discernment.

*El Fósforo*, in its issue No. 16, was quite right to say that there would be no hint of inquisition in such an establishment, since the accusing party would always be public outrage, and the very fact that public outrage is public opinion horrified by crime means there would indeed be no such inquisition. My dear friend, I ask you to come out in favour of my Moral Power. I who am its author do not hope that anything will make me good except a court which condemns what the laws cannot prevent; by this I mean that I cannot hope that my own shortcomings will be corrected except by a court which will make me feel ashamed. The feeling of shame is the hell of all who have no principles, or who call themselves philosophers and men of the world. Religion has lost much of its influence, and will not, perhaps, recover it for a long time, since customs are nowadays in opposition to the holy doctrine. Consequently, if we do not set up in society a new system of penalties and punishments of wrongs and offences, in order to improve our morality, we will probably be rushing headlong towards universal moral dissipation. All the world knows that religion and philosophy hold men back, the first by the penalties it threatens and the second by hope and persuasion. But religion is full of indulgence towards evil-doers, and philosophy offers many conflicting systems, some of which tolerate one type of wrongdoing and some another. The first has stable laws and tribunals; the other has only professors without any fixed codes or bases, and without any endorsement from any political institutions.

I, therefore, conclude that we should seek a mean between these two extremes, and set up an institution endorsed both by the fundamental laws and by the irresistible force of opinion.

52

# Best wishes for the freedom of Peru

*Words of gratitude and promise sent to the Congress of Peru in Lima on 13 September 1823.*

The Constituent Congress of Peru has overwhelmed me by the extent of its goodness; and my gratitude will never match its great confidence. Nevertheless, I shall make good this shortcoming with the sacrifices of my life: for Peru, I shall do more than my own capabilities would allow, since I count upon the efforts of all my generous comrades. The wisdom of the Congress will be my guiding light amidst the chaos of difficulties and dangers in which I am submerged. By service, patriotism and virtue, the President of the state would have liberated the country alone if such a glorious undertaking had been entrusted to him; the executive power shall be my right hand, and the instrument of all my actions. I also count upon the talents and virtues of all Peruvians, who are eager to raise the edifice of their fair republic; they have placed upon the altar of their homeland all their offerings; all they have left is their hearts but, for me, those hearts are the champions of their freedom. The soldiers of liberation, who have come from the Plate, the Maule, the Magdalena and the Orinoco, will not return to their native lands until they are crowned with laurels, marching under triumphal arches and bearing as trophies the standards and pennants of Castile. They will win and will restore freedom to Peru, or they will all perish: this, sir, I promise you.

I offer victory, confident of the valour of the united army and of the good faith of the Congress, the executive power and the people of Peru. Thus, Peru will remain independent and sovereign throughout all the centuries which Divine Providence vouchsafes to her.

## 53

# Praise for the learning of Humboldt and Bonpland

*On 22 October 1823, the Liberator writes from Lima to Gaspar Rodrí-guez de Francia, Dictator of Paraguay, to intercede for the release of the French scholar, Aimé Bonpland. Bolívar demonstrates there his high esteem both for friendship and for learning.*

Sir,

Ever since my earliest youth I have had the honour to enjoy the friendship of Mr Bonpland and Baron von Humboldt, whose learn-ing has done more good for America than all the conquerors to-gether.

I am now led to believe that my good friend Bonpland is being detained in Paraguay for reasons I do not know. I suspect that this honest scholar has been maligned in certain false reports and that the government over which you preside may have allowed itself to be misled with regard to this gentleman. Two considerations lead me to appeal to your goodwill to secure the release of Mr Bonpland. First, I am the reason for his coming to America, since I invited him to Colombia; and once his journey had been decided upon, the cir-cumstances of the war inevitably led him to Buenos Aires. Secondly, this man of letters has the ability to enlighten this land of mine with his knowledge, once you have been so good as to allow him to come to Colombia, over whose government I preside by the will of the people.

You will doubtless be unaware of my name or of my services to America's cause; but if I were permitted to bring to bear all the influence I can command for Bonpland's release, then I would cer-tainly venture to submit the following request to you. May it please you to heed the appeal of 4 million Americans liberated by the army I command, all of whom are at one with me in imploring your clemency in the name of humanity, wisdom and justice, and out of consideration for Mr Bonpland. Mr Bonpland can give you his word, before departing from the territory under your authority, that he will leave the provinces of the River Plate, in order not to cause any possible prejudice to the province of Paraguay. Meanwhile, I await him with the anxiety of a friend and the respect of a disciple; I would be capable of marching to Paraguay alone to release the best of men and the most celebrated of travellers.

Sir, I trust that you will not leave my most urgent request

unanswered and I hope, too, that you may count me among your most trusted and grateful friends, provided that the innocent man who is so dear to me is not the victim of injustice.

I am, sir, your obedient servant,

*Bolívar*

## 54

# '. . . and then I sought to ascend to the pinnacle of the Universe'

*Literary text by Bolívar, known as 'My delirium on Chimborazo', a fantasy on eternity, infinity and the ages. Believed to have been written in 1823.*

I am cloaked in the mantle of Iris, from where the majestic Orinoco pays tribute to the God of the waters. I had explored the mysterious sources of the Amazon, and then I sought to ascend to the pinnacle of the Universe. I strove bravely forward in the footsteps of La Condamine and von Humboldt, and nothing could hold me back. I reached the icy region where the thin air made me gasp for breath. No foot of man had yet defiled the glittering crown which the hands of Eternity had placed upon the lofty temples of the Andean peak. And to myself I said: the mantle of Iris which has served as my banner has in my hands passed through infernal regions, crossed rivers and seas, and mounted the giant shoulders of the Andes; the land levels off at the feet of Colombia, and time has not held back the onward march of liberty. Bellona has been shamed by the radiance of Iris. Then should not I scale the snow-capped grandeur of this giant of the world? Yes, yes, I can! Seized by an unknown and seemingly divine spirit, I left behind the trail of Humboldt, tarnishing the everlasting crystals which encircle Chimborazo. As if driven on by the spirit which inhabited me, I reached my journey's end, and was stunned as my head touched the dome of the firmament, my feet coming to rest at the very edge of the abyss.

A feverish delirium seizes my mind; I feel consumed by some strange and overwhelming fire. The God of Colombia possesses me. And suddenly Time appears before me, in the venerable form of a bald old man, his grim face racked by the ravages of time, his shoulders stooping under the burden of the ages, carrying a sickle in his wrinkled hands. . . .

'I am the Father of the Centuries,' he said, 'the mysterious repository of fame; and the unknown Eternity was my mother; Infinity marks the borders of my realm; no sepulchre will ever hold me, for I am mightier than Death; my vision scans the past and the future, and through my hands the present flows. Why do you take pride in childhood or old age, man or hero? Do you think your Universe is anything, or that to stand atop an atom of creation is a noble act? Do you think that the moments you call centuries can serve to measure my mysteries? Do you imagine that you have witnessed the Holy Truth? Do you foolishly suppose that your deeds have any value to me? They are all but specks of the tiniest matter in the presence of Infinity, who is my brother.'

Overcome by holy terror, I reply: 'How, O Time, can the wretched mortal who has climbed so high fail to be proud? I have surpassed all honours, for I have raised myself above the heads of all men. I command the land beneath my feet; I stretch out my hands and touch Eternity; I sense the prisons of the underworld stir beneath my every stride; beside me I behold the shining stars and the suns of the infinite; I look without wonderment at the vastness of the space which encircles matter, and on your face I can read the History of things past and the thoughts of Destiny.'

He answers: 'Observe, and keep in your mind all that you have seen. Paint for the eyes of your fellow-men the picture of the physical Universe and the moral Universe; do not keep to yourself the secrets which the heavens have revealed to you, but proclaim the truth among men.'

The apparition vanished.

Entranced, as if turned into stone, I lay motionless, stretched out upon the huge diamond which was my bed. At length, the thundering voice of Colombia calls me back to reality, to my own flesh and blood, and with my own hands I open my heavy eyelids. I am a man once more, and I write down this account of my delirium.

55

# Two decrees for administrative morality

*In Lima, on 12 January and 31 May 1824, the Liberator promulgated these two decrees which reaffirm his determination to put an end to corruption by civil servants and to promote public morality. These legal instruments, designed for the difficult situation which existed in Peru, are marked by extreme severity combined with a clear expression of a rule of criminal law and a precise attribution of responsibilities.*

## SIMÓN BOLÍVAR
### Liberator President, etc., etc., etc.

Considering:

(1) that one of the main causes of the disasters which have befallen the Republic has been the scandalous squandering of its funds by certain officials who have misappropriated them; and (2) that the only way to stamp out these irregularities once and for all is by ordering strong and extraordinary measures,

I have decided to decree, and I do so decree as follows:

*Article 1.* Any public official convicted by summary judgement of having misappropriated public funds in excess of ten pesos, or of having appropriated such funds for his own use, shall be liable to the penalty of death.

*Article 2.* Any judges who, by law are required to render such judgements but fail to proceed in accordance with this Decree, shall likewise be sentenced to death.

*Article 3.* Any private citizen shall be entitled to accuse public officials of the offence referred to in Article 1 above.

*Article 4.* This Decree shall be posted in all government offices of the Republic and shall be communicated to all other offices occupied by officials who are in any way involved in the handling of public funds.

This Decree shall be printed, published and circulated.

Done in the Palace of the Chief of State, Lima, this twelfth day of January 1824, Year I of the Republic.

*Simón Bolívar*

By order of H.E.
*José Sánchez Carrión*

## SIMÓN BOLÍVAR
Liberator President of Colombia, and invested with the Supreme Power in the
Republic of Peru, etc., etc., etc.

Considering:

(1) that nothing contributes more to the proper administration of justice and to the correct performance of their duties by all public servants, than that they should be effectively called to account whenever they have failed to fulfil such obligations;

I have decided to decree, and do so decree as follows:

*Article 1.* Any judge who knowingly and through favourable or unfavourable predisposition towards any of the parties to a dispute, passes judgement contrary to the law shall be deemed to have acted wrongfully in the performance of his duties.

*Article 2.* Any judge or magistrate who commits this offence shall be relieved of his post and disqualified from obtaining any other post whatsoever; in addition he shall pay to the aggrieved party all costs and damages. If the fault in the performance of his duties is committed during criminal proceedings, he shall in addition be subjected to the same penalty as that unjustly imposed upon the accused.

*Article 3.* Any magistrate or judge who knowingly renders a judgement contrary to the law as a result of corruption or bribery, i.e. because he or his family have been given or promised something, be it money or other effects, or hopes of better fortune, shall in addition to the penalties provided for in the above article suffer public disgrace and shall pay four times what he received, half to be allotted to public educational establishments and half to be awarded to the accuser.

*Article 4.* Any magistrate or judge who knowingly receives or agrees to receive either for himself or for his family any gift from the parties to a dispute, or on their behalf, even if he does not subsequently render a judgement contrary to the law, shall also pay four times what he receives, and the amount shall be applied for the same purposes as stipulated above; he shall likewise be removed from his post and disqualified from the discharge of any further function in the administration of justice. All gifts which certain corporations, communities or private persons have been accustomed to give— whether they are known as *tablas* or under any other name—shall be strictly prohibited.

*Article 5.* Any magistrate or judge who seduces a woman who is party to a dispute, or is accused before him, or is a witness in a case, shall for that reason be removed from his post, and disqualified from obtaining any other post in the administration of justice, without prejudice to any further penalty to which he might be liable as a private person in regard to his offence. Furthermore, if he seduces or consorts with a convicted woman, he shall be declared incapable of holding any other post or responsibility of any kind whatsoever.

*Article 6.* Any magistrate or judge convicted of sacrilegious behaviour, public incontinence, repeated drunkenness, or scandalous immorality on any other grounds, or of notorious ineptitude or habitual neglect in the discharge of his duties, shall lose his employment and shall take no further part in the administration of justice, without prejudice to any other punishment or penalty to which he may be liable as a private person for such dissolute conduct.

. . . . . . . . . . . . . . . . . . . . . . . . . . . . . . . . . . . . . .

*Article 17.* When a complaint is lodged against a magistrate of a higher court, or a judge of the courts of first instance, the accused shall not reside in the locality where his case is heard, nor within a radius of six leagues.

. . . . . . . . . . . . . . . . . . . . . . . . . . . . . . . . . . . . . .

*Article 22.* Public officials of all categories shall also be responsible for wrongful acts committed in the course of duty by their respective subordinates, if such wrongful acts are due to their own oversight or indulgence or if they themselves fail to take appropriate remedial action immediately.

*Article 23.* Any delay or hesitation in the implementation and enforcement of all laws, decrees and government orders shall be published as an intentional act of disobedience.

56

# 'You formed my heart for freedom, justice, greatness and beauty. I have followed the path which you marked out for me'

*This, one of Bolívar's most famous letters, is addressed to Don Simón Rodríguez, the most influential of all his teachers. It was written from Pativilca on 19 January 1824.*

O my master! My friend! My Robinson, you are here in Colombia! In Bogotá, without a prior word or letter to me! You really are without a doubt the most extraordinary man in the world; you may deserve many more titles, but I do not wish to write them down so as not to be discourteous as I greet a guest from the Old World, come to see the New—come, indeed, to see his country as yet unknown to him, forgotten not in his heart but in his memory. I more than anyone know how much you love our beloved Colombia. Do you recall when we went together to the Monte Sacro in Rome, there to swear on its holy soil to the freedom of our homeland? You will certainly never have forgotten that day of everlasting glory for us both, a day on which prematurely—so to speak—we swore a prophetic oath, for that very hope we ought not then to have had.

Master, how closely you must have been thinking of me, even though you were so far away. How keenly you must have charted my progress, each step of which you yourself had long ago envisaged. You formed my heart for freedom, justice, greatness and beauty. I have followed the path which you marked out for me. You have been my pilot though you stood on the far-off shores of Europe. You cannot imagine how deeply your lessons have been engraved on my heart; I have never managed to erase even the merest comma of the great lessons you imparted to me. They are ever present before my mind's eye, and I have followed their infallible directions. In short, you have been my guide. You have seen my writings, the thoughts of my soul put down on paper, and you must constantly have reflected: all this is mine, I sowed this plant, I watered and tended it, I nourished it when it was young and weak, and now that it is healthy, strong and fruitful, I reap those fruits. They are mine, I shall savour them in the garden I planted; I shall enjoy its friendly shade, I have a prescriptive and exclusive right to everything.

Yes, my dear friend, you are here among us; blessed a thousand times is the day you first stepped on to the shores of Colombia. Another wise and just man crowns the proud head of Colombia. I am at a loss, for I know neither your intentions nor your destination; and above all, I am desperately impatient for I cannot embrace you in my arms. Since I cannot hurry to meet you, hasten to me; it will not be a waste of your time. You will behold, enchanted, the immense homeland that is yours, chiselled out of the hard stone of despotism by the liberators, your brothers. No, your eyes will never have their fill of the landscapes, the colossi, the treasures, the secrets and the marvels our grand Colombia holds within her borders. Come to Chimborazo; profane with your bold footstep the ladder of the Titans, Earth's crown, the impregnable fortress of the New Universe. From such heights you will have a magnificent vantage point: and, observing the skies and the land, gazing in awe at Earth's creation, you may say: here, two eternities look upon me: that now past and that to come; and this throne of nature, like its Maker, shall be as enduring, indestructible and everlasting as is the Father of the Universe.

From where else could you make so proud a claim? Friend of Mother Nature, come, inquire of her age, her life and her primitive origins; in that aged world of yours, you have seen nothing but the relics and vestiges of her fine works; she is bent under the burden of the passing years, the diseases and the foul breath of men. Here, she is still an innocent young woman, her maidenly beauty enhanced by the hand of the Creator himself. No, the profane contact of man has not yet faded her divine allure, her wondrous grace and unsullied virtue.

Friend, if so many irresistible attractions do not entice you to hasten to my side, then I shall invoke a far stronger motive: I invoke our friendship.

Present this letter to the Vice-President, ask him for funds on my behalf, and come and see me.

*Bolívar*


57

## To a soldier of justice and of law

*Letter to his English friend Sir Robert Wilson—father of his aide-de-camp Belford Wilson—written on 28 January 1824 from Pativilca.*

Distinguished General and friend,

It was with great pleasure that I received your esteemed letter, with which you did me the honour of sending to me part of your own heart in the person of your fine and worthy son. I appreciate this noble trait of character which has always been your mark of distinction. If history correctly records the excellence of men's acts, it will not relate many finer things than this. Thus, whatever the achievement of young Wilson in our struggle, and whether it is a laurel or a cypress that will crown the head of Spain, both father and son are assured of triumph on the field of liberty. The press, which recounts and publicizes all events, has already printed all that can be printed in honour of a warrior: it has depicted you attacking the walls of Dresden, and tearing from your noble breast the insignia of your former glories. But your supreme glory is to have left for Spain to water with your blood the tree of liberty, and to have sent your beloved son to fight the Spanish oppressor; since a soldier of justice and of law is far greater than the conqueror of the universe. I ask you therefore, General, to accept my congratulations in advance.

It was with real pleasure that I beheld the fine scion of the Wilson family: I have taken him to myself as part of the family, and would be as a father to him.

I was also extremely pleased to learn of Mr Zea's great soundness of judgement in confiding in you the noble task of defending the rights of our emancipation in Madrid before the Spanish Government. I like to think that if the government had heard the cry for freedom from the mouth of a hero, it would not have remained deaf to his proud appeal; the impact of the aura of victory which great men spread around them would have given yourself and all of us a day to be remembered for ever; you would have closed, with your name, the doors of death on this continent and opened those of health and long life for an entire new world.

We learned with deep regret that the good cause in Spain has been betrayed: you will therefore probably have returned home. I would not presume to recommend you to visit Colombia, since we have little to attract an inhabitant of the court of Neptune, and yet pure nature and liberty have an irresistible charm for worthy souls, and that is why I dared to speak to you of Colombia.

May I take this pleasurable opportunity, dear General, of reiterating the assurance of the highest consideration and respect, in which I have always held you.


58

# Decree establishing the University of Trujillo

*An important document in the series of Bolívar's papers concerning education and culture. Promulgated at General Headquarters at Huamachuco (Peru) on 10 May 1824.*


### SIMÓN BOLÍVAR
Liberator President of Colombia, and invested with the Supreme
Power in the Republic of Peru

Considering:
1. That in accordance with article 184 of the Political Constitution

of the Republic, universities are to be set up in the capitals of each department, this being one of the most effective ways of promoting public instruction, on which the advancement and protection of social rights largely depends;

2. That, nevertheless, the people of the department of Trujillo have no opportunity for education except the schooling which may be obtained at the expense of considerable time and effort in the Seminary of their capital city;

3. That the provinces of the aforementioned department deserve much from their country in return for their fidelity to the cause, and for the many important services they rendered to the army of liberation during the most dangerous times in the life of the Republic;

I have decided to decree, and I do so decree as follows:

*Article 1.* The University to be opened in accordance with Article 184 of the Constitution in the city of Trujillo, as the capital of one of the departments of the Republic, is hereby declared established.

*Article 2.* The Colegio del Salvador, together with its chapel, shall be assigned for use by this establishment, and the Rector of the said university, who shall be the Archdeacon Don Carlos Pedemonte, shall indicate the classrooms to be used for its various activities.

*Article 3.* The Rector, together with Don Hipólito Unanue, Don Manuel Lorenzo Vidaurre and Don Manuel de Villarán, shall prepare the statutes of the University and submit them at the earliest possible moment to the government. It shall be understood that education is to be imparted in ecclesiastical studies, pure and applied science, public and national law, and philosophy and the humanities, and that the most efficient curriculum and organization is to be adopted, in conformity with sound principles and modern discoveries.

*Article 4.* The funds for this university shall be constituted from: the revenues of the Jesuits in the Department of Trujillo which have been allocated by the Supreme Government for other purposes; the lay foundations financed by the State in the Diocese, for defraying the costs of the designated masses; the legacies bequeathed within the District of Trujillo for educational establishments; the deposits or fees paid by students; and any special contributions which the lay and regular clergy of the bishopric, the municipalities and heads of family may care to make because of their patriotism and desire for their country's enlightenment. The names of all such persons and their corresponding donations shall be published in the *Gaceta*.

*Article 5.* Without prejudice to the provisions of Article 4 above, the Ecclesiastical Council and the municipality shall each be authorized to submit a project for increasing these funds, so that the teaching staff may be well remunerated, and all other requirements of the institution can be covered.

*Article 6.* The Rector shall proceed with the organization and opening of the university in accordance with the usual practice in these cases and shall for this purpose be entrusted with wide powers; he shall at the same time be obliged to render account of the successful completion of such work to the government, which is particularly concerned with this project.

This Decree shall be printed, published and circulated.

Done at General Headquarters, Huamachuco, on 10 May 1824—Year III of the Republic.

*Simón Bolívar*

By order of H.E.
*José Sánchez Carrión*

## 59
## 'The hope of the Universe'

*Prophetic proclamation to the soldiers of the United Army of Liberation in Pasco on 29 July 1824 before the decisive and final battles of Junín and Ayacucho, which brought freedom to Peru and Bolivia, and set the seal on Latin America's independence.*

### SIMÓN BOLÍVAR
Liberator President of Colombia and invested with the
Supreme Power in Peru, etc., etc., etc.

Soldiers!

You are about to complete the greatest task that Heaven has entrusted to men, the task of liberating an entire world from slavery.

Soldiers! The enemies you have to destroy boast of their fourteen years of triumphs; they will, therefore, be well placed to match their weapons against your own, which have excelled in a thousand battles.

Soldiers! Peru and the whole of America place in you their hopes for peace, the daughter of victory. Liberal Europe, too, is watching you, spellbound, since the freedom of the New World is the hope of the Universe. Would you dash such hopes? No, no, no! You are invincible.

General Headquarters of the Liberation, Pasco, 29 July 1824.

*Bolívar*

## 60

# 'True glory lies in being great and useful'

*Letter to General Antonio José de Sucre—soon to be named Grand Marshal of Ayacucho—from Huamanga, dated 4 September 1824. Bolívar's aphorism, 'True glory lies in being great and useful', is one of the most frequently quoted and representative examples of his thought.*

My dear General,

I answer the letter brought to me by Escalona with an expression of Rousseau's—when Julia's lover complained of the slander to which he was subjected for the money she sent to him—'This is the only thing you have ever achieved in your unaccomplished life.' I believe you have badly misjudged me in thinking that I could have possibly wished to offend you. I am sorely aggrieved to learn of your distress, but I do not have the least feeling that I have offended you. I had wanted to perform this task myself; but, thinking you would do a better job than I because of your great energy, I entrusted it instead to you, more as proof of preference than from any desire to humiliate. You know that I cannot lie, and you also know that the honesty of my soul would never lower itself to falsehood and pretence; in this you must believe me.

The day before yesterday, before knowing anything at all of the existence of such feelings in you, I informed General Santa Cruz that we would be staying behind to lead the rearguard, since it would have been a dishonour for you to do this, and that you would press ahead with the main army to the area of Cuzco or Arequipa, depending on the direction the enemy took. In all this I saw nothing and see nothing other than service, since glory, honour, ability and ingenuity are all applied for the single and sole purpose of bringing triumph to Colombia and its army and freedom to America.

My appreciation of you was never so unfavourable that I could imagine that you would take offence at being entrusted with the supervision of the army's administration and at the accomplishment of a valuable task.

If you wish to know whether your presence was necessary with the rearguard, take a glance at our finances, our reserves, our supplies, our hospitals and Zulia's column—all in total disarray, lost in enemy country, incapable of surviving or moving on.

And what is this vanguard I am supposed to have led? It was Colonel Carreno who did so. General Santa Cruz arrived six days before me. The enemy need not expect us now, or even in a month. The army required and requires *everything* you have gone to collect and much more. If the salvation of Colombia's army is a dishonourable thing, then I understand neither words nor ideas. I therefore conclude, my dear General, by saying to you that your feeling of distress should become one of regret for the harm *you* have caused yourself in considering yourself offended unduly, and also in having offended *me* with your grievances.

Such touchiness and attention to tittle-tattle are for common people and are not worthy of you; true glory lies in being great and useful. I have never refused tribulation, and have always believed that what was not unworthy of me was not unworthy of you, either.

Lastly, I may say to you that I am so certain of the choice you yourself will make—between coming to perform your duty or returning to Colombia—that I do not hesitate in leaving you the opportunity to decide. If you leave, then you are not the person I thought you were. If you wish to come and lead the army, I shall remain behind, and you shall march forward so that all can see that the task I have assigned to you is no rebuff on my part. This is my answer.

Yours very truly,

*Bolívar*

61

# Two books from Napoleon's library

*Interesting obiter dicta on culture in these paragraphs from two docu-
ments: a letter to General Sir Robert Wilson, dated Chancay, 15
November 1824, and the Testament of the Liberator, made while he
was staying on the Estate of San Pedro Alejandrino, Santa Marta
(Colombia), on 10 December 1830.*

The Vice-President of Colombia has written to inform me that you
have had the goodness to present me with the rare gift of two books
of inestimable value on law and warfare—*The Social Contract* and
Montecuccoli—both of which were used by the great Napoleon.
Both these works will give me great pleasure in all respects. Their
authors are highly regarded both for the good and for the harm they
have done; their first owner is the honour and the despair of the
human spirit, and the second, who has honoured me by giving them
to me, is worth more than any other to me, for he has traced with
his sword the precepts of Montecuccoli and *The Social Contract* is
engraved on his heart not with theoretical characters but with deeds
in which heroism and benificence have an equal share. I am speaking
of General Wilson, that wonderful man who, like Caesar or Titus,
has travelled the world sword in hand; he has defended in Parliament
the rights of men with an eloquence worthy of the victor of Phar-
salus, and not a day in his life has passed without him doing a good
deed for mankind, like the man who called himself 'the delight of
mankind'.

LETTER TO GENERAL SIR ROBERT WILSON

... 7. It is my wish that the two works presented to me as a gift by
my friend General Wilson, which formerly belonged to the library
of Napoleon—namely Rousseau's *Social Contract* and Montecuccoli's
*Military Art*, be given to the University of Caracas.

Testament of the Liberator

62

'The day our plenipotentiaries exchange their
credentials will remain immortal in the
diplomatic history of America. . . . What then will
the Isthmus of Corinth be by comparison
with the Isthmus of Panama?'

*On 7 December 1824, Bolívar, believing that 'the time has come for
the interests and relationships which unite our republics' to consolidate
their destinies, convenes the Amphictyonic Congress of Panama. The
circular was sent from Lima, on behalf of Peru, to the Governments of
Colombia, Mexico, the River Plate, Chile and Guatemala.*

Sir,

Great and dear friend,

After fifteen years of sacrifices for the freedom of America, in
order to secure a system of guarantees which would be the shield of our
new destiny, be it in peacetime or war, the time has come for the
interests and relationships that unite the American republics, which
were formerly Spanish colonies, to be given secure foundations that
will, if possible, ensure the stability of their governments forever.

The establishment of such a system and the consolidation of the
power of this great body politic are tasks for a single supreme
authority which should direct the policy of our governments, which
should use its influence to maintain the constancy of their principles,
and whose name alone should be capable of settling our differences.
Such a respectable authority can exist only in an assembly of plenipotentiaries appointed by each of our republics, and meeting under
the auspices of victory, the victory won by our armed forces over
the rule of Spain.

Deeply convinced of these ideas, as President of Colombia, in
the year eighteen hundred and twenty two, I invited the Governments of Mexico, Peru, Chile and Buenos Aires to form together a
confederation; and I proposed the convening, at the Isthmus of
Panama or any other mutually acceptable place, of an assembly of
plenipotentiaries from each state 'to act as counsel in major conflicts,
as a place of contact during periods of common danger, as faithful
interpreter of public treaties whenever difficulties should arise and,
lastly, as conciliator in our disputes'.

The Government of Peru entered into a treaty of alliance and
confederation with the plenipotentiary of Colombia on the sixth day

of July in that year; by that treaty, both parties committed themselves to use their good offices with the governments of the former Spanish America to ensure that such governments entered into the same pact and that the meeting of the general assembly of the confederate parties could be held. An identical treaty was concluded in Mexico on the third day of October in the year eighteen hundred and twenty-three by the Envoy Extraordinary of Colombia to that state; and there are sound reasons for hoping that other governments may also heed the dictates of their supreme interests.

Any further delay in convening the general assembly of the plenipotentiaries of those republics which have already joined the confederation—until such time as the other states have acceded—would result in our depriving ourselves of the advantages which that assembly will provide immediately it is established. These same advantages are multiplied considerably when one considers the present political situation in the world, and particularly on the continent of Europe.

The meeting of the plenipotentiaries of Mexico, Colombia and Peru will, if it is not now proposed by one of the contracting parties, be delayed indefinitely unless we are to await the conclusion of a special convention on the date and place for this important event. In view of the difficulties and delays caused by the distance which separates us, and also for other compelling reasons relating to general interest, I have decided to take this step and propose the immediate convening of our plenipotentiaries, pending the conclusion by the other governments of the preliminary arrangements, such as we have already made ourselves, regarding the appointment and incorporation of their representatives.

With regard to the date for the convening of the Assembly, I make so bold as to suggest that there is no obstacle to its meeting within six months from the present date; I also take the liberty of believing that the earnest desire of all Americans to enhance the power of Columbus's world will reduce the difficulties and delays required for ministerial preparations and will shorten the distance between the capitals of each state and the place of the meeting.

It would seem that if the world were required to choose its capital city, the Isthmus of Panama would be the perfect place for such a destiny, situated as it is in the centre of the globe between Asia on the one side and Africa and Europe on the other. The Isthmus of Panama has been offered for this purpose by the Government of Colombia in existing treaties. It is at an equal distance from all furthest points and might for that reason become the provisional meeting place for the first assembly of the confederate states. For my part, for all these reasons, I feel a great inclination to dispatch the deputies of this republic to Panama as soon as I have been honoured with the impatiently awaited reply to this circular. Nothing indeed could better fulfil my heart's desire than agreement by the confederate governments to organize now this solemn event in America's history.

If you do not wish to be party to this event, I foresee delay and great harm in these times when events of the world are accelerating, and may be doing so indeed to our detriment.

Once the first meetings of plenipotentiaries have been held, the seat of the Assembly and its powers can be determined officially by mutual agreement; and then all will have been achieved.

The day our plenipotentiaries exchange their credentials will remain immortal in the diplomatic history of America. When, in ten centuries' time, posterity looks for the origins of our public law, and the pacts which consolidated its destiny are recalled, the protocols of the Isthmus will be held in great respect. In them will be found the design of the first alliances which mapped out the path of our relations with the Universe. What then will the Isthmus of Corinth be by comparison with the Isthmus of Panama?

God be with you,

Your great and good friend,

*Bolívar*

The Minister of Government and Foreign Relations,
*José Sánchez Carrión*

## 63

## A Lancastrian school in each capital

*Decree establishing and officially imposing the system of Monitorial Schools in Peru. This system, originated by Joseph Lancaster, was regarded at that time by Bolívar as 'the only method of promoting public education swiftly and efficiently'. Lima, 31 January 1825.*

### SIMÓN BOLÍVAR
Liberator President of the Republic of Colombia
and invested with the Supreme Power in the
Republic of Peru

Considering:
I. That the Lancastrian system is the only method of promoting public education swiftly and efficiently;

II. That, if this system is extended to each department, it will without delay become disseminated throughout the territory of the Republic;

I have decided to decree, and I do so decree as follows:

1. A school organized according to the Lancastrian system shall be established in the capital city of each department.
2. The prefects shall, by agreement with the municipalities of their respective cities, determine exactly the moneys necessary for establishing such schools.
3. Each province shall send to the school in its department six children at least, so that these children may subsequently disseminate this system of education throughout the capital city and other towns and villages of the province concerned.
4. The administrators, in conjunction with the municipalities, shall designate the most able children to be sent to the school. From the funds allocated for public instruction, provision shall be made for the subsistence of children of poor families.
5. The Minister of State in the Department of Government and Foreign Relations shall be entrusted with the execution of this decree.

This decree shall be printed, published and circulated.

Done in the Palace of the Chief of State, Lima, on 31 January 1825—Year IV of the Republic.

*Simón Bolívar*

By order of H.E.
*José Sánchez Carrión*

64

# Encouraging prospects
## after the liberation of Peru

*A speech typical of Bolívar, made to the Sovereign Constituent Con-*
*gress of Peru. Dated Lima, 10 February 1825.*

Gentlemen,

The representatives of the people of Peru meet today under the
auspices of the magnificent victory of Ayacucho which has for ever
settled the destinies of the New World.

A year ago, the Congress proclaimed dictatorial powers for the
purpose of saving the Republic, which was then weighed down
under the burden of the most dreadful calamities. However, the
providential hand of the army of liberation has now healed the
wounds in the country's heart: it has broken the chains that Pizarro
had forged around the sons of Manco Capac, founder of the Empire
of the Sun; and it has brought all Peru back under the hallowed
régime of its former rights.

My administration cannot properly be described as anything
but a campaign; we barely had time to arm ourselves and fight,
when the onrush of disasters left us no other alternative but to defend
ourselves. Now that the army has triumped with so much glory for
Peruvian arms, I feel obliged to appeal to the Congress duly to
reward the valour and virtue of the country's defenders.

Courts have been set up in accordance with the fundamental
law. I have ordered that hidden merit be sought out and given its
place in the courts, and I have carefully endeavoured to recruit those
who modestly professed the cult of conscience—the religion of the
law.

National revenues did not exist; fraud was rife in every department; disorder increased the misery of the state. I felt compelled to
order essential reforms and to issue severe decrees in order to ensure
survivial of the Republic. Social life can prosper only if gold runs
through its veins.

The crisis in the Republic gave me a chance which may not
perhaps arise again for centuries—to introduce a valuable reform.
The political edifice had been destroyed by crime and war; I found
myself in a field of desolation, but with the advantage of being able
to build sound government in that field. Despite my earnest desire
for the well-being of Peru, I cannot assure the Congress that this
endeavour has resulted in improvements to the extent I had been led

to expect. The Congress in all its wisdom will need to make every effort to endow the country with the organization it requires, and the good fortune that freedom promises. Let me confess that, as I am not a Peruvian, it has been all the more difficult for me to succeed in such a difficult task.

Our relations with the Republic of Colombia have provided us with powerful support. Our ally and confederate has withheld nothing from us; it has used its wealth, its navy and its army to fight the common enemy, as if it were fighting for its own cause.

The Congress will note, from these gestures by Colombia, the infinitely great value—in our situation here in America—of close confederation between the new states. As I am personally convinced of the benefits which would be derived from a meeting of the Congress of Representatives, I have taken the initiative of inviting our fellow confederates, on behalf of Peru, to hold this august assembly without delay in the Isthmus of Panama, in order to seal our everlasting alliance.

The Republic of Chile has placed under the orders of our government part of its navy, commanded by the gallant Vice-Admiral Blanco, and these units are now blockading the fortified town of Callao with Chilean and Colombian forces. The states of Mexico, Guatemala and Buenos Aires have offered us their services, although this has been of no avail owing to the rapidity of developments. These republics have established and are maintaining peace within their borders.

The diplomatic agent of the Republic of Colombia is the only representative under present circumstances to have been accredited to our government. The consuls of Colombia, the United States of America, and of Great Britain have arrived in our capital to take up their functions. The last-mentioned consul unfortunately died in most regrettable circumstances; the other two have obtained the *exequatur* to take up their duties in their posts.

When the military events in Peru become known in Europe, it seems likely that the governments there will finally decide on the policy they are to adopt. I am delighted that Great Britain is to be the first to recognize our independence. If we are to believe the statements being made in France, that country too cannot be far behind England in taking this liberal measure; perhaps the rest of Europe will also follow the same path. Even Spain, if she were to act in her own interests, would no longer oppose the existence of the new States that have come to join the world community.

Legislators! As I hand back to the Congress the supreme powers it bestowed upon me, may I be allowed to congratulate the people, which has rid itself of the most terrible things in this world—of war, through the victory at Ayacucho, and of despotism through my resignation. I implore you to ban forever such awesome authority— such authority as dug the grave of Rome. It was no doubt praise- worthy that the Congress, in its efforts to cross terrible chasms to ride the fury of the storms, should have spiked its laws on the bay- onets of the liberation army; but now that the country has recovered its internal peace and political freedom, the Congress should insist henceforth that only laws should hold sway.

Gentlemen, the Congress is now opened.

My other destiny as a soldier bids me now to help to secure the freedom of Upper Peru, and the surrender of Callao, the last outpost of the Spanish Empire in South America. I shall then return im- mediately to my country to report to the representation of the Colombian people on my mission in Peru, on your freedom and on the glory of the army of liberation.

*Bolívar*

65

# Unlimited support for the educationalist Joseph Lancaster

*An effusive letter, expressing 'admiration, respect and gratitude' to the English educator, inventor of the teaching method which Bolívar de- scribed as a 'magnificent work' and undertook to spread throughout America, dated Lima, 16 March 1825.*

Dear Sir,

I was honoured to receive your kind letter from Baltimore, the reply to which was forwarded to the United States of America via a whole series of roundabout routes which must have considerably delayed its arrival in your hands. I am now delighted to learn from your letter from Caracas how determined you are to remain in our midst with the laudable objective of promoting and perfecting the mutual education that has done and will go on doing so much good to mankind; a magnificent achievement which we owe to the out- standing genius of a man who has been good enough to devote himself to the instruction of my untutored fellow citizens.

You would seem to need some support in order to carry out your beneficent projects; and I therefore propose to offer you 20,000 duros to be used for the instruction of the children of Caracas. The 20,000 duros will be made available in London by the agents of Peru there, on whom you will be able to draw this amount within three or four months. The agents will be instructed to remit this sum to any person you may ask to collect it. Should you not deem it necessary to draw the full amount available in London, nothing will be easier than to transfer to Caracas that portion which you do require.

I would add that I will gladly advance further sums of money for the same purpose if you think additional sums are needed. In order to avail yourself of this offer, kindly let me know in the manner you think best.

The Government of Peru has been generous to me in a thousand ways; and it has also placed at my disposal the sum of 1 million pesos for the benefit of the people of Colombia. Public education will have first priority in the allocation of these funds. Consequently, I would be happy to contribute to improvements in the educational establishments you direct with such remarkable genius.

Accept the assurance of my admiration, respect and gratitude for choosing the country of my birth as your home.

Your affectionate and humble servant,

*Bolívar*

## 66

# A romantic heart

*From Ica, on 20 April 1825, Bolívar writes to his faithful mistress Manuela Sáenz, 'Manuelita', his loyal and devoted companion since 1822. Most of Bolívar's love letters were lost with the burning of Manuela Sáenz's papers when she died of diphtheria in Paita in 1856.*

My fair and lovely Manuela, I am constantly thinking of you and your fate. I see that nothing in the world can bring us together in conditions of innocence and honour. I can see it clearly, and I shudder at the thought of such a terrible situation for you, because you have to reconcile yourself to someone you have never loved, because I must be separated from the one I worship and adore! Yes, indeed, I worship you now more than ever. Having wrenched myself away from your love and your presence, I feel a thousand times more strongly the enchantment of your soul and of your divine heart, a heart that has no peer.

When you were mine, I loved you more for your captivating nature than for your irresistible charms. But now, it seems as if an eternity has come between us, since my own will has imposed on me the torment of wrenching myself away from your love and your faithful heart keeps us apart, since we are now tearing out the soul which gave us life and our pleasure in living. In time to come, you will be alone, even with your husband at your side. And I shall be alone in the midst of the world. Our only consolation is the thought that we have mastered our feelings. Duty tells us that we are guilty, no more, and we shall never be guilty again.

*Bolívar*

67

# Selection of students for training in public affairs in Europe

*In an attempt to improve efficiency in state administration, and desiring to seek out knowledge and experience wherever it was to be found, Bolívar gave the following instructions to the Government Council of Peru in May 1925.*

18. The Government Council shall send to England ten young men, either with the commissioners or travelling separately, to receive instruction in European languages, public law, political economy and all other branches of knowledge necessary for training statesmen. These young men shall be between 12 and 20 years of age. They shall be selected from the students who are most outstanding for their natural talent, application, good behaviour and intellectual ability. Account will also be taken of their general demeanour, a necessary quality for those appointed to posts in foreign relations: four of these young men shall be selected from the Department of Lima, two from Trujillo, two from Cuzco and two from Arequipa.

The Government Council shall enact the necessary measures for their subsistence and education in England, and shall take any other steps it considers advisable in this connection.

68

# The intelligent practice of literary criticism

*Letter to the Ecuadorian poet José Joaquín Olmedo, author of the famous* Canto a Junín, *written from Cuzco on 27 June 1825.*

Dear friend,

A few days ago, when I was travelling, I received two letters and one poem from you: the letters are those of a politician and a poet, but the poem is the work of an Apollo. All the heat of the arid deserts, all the fire of Junín and Ayacucho, all the rays of the Father of Manco Cápac have never produced a greater or more intense flame in the mind of a mortal. You unleash emotions as yet unknown, you scorch the earth with the sparks of the axle and the wheels of a chariot of Achilles which has never before driven over the soil of Junín. You are master of all the characters, making me a Jupiter, Sucre a Mars, La Mar an Agamemnon and a Menelaus, Córdoba an Achilles, Necochea a Patroclus and an Ajax, Miller a Diomedes and Lara a Ulysses. We each have our divine or heroic shadow, which covers us with its protective wings like a guardian angel. In your fashion you make us figures of poetry or fantasy, and—to continue in the realm of poetry, fiction and fable—you elevate us to false divinity, as Jupiter's eagle lifted the tortoise up to the skies, only to drop it on a rock and break its stunted limbs. You have elevated us so much that you have cast us also into the abyss of nothingness, covering the pale radiance of our obscure virtues with myriads of shining lights. Thus, my friend, you have atomized us with the bolts of your Jupiter, the sword of your Mars, the sceptre of your Agamemnon, the lance of your Achilles, and the wisdom of your Ulysses. If I were less charitable, and you were not such a good poet, I would be inclined to think that you had wished to write a parody of the Iliad with the heroes of our feeble masquerade. But no, this I would not believe. You are a poet, and, like Bonaparte, you know that there is only one step from the sublime to the ridiculous, and that Manolo and El Cid are brothers, though of different fathers. An American will read your poem as if it were a canto by Homer, and a Spaniard as if it were a canto from Boileau's *Facistol.*

For all this, allow me to express my unbounded gratitude.

I do not doubt that you will worthily perform your mission in England: I was indeed so convinced of this that, having looked over the length and breadth of the Empire of the Sun, I could find no diplomat capable of representing and negotiating for Peru to better advantage than yourself. I have sent a mathematician with you so that, once removed from the truth of poetry, you might not come to think that two and two made 4,000; and so our Euclid has departed to open the eyes of our Homer so that he can see not with his imagination but with his senses, to present him from falling under the charms of harmony and metre, and to induce him to pay heed only to the tough, harsh and soul-searching prose of politicians and public figures. Yesterday I reached the classic country of the sun, of the Incas, of fable and history. Here the real sun is gold; the Incas are the viceroys and prefects; the fables are the stories of Garcilaso; history is the tale of the destruction of the Indians by Las Casas. Poetry aside, everything here sets my mind to high ideas, deep thought; my soul is spellbound by the presence of primitive nature unfolding through its own endeavour, creating from its own resources, inspired by its own inner patterns, having no compound with the foreign works, alien advice and whims of the human mind, and not tolerating contagion by the history of mankind's crimes and absurdities.

Manco Cápac, the Adam of the Indians, came down from his paradise in Titicaca to set up a historic society, untroubled by either sacred or profane fabrication.

God made him man; he built up his kingdom, and history tells the truth, in the monuments of stone, the straight wide roads, the innocent customs and the genuine traditions which all bear witness to a social creation of which we have no notion, no model and no replica. Peru is unique in the annals of mankind. This is how I see it, because I am here where all that I have described to you, poetically or not, is clear and directly perceptible.

Please be good enough to present this letter to Mr Paredes, and accept the most sincere assurance of my friendship,

*Bolívar*

69

# In defence of nature

*Two decrees promulgated on 5 July 1825 from Cuzco, concerning the taming of the useful and necessary vicuña* (Vicugna vicugna) *and measures to increase the numbers of these animals.*

## SIMÓN BOLÍVAR
Liberator President
of the Republic of Colombia, Liberator of the Republic of Peru and
invested with the Supreme Power therein, etc., etc.

Considering:

That there is an urgent need to do everything possible to increase the numbers of vicuña;

That this fine and unique specimen of the fauna of Peru has hitherto been neglected;

That this animal would have eventually become extinct if the yearly massacres which took place in order to supply the wool industry had been allowed to continue,

I have decided to decree, and do so decree as follows:

1. From this day forward the slaughtering of vicuña in whatever numbers shall be prohibited.

2. No one shall be permitted to slaughter the animals, even on the pretext of hunting.

3. Whoever may wish to use the wool for commercial purposes or any other purpose or advantage may do so during the shearing season, i.e. during the months of April, May, June and July, so that the mildness of weather may make up for the warmth previously provided by the coat the animals have lost.

4. Any person violating this decree shall be liable to a fine of four pesos for each vicuña slaughtered, and this fine shall be imposed on the person committing the offence.

5. All prefects, administrators and governors shall exercise the greatest conscientiousness and vigilance in this matter.

6. The Secretary-General shall be entrusted with the implementation and execution of this decree.

This decree shall be printed, published and circulated.

Done in Cuzo, this fifth day of July 1825.

## SIMÓN BOLÍVAR
Liberator President
of the Republic of Colombia, Liberator of the Republic of Peru and
invested with the Supreme Power therein, etc., etc.

Considering:

That great advantages would accrue for Peru if vicuña were raised in herds;

That experience shows constantly how easily these animals can be tamed;

That in the areas where these animals are raised, as well as in others of milder climate, there are great expanses of land which naturally provide the fodder on which they feed;

I have decided to decree and do so decree as follows:

1. Any person breeding tame vicuña shall receive for each head one peso, to be deducted from the taxes to which he is liable, unless he is so poor that he pays no taxes, in which case this bonus shall be payable in cash from the treasury of his department.

2. This bonus shall be payable for a period of ten years from the date of this decree.

3. Prefects of departments shall establish special regulations determining and specifying the formalities to be observed in order to certify that the terms of Article 1 above are being complied with.

4. Prefects, administrators and governors shall bring all their authority and influence to promote and encourage this new branch of the country's industry.

5. The Secretary-General shall be entrusted with the implementation and execution of this decree.

This decree shall be printed, published and circulated.

Done in Cuzco, this fifth day of July 1825.

*Simón Bolívar*

By order of H.E.
*Felipe Santiago Estenós*

70

# In the vanguard of education for women in America

*Bolívar promulgated this decree on the education of women—at the time a neglected subject—from Cuzco on 8 July 1825. The Liberator's administrative activity was very productive during his one-month stay in the city which was once the capital of the Empire of the Incas.*

## SIMÓN BOLÍVAR
Liberator, President of the Republic of Colombia,
Liberator of the Republic of Peru, and invested with the
Supreme Power therein

Considering:

1. That education of girls is the basis of family morality, but has in this city been totally neglected;

2. That measures should be taken to open a much-needed institution for this purpose as soon as possible;

I hereby decree:

1. That in the building of the college of S. Bernardo there shall be founded another school to be known as Educación del Cuzco, and that girls of all classes—both from the city and from the department—who are able to profit from education, shall be admitted to this new school;

2. That the funds for this school shall be provided from the surplus apportioned by decree of this date to the Cuzco School of Science and the Arts;

3. That the wealthy citizens of the department shall pay for their daughters' board, an amount to be announced in due course, in order to augment the school's funds;

4. That the benefit of education be extended to young girls of other departments, in accordance with the terms of the school regulations;

5. That the methods to be followed in the education provided by, and in the economic administration of, this school shall be the subject of a separate set of regulations;

6. That the prefect of the department shall, with great care and vigilance, supervise compliance with this decree;

7. That the acting Secretary-General shall be entrusted with the implementation and execution of this decree.

This decree shall be printed, published and circulated.
Done in Cuzco, this eighth day of July 1825.

*Simón Bolívar*

By order of H.E.
*Felipe Santiago Estenós*

---

71

# Another higher educational establishment to disseminate enlightenment

*Decree establishing a College of Science and the Arts in Cuzco, where Bolívar was given a specially warm welcome by the humble half-castes and Indians. This decree also dates from 8 July 1825.*

## SIMÓN BOLÍVAR
### Liberator of Colombia and of Peru, etc.,

Considering:

1. That the education of young people has been almost totally neglected as a result of the insufficient number of places for such an important purpose;

2. That the enlightenment of this important department depends on the reform of its age-old education system;

3. That it is necessary for this purpose to set up a public educational establishment in which all branches of education are taught;

I decree:

1. That there shall be established in this city a Colegio de Estudios de Ciencias y Artes with the title of Colegio de Cuzco;

2. That the premises of the banished Jesuits, including their church, shall be used for this establishment;

3. That the colleges of S. Bernardo and El Sol shall be combined within these buildings into a single entity;

4. That the revenues hitherto accruing to the Bethlemites of this city, the revenues of the colleges of S. Bernardo and El Sol, the local taxes and all other revenues of this department shall be applied to the establishment of the new Colegio de Cuzco;

5. That the cost of refurbishing the buildings shall be drawn from these funds now, so that the Colegio de Estudios del Cuzco can be opened as soon as possible;

6. That, pending the elaboration of the general curriculum by the Sovereign Congress, this establishment shall be governed by provisional regulations, concerning its economic administration and the method of education to be followed;

7. That the prefect of the department will rigorously ensure that this decree is strictly complied with;

8. That the acting Secretary-General shall be entrusted with the implementation and execution of this decree.

This decree shall be printed, published and circulated.

Done in Cuzco, on this eighth day of July 1825.

*Simón Bolívar*

By order of H.E.
*Felipe Santiago Estenós*

72

# 'I have represented them before mankind and I will represent them before posterity'

*Recollections of Caracas, in another memorable letter, known as the 'Elegy of Cuzco'. Written to Don Estebán Palacios, on 10 July 1825.*

Dear Uncle Estebán and gracious godfather!

How pleased I was when you came back to life for me yesterday! Yesterday, I learnt that you were alive, and living in our beloved homeland. Imagine how many memories suddenly flooded my mind! My mother, my good mother who was so like you, came back from the grave and appeared in my mind's eye. My tender infancy, my confirmation, my godfather, all came together to tell me that you were my second father. All my uncles and aunts, my brothers and sisters, my grandfather, my childhood games, the gifts you gave me when I was still innocent . . . all these pictures rushed into my mind and recalled to me my earliest emotions . . . the feelings of youthful sensibility.

Yesterday, everything that is human in me was stirred—by 'human' I mean what is closest to nature and to our earliest impressions. You, my dear uncle, have given me the deepest sense of joy, now that I know you are back in your home, with your family, your nephew and your country. Enjoy, therefore, as I do, this genuine pleasure, and live with your people for the remaining days that Providence has given you, so that it will be a brotherly hand that closes your eyelids and takes away your remains to place them together with those of the fathers and brothers who are at rest beneath the earth on which we were born.

Dear Uncle, you have dreamed the dream of Epimenides: you have returned from the land of the dead to witness the ravages of inexorable time, cruel war and savage men. You must find yourself in Caracas, like a phantom spirit come from the other life, and seeing that nothing is as it was before.

You left behind a large and happy family: and it was cut to pieces by a bloody sickle. You left behind a new-born country, unfolding the first seeds of its creation and the first elements of its society, and you return to find it in ruins . . . nothing but memories. The living are no longer here: the work of men, the houses of God and even the fields and meadows have felt the havoc wrought by the tremors of nature. You will be wondering where your fathers, brothers and nephews may be. . . . The fortune were entombed within the protective walls of their domestic mansions, and the unlucky had their bones strewn across the fields of Venezuela, after watering them with their blood . . . their only crime was that they had loved justice.

The fields irrigated by the sweat of thirty years' toil have been parched by a fatal combination of meteors and crimes. You will ask—where is Caracas? It does not exist. But its ashes, its monuments, the land on which it was built, all have remained, respondent in their freedom; and they are covered with the glory of martyrdom. This consolation makes up for all losses; at least, this is my consolation. I should also like it to be yours.

I have commended to the Vice-President the talents and virtues I have recognized in you. My commendation was as impassioned as I am myself towards you, my Uncle. Direct your attention to the executive authorities; it will be rewarded. I have asked these same authorities to have remitted to you the sum of 5,000 pesos in Caracas, so that you will be able to live until we meet, which will probably be next year. My instructions to the Minister of Finances were that the letter of credit should be sent to you from Bogotá.

Goodbye, dear Uncle. Console yourself in your homeland with those of your family who still remain: they have suffered much, but theirs has been the glory ever to have remained faithful to their duty. Our family has shown itself worthy of us, and its blood has been avenged by one of its members. I have had the fortune to be that member. I have reaped the fruit of all the services of my fellow countrymen, relatives and friends. I have represented them before mankind, and I will represent them before posterity. This has been unbelievable good fortune. Fate has punished all; only I have received its favours, and so I offer them to you with my most heart-felt sincerity,

*Bolívar*

## 73

# For the conservation of monuments of Indian culture

*Memorandum to the prefect of the Department of Cuzco from Uru-bamba, dated 18 July 1825. It illustrates the Liberator's concern for the care of cultural property.*

To the Prefect of the Department of Cuzco,

His Excellency the Liberator has given instructions that you are to use your full authority to ensure that ancient monuments which—despite the ravages of time and the determined attempts of the Span-iards to destroy them—are still to be found in your Department are conserved in their existing state. The glory their creators have acquired through the very efforts to destroy them must not be hidden. Now that the natural rights of the Indians have been restored by the present system, it is fitting that their ancestors should be immortalized through their works. For this most important objec-tive, you are required to make known through the press whatever measures are to be taken in this respect.

By order of His Excellency, I assure you of my highest con-sideration.

Urubamba, 18 July 1825

*Felipe S. Estenós*

74

# 'The Argentine people shall be assured for all time that our heart will never be dissociated from their future well-being'

*Address to the envoys from the River Plate, General Carlos de Alvear and Dr José Miguel Díaz Vélez, in Potosí, on 16 October 1825. The Argentine diplomats proposed to Bolívar that he should declare himself 'Protector of America's Freedom'.*

Gentlemen,

The Government of the United Provinces of the River Plate has honoured us with a mission that is most flattering, both by its truly magnificent purpose and by the eminent personalities which compose it.

Thus, the Argentine people shall be assured for all time that our heart will never be dissociated from their future well-being; our most earnest concern and most heart-felt affection go out to that people, which set off with us along the splendid road to freedom, the end of which we now have reached.

We would not have wished to mention our regrettable grievances; but when scandal makes them known why should they be passed over in silence? In truth, we have the most unchallengeable right to be surprised that an American prince recently independent from Europe, who is involved in our noble uprising and has established his throne not on flimsy foundations but on the indestructible bases of the sovereignty of the people and of their laws—we have a right to be surprised that this prince, who seemed destined to be the friend of neighbouring republics, should still be occupying a province and a military stronghold which do not belong to him and which are holding in subjection one of our most distinguished nations.

Furthermore, his troops recently invaded our province of Chiquitos, laying it waste and insulting us with barbarous threats; and when the terror of our armies put his troops to flight, they seized our property and citizens as they went. And yet these clear violations of international law have gone unpunished; our peoples are humiliated, our glory offended. However, we give thanks for the events that have brought new ties to our relations and which draw us closer, so that we can claim our rights and at the same time secure them.

*Bolívar*

75

## 'In fifteen years of a titanic struggle, we have demolished the edifice of tyranny that has been built up over three centuries'

*Words spoken at Potosí, before the flags of Colombia, Peru, Chile and Buenos Aires, to Bolívar's companions-in-arms and to the Argentine mission led by General Alvear, on 26 October 1825.*

From the shores of the Atlantic we have pursued our path of victory, and in fifteen years of a titanic struggle, we have demolished the edifice of tyranny that had been built up over three centuries of usurpation and violence. The poor remnants of the true masters of this world were doomed to the most debasing slavery. Our joy is unbounded, now that so many millions of men and women have recovered their rights through our perseverance and endeavour! And I, as I stand here on this vast mass of silver called Potosí, the overflowing wealth of whose veins were for 300 years the treasury of Spain, I regard it as worthless when I compare it with the glory of carrying the banner of freedom to victory from the burning shores of the Orinoco, and planting it on the summit of this mountain, which contains the object of the wonder and the avarice of the whole world.

76

# A many-sided initiative: duties and powers of the Director-General of Public Education; a graded primary school in each department; a military college in the capital of the Republic; a college of science and the arts in Chuquisaca; all the savings achieved in public administration to be allocated to education

*Decree promulated in Chuquisaca (Bolivia) on 11 December 1825. Now at the frontier with Argentina, Bolívar demonstrates once again his characteristic concern for education in this decree, which contains so many essential provisions.*

## SIMÓN BOLÍVAR
Liberator of Colombia and Peru, etc.

Considering:

1. That the first duty of the government is to provide education for the people.

2. That this education should be uniform and general.

3. That educational establishments should be organized in accordance with the laws of the State.

4. That the well-being of a republic depends on the sense of morality acquired by citizens through education in their childhood.

And having also heard the views of the Standing Committee, I decree:

1. That the Director-General of Public Education shall assess the information on the education establishments that exist throughout the Republic and shall report to the government on the state of the schools and colleges and the funds which support them.

2. That the Director shall for this purpose be empowered to request from the relevant sources all the information and documents he may require.

3. That the Director shall submit to the government a plan for the establishment of an educational system which covers all branches of instruction, and ensures that education is available to all peoples of the Republic.

4. That in the meantime, and without delay, he shall establish

in each departmental capital a primary school with the different grades necessary for receiving all children of both sexes who are in a position to attend school.

5. That a military college shall be established in the capital of the Republic.

6. That the College of San Juan in this city shall be repaired and reorganized appropriately as a college of science and the arts.

7. That, during the period of construction of the buildings for the primary school and the military college, the latter shall also be installed in the College of San Juan.

8. That, in the course of the visit which the Director shall be required to make to each departmental capital, he shall, after consultation with the Presidents, assign the best premises for the colleges of science and the arts and the primary school, which are to be established on the same basis as those at Chuquisaca.

9. That to fund these establishments, the following shall be allocated in each department: (i) all real estate, levies, revenue and shares of lay foundations, allocated to public establishments by decree of this day; (ii) the duty levied on each measure of flour at the city gates, until such time as this duty is abolished.

10. That not only estates subjected to taxation but also the proceeds from: (i) tax accounts; (ii) the Paria religious foundation established by Lorenzo Aldana; and (iii) monasteries that are abolished, shall be used for funding these establishments.

11. That all these funds shall be centralized under a single administration in each department under the authority of a directorate-general.

12. That for each administration the government shall nominate responsible citizens with reliable guarantees, who shall have the task of renting the estates and collecting the rents they yield, and shall receive in remuneration for their work 5 per cent of the total amounts of rent collected.

13. That the Directorate-General shall be staffed with competent persons.

14. That the administrators shall deposit forthwith in the public treasury all rents in their possession, and shall collect all instalments of rent as they fall due.

15. That these funds shall be totally separate from all other funds, and shall under no circumstances be used for any purpose other than that for which they are intended.

16. That the government shall undertake to allocate to public education all savings henceforth achieved in other branches of public administration.

17. That the acting Secretary General shall be entrusted with the execution of this decree.

This decree shall be printed, published and circulated.

Done in the Palace of Government in Chuquisaca, this eleventh day of December 1825.

*Simón Bolívar*

By order of H.E.
*Felipe Santiago Estenós*

77

## Justice in the distribution of land to peasants

*This decree for the strengthening of economic and social justice was promulgated in Chuquisaca on 14 December 1825. Bolívar reiterates and confirms his resolutions of September 1817, May 1820, April 1824 and July 1825.*

SIMÓN BOLÍVAR
Liberator of Colombia and Peru, etc.

Considering:

1. That agriculture in the Department of Santa Cruz has been gradually run down owing to the neglect to which it was previously subjected by the Spanish Government.

2. That the fertility of its soil offers industrious men the promise of certain wealth.

3. That, in the absence of provisions guaranteeing rights of ownership and ensuring conservation of the land, the inhabitants of the department have totally abandoned it.

And having also heard the views of the Standing Committee, I decree:

1. That rights of ownership acquired in the Department of Santa Cruz by just title and in accordance with the laws shall be protected by the government.

2. That lands belonging to the State shall be divided up among the inhabitants whose allotments shall, after they have been surveyed and their boundaries determined, be transferred into their ownership.

3. That every individual, irrespective of sex and age, shall

receive one-and-a-half acres of land in rich and well-watered places, and three acres in barren areas without irrigation.

4. That priority in this distribution shall be given to Indians and to those who have most vigorously supported the cause of independence or have suffered for supporting it.

5. That if, at the end of the year following the allocation and demarcation of the land, the recipients have failed to start the work appropriate for the season of the year and have shown no signs of interest in such work, they shall be dispossessed of the said land, which shall be allocated to others who will cultivate it properly.

6. That fields intended for use as pastureland shall be jointly owned by all the inhabitants of the provinces or districts, or by the groups which occupy the said areas, as long as they are not distributed as above.

7. That ownership accorded in accordance with Article 2 shall be subject to the restriction that the land allocated cannot be transferred until the year 1850, and never as mortmain on pain of nullity.

8. That surveying and distribution of land shall be effected by a body of three persons of probity and intelligence, proposed by the President of the department by the municipalities concerned, which shall also fix the scale of the fees and charges to be paid to such persons for their services.

9. That the measurement and distribution of land shall be effected with the consent of the Director-General of Agriculture on his arrival in the department.

10. That the President of the Department of Santa Cruz shall ensure that an accurate list of the remaining lands, which shall be declared to be the property of the government, is submitted to the Supreme Government together with any remarks and any information he may obtain concerning the implementation and fulfilment of the objectives contained in this decree.

11. That the acting Secretary-General shall be entrusted with the execution of this decree.

This decree shall be printed, published and circulated.

Done in the Palace of Government at Chuquisaca, on 14 December 1825.

*Simón Bolívar*

By order of H.E.
*Felipe Santiago Estenós*

78

# Pioneer in ecological matters: conservation and proper use of water resources

*Decree promulgated in Chuquisaca on 19 December 1825. This is in addition to the rules on the care and exploitation of forests and the protection of livestock.*

## SIMÓN BOLÍVAR
### Liberator of Colombia and Peru, etc.

Considering:

1. That much of the territory of the Republic lacks water and consequently the plants needed in everyday life.

2. That the barrenness of the soil is an obstacle to population growth and at the same time deprives the present generation of many amenities.

3. That, owing to lack of fuel, the extraction of metals and the manufacture of many mineral products which constitute virtually the only wealth of the soil, cannot be undertaken or are undertaken incorrectly and imperfectly.

And having heard also the views of the Standing Committee, I decree:

1. That the banks of rivers shall be inspected, and the course of rivers observed, so that it can be determined at what points water may be channelled to land now deprived of it.

2. That wherever the soil is such that large species of plants are likely to flourish, organized planting shall be undertaken at the expense of the state, of up to 1 million trees, preferably in the places most in need of them.

3. That the Director-General of Agriculture shall propose to the government any instructions he considers necessary for the creation, the prosperity and the future of forests in the territory of the Republic.

4. That the acting Secretary-General shall be entrusted with the execution of this decree.

This decree shall be printed, published and circulated.

Done at the Palace of Government in Chuquisaca, on 19 December 1825.

*Simón Bolívar*

79

# 'Nations march towards greatness at the same pace as education advances'

*The statesman's considered reflections on 'the primary task of government', public education, in this newspaper article written in 1825.*

A government shapes the morality of peoples and guides them to greatness, prosperity and power. How? By establishing and directing public education, since it is responsible for all the various elements in society. A nation will be wise, virtuous and warlike if the principles of its education are wise, virtuous and warlike; it will be foolish, superstitious, effeminate and fanatic if it is reared in the school of these errors. This is why enlightened societies have always placed education among the bases of their political institutions. Think of Plato's *Republic*. But why bother to examine theories? Think of Athens, the mother of the sciences and the arts; Rome, the mistress of the world; virtuous and invincible Sparta; the Republic of the United States, throne of liberty and sanctuary of the virtues? Where did they find what has made them and what they are? Nations march towards greatness at the same pace as education advances. They fly if it flies; they retreat if it retreats; they rush headlong into obscurity if it is corrupted or totally neglected. This principle, dictated by experience and taught by philosophers and politicians, ancient and modern, is now such a truism that there can be no one alive who is not aware of it.

Happily, we are influenced by a government as enlightened as it is paternal, a government which, amid the persecution and penury thrust upon us by the King, amid the upheaval and the agitation caused by a war of extermination, turns its benevolent gaze from the heart of its trouble towards the people. It sees their poverty, shares their distress and, notwithstanding the scarcity of resources, seeks to remedy their condition by every means philanthropy can supply. It has chosen to focus its attention on the most significant point, on the true foundation of happiness; education.

It is not my intention here to discuss curricula, the establishment of schools, the encouragement of the arts and the sciences, the encouragement and appreciation of men of letters, or practical regulations. The public have seen with their own eyes that this system of moral regeneration now works, and no one can fail to feel its salutary effects.

I will confine my remarks to the school opened here on 1

October of this year. What a difference! To see those groups of youths who were reduced to idleness, the plague of the streets, a public nuisance and a burden to their parents—to see them now, an orderly and decent company, to hear them argue with conviction about the history of religion, the rudiments of arithmetic, drawing and geography: to see them write elegantly to Carver's style, ever eager for knowledge, excited at the thought of a prize, and rejecting the attractions of leisure. This is what makes happiness today, and provides blessings for the people: if there be any who do not experience similar feelings, then they must be insensitive to good. But I, who experience them now, wish to display my interest in such a useful establishment by venturing a few remarks which may be put to any use they deserve.

The principal of a school, or rather the generous man who loves his country and sacrifices rest and freedom to devote himself to the painful exercise of creating citizens who will defend, dignify, sanctify and embellish the state and inspire others as worthy as himself, is doubtless to be blessed . . . he deserves the veneration of the people and the respect of the government. The government should encourage him and award him honourable distinctions.

Clearly, I am not referring to those who are called schoolmasters—those common men who, armed with whip, and with frowning brow, declaim perpetually and bear more resemblance to Pluto than to a benign philosopher.

They teach cares rather than truths: theirs is the school of servile minds, where dissimulation and hypocrisy are learnt together with other vices, where fear prevents the heart from enjoying any other sensation. Away with such tyrants: let them go to Salamanca where there will be room for them.

The government should proceed thus: choose from among the crowd not a scholar but a man distinguished for his good breeding, for the purity of his ways, for his natural demeanour, jovial, open, gentle, frank; in a word a man in whom there is much to imitate and little to correct.

Terms, no matter how attractive the ideas they represent in the first place, degenerate later by misuse and call up different images: this seems to be the case with the words 'master' and 'school'. Under the barbarous foot placed upon educational establishments in the days of Spanish rule, these words produced only disagreeable sensations. To say to a child, 'We are going to school or to see the master', was the same as saying, 'We are going to prison or to your worst enemy.' To take him there and make him the poor slave of fear and boredom was one and the same thing. So I think that these names should be replaced by others which do not produce aversion. Some will say that names have no significance, but experience has shown that they directly influence our judgement. How many quarrels, disputes and wars just because of a name! Think of the dread of our descendants in 100 years' time when they hear the word 'Spanish'. So let the master be called by a different name such as 'principal', and let the school be called 'the society'.

The principal must use his skill to train the minds and the hearts of young people. When, by his wisdom and ability, the cardinal principles of virtue and honour have been engraved on children's souls; when he has succeeded in influencing them by means of examples and simple demonstration, so that they are more stirred by the sight of a badge of honour than by the offer of an ounce of gold; when the thought of failing to deserve the prize or to receive it with a blush distresses more than being deprived of toys and favourite amusements; then he will have laid the solid foundations of society. He will have applied the spur that inspires noble valour and gives children the strength to confront the temptations of idleness by devotion to work. Youth will make unparalleled progress in the arts and the sciences.

Fortunately our society is now in this position; children stay up late to study, talk only of what they have learned, and are disconsolate on the day when the school is closed.

Moral inducements and penalties should be the spur for gentle rationalists; and rigour and the whip the spur for animals. This system elevates the mind, produces nobleness and dignity of feeling, and decency in action. It contributes greatly to the formation of a man's morality, creating within him that inestimable treasure which will enable him to be fair, generous, human, gentle, moderate; in a word an honourable man.

Like the principal, the disciple must possess certain qualities at the time when he enters the society: physical and moral readiness to be taught, at least two suits of clothes, a bow-tie, a hat and a book.

Teaching is nothing more, shall we say, than the training of a military corps, with the difference that soldiers are drilled physically, and children both physically and morally. But, just as the former are given instruction, from the moment they rise to the moment they go to bed, to impart regularity, timing, order and duration to all their movements and duties, in order to produce a rounded whole, so children must be instructed to follow a regime every hour of the day.

The first maxim to be inculcated is that of hygiene. When the importance of respecting this principle is thoroughly examined, no one will doubt its value. There is no more agreeable sight than that of a person with clean teeth, hands, face and clothes: when these are combined with fine and natural manners, we have here the best promise of a warm welcome in men's minds. The principal's first task should be to hold a daily inspection so as to note everything that needs to be pointed out and corrected in this respect. A prize or a distinguishing mark as a reward for this virtue will be sufficient incentive to practise and emulate it.

At the same time, practical instruction should be given in etiquette and the ceremonies and compliments due to persons according to their station. This is no frivolous matter; indeed, its importance is such that failure to observe it may produce displeasure, enmity and duels. There are some so refined and sensitive about these matters, especially foreigners, that they do not tolerate the slightest fault: I have seen men reproved because they lingered at table, smoked in company or wore their hat. This is not surprising: educated men take it as an insult when any irregularity occurs in their presence. What should we say of our social occasions, our banquets? How provincial! What a disgrace! They are more like pigsties than the gatherings of rationalists.

It is also necessary to avoid going to the other extreme, which is over-fastidiousness in the observance of rules, producing affectation so offensive and ridiculous that such persons seem more like men written into precepts than precepts written into men.

Since speech is the vehicle of instruction, one of the principal's first concerns must be to see that diction is pure, clear and correct: that there are no barbarisms or solecisms; that importance is given to accents, and that things are called by their proper names without alteration.

Once the society has been assembled, it would be prudent to divide it into classes—Class I, Class II and Class III—composed of beginners, advanced pupils and very advanced pupils, and to place a boy at the head of each class as a monitor capable of directing it. The monitors should be elected and wear special badges to inspire the ambition of the rest. Boys should grow accustomed to conducting these elections in a manner so orderly and impartial that it will familiarize them with decency and fairness and the pursuit of merit alone.

Children when they are talking together, will address each other as '*tú*'; but, in the presence of the principal, they should use the word '*señor*'.

Quintilian preferred public education to private teaching

because, in addition to the advantages to be derived from acquaintance and contact with persons of different temperaments, public education was where true friendships were formed, those which lasted for life. Bearing this in mind, I would wish every boy to choose another he likes and to form a closer friendship with him than with anyone else. The purpose of such a friendship may be to defend each other before the principal or on any other occasion, for the boys to help each other, to share benefits, to correct each other and to be loyal.

The principal may teach everything his time and ability and the ability of his pupils permit. But the chief subjects should be reading, writing, the priciples of religion, arithmetic and geography. The easiest method of teaching children how to read seems to me, first, to make sure that the pupils are skilled in the knowledge of the alphabet, then in the pronunciation of syllables, but without spelling them out, then going on to read any book whatsoever. This operation includes instruction in the rudiments of Spanish grammar.

For learning to write, Carver's system would appear to be the best method, because it is simple, easy and beautiful. This exercise should include practice in spelling and learning how to read handwriting.

In teaching the principles of the scriptures and religion, the Catechism of Fleuri and Padre Astete may be used with advantage.

For arithmetic, the exercise-book used in class is best.

For universal geography and the geography of the country, a full summary drawn up for the purpose is useful. The lessons given on each of these subjects should take place at a definite hour, should be very clear and should last as long as the average ability of the pupils will allow; there should be special and general examinations at certain periods and, finally, prizes.

A man of character who knows the human heart and directs it wisely, and a simple system and a clear and natural method, are wholly adequate; and the society should make outstanding and brilliant progress in a few days. Without these requirements, precepts and studies will be accumulated in vain; all will be trouble and confusion.

Games and recreation are as necessary to children as food: their physical and moral condition demand them. But such outlets must be channelled to some useful and honest end: the principal may decide on these as he thinks fit, and should supervise them if possible. Games acknowledged as useful and honest are pelota, tennis, skittles, kites, air-balloons, draughts and chess.

The winning of prizes, and outstanding performances in application, honour or any other noble sentiment must not be consigned to oblivion but commanded to memory with esteem. A register should be kept for listing the most noteworthy deeds and recording who did them and the day when they were done. The register should be placed in the charge of an elected secretary who will record and approve the act; the book should be decorated and kept with care in a public place. On the day of great national holidays, the society and some of the leading figures in the country should assemble, and one of the most distinguished persons present should recount the glories and triumphs of youth. Records should be kept of the ceremony, and those whose names are written in the hallowed book should be acclaimed and praised. That day will be a day of festivity and rejoicing for the society.

## 80

# Strict and inflexible republicanism

*Another categorical rejection of monarchist ideas and reaffirmation of the old saying: 'Liberator or dead'. Letter to General F. de P. Santander from La Magdalena (Lima), dated 21 February 1826.*

My dear General and friend,

I have already told you that I came here intending to relinquish my command to the Peruvian Congress, but I am now resolved to do no more to contribute to the well-being of these peoples than use my influence. I find the machinery of government extraordinarily distasteful and, what is more, my enemies will not believe that I detest authority. As proof of this, I shall recount to you a very strange thing later.

Lima has given me a wonderful welcome; these gentlemen vie with the Colombians in their love for us, and they want to force me to be their ruler. General La Mar is sick and no longer wishes to serve in the government, so my position is very difficult. The Congress will meet this week to decide this and others matters, which will certainly give them much to think about. However, I shall tell them that under no circumstances can I be their constitutional leader and that, moreover, Colombia is waiting for me. I have no other command but the military command; and that I shall keep until I leave the country. Many members of the Congress are thinking of proclaiming a Bolivian republic, like the republic of Upper Peru, after concluding a treaty with that country. They aim to detain me by such flattery, choose Sucre as leader and adopt the Constitution I have drawn up instead of the bad one they have now. If this operation succeeds, both peoples will need us to settle their affairs. Then there are others who would like me to become absolute leader of the south, assuming that Chile and Buenos Aires are going to need my protection this year because war and anarchy are devouring them.

Of course, I refuse such a role outright because it does not enter into my ambitions.

With regard to the government's proposals concerning the federation, I tactfully refrained from taking part in its deliberations. I imagine that in this case they will not wish to rush headlong into a very narrow federation for various reasons: those they have given me are to my credit, but there will always be an ulterior motive. Also, they are afraid of the cost, as they are very poor and very deeply in debt: here a great deal is owed to everyone. They do not want to go to Havana because they have to go to Chiloé which belongs to them and they can pay Chile off with that island. They have more of a navy than they can use, and so will not want to buy more ships. They are too afraid of the English to join up with them, but have no fear of a revolution by the coloured population because that population is very submissive. I am telling you all this so that you will be aware of the main ideas that may be put forward in opposition to those of Colombia.

*Highly confidential*

I have recently received letters from various friends in Venezuela proposing Napoleonic ideas to me. General Páez is behind these ideas, which were suggested by his friends, the demagogues. A private secretary and editor of *El Argos* came to deliver the project to me. You will find the original concealed in the letter I am enclosing, and you should guard it with infinite care so that no one may set eyes upon it. It was Carabeño who wrote the letter. General Briceño sent me a message saying that he had to restrain those who were in favour of a coup d'état in Venezuela, and had advised them to consult me. General Mariño also wrote, as have other less important but even wilder demagogues. Of course, you will have guessed what my answer will be. My sister says that there are three parties in Caracas, monarchists, democrats and the mixed bloods; and her advice is that I should be *Liberator or dead*. That is the advice I shall follow, even if I knew that, by doing so, I would cause the whole of mankind to perish. I shall answer General Páez by sending him my projected Constitution for Bolivia, so that he may examine my ideas on stability combined with freedom and the maintenance of the principles we have adopted. I shall also add that he should not drive his friends to despair, lest they swing to another extreme more cruel than this, since the only one left to them is pure anarchy. You should bear in mind that these gentlemen were federalists first, then constitutionalists and are now Bonapartists, so their next titles can only be anarchists, *pardocratas*, or hangmen. At the moment, they say they are moderates and regret their former ideas, but Briceño adds that all this is doubtful until I decide. After losing the first battles, they want to win or die at all costs in the last one.

I shall tell General Páez that he should channel opinion towards my Bolivian Constitution, which unites extremes and everything that is good, since even the federalists find that it meets their wishes in a very great measure; that in 1831 a reform can be introduced to ensure the stability and preservation of the Republic; and that he should also fear what Iturbide suffered for placing too much trust in his supporters, and he should likewise be wary of a terrible reaction from the people for rightly suspecting the advent of a new aristocracy which would destroy equality. I shall say all this and more to erase any thought of a plan so fatal, so absurd and so inglorious; a plan which would attract the hatred of the liberals and the contempt of the tyrants; a plan which is repugnant to my principles, my prudence and my pride. This plan offends me more than all the insults of my enemies, since it assumes that I am a man of vulgar ambition and of infamous heart, capable of lowering myself to the level of Iturbide and those other wretched usurpers. According to these gentlemen, no one can be great except in the manner of Alexander, Caesar and Napoleon. I desire to outdo them all in disinterestedness, since I cannot match them in deeds. My example may do some service to my country, since the moderation of the first Chief will spread even to the last, and my life will be an example. The people will adore me and I shall be as the Ark of their Covenant.

I am yours with all my heart,

*Bolívar*

81

## 'The title of Liberator
## is superior to all those
## bestowed on human pride'

*A further condemnation of absolutism. 'Colombia is not France and I am not Napoleon ... I am not and do not want to be Napoleon.' Letter to General-in-Chief José Antonio Páez, written on 6 March 1826 from La Magdalena.*

My dear General and friend,

I have received your very important letter of 1 October last year, which you sent through Mr Guzmán whom I saw and heard with not a little surprise, since his mission is extraordinary. You say that the position of Colombia is very like that of France when Napoleon was in Egypt and that I should say, as he did, that 'the intriguers are going to ruin the country, and we will save it'. Indeed, almost everything you write bears the stamp of truth, but truth alone is not enough for a plan to achieve its effect. I feel that you have not been impartial enough in judging the condition of things and men. Colombia is not France, and I am not Napoleon. In France, they think a lot and know even more, and the population is homogeneous and also war had brought the country to the brink of a precipice. There had never been any republic as great as France; and France had always been a kingdom. The Republican Government had discredited itself and reduced itself to an object of abysmal execration. Each of the monsters who ruled France was a cruel and as inept as the other. Napoleon was great and unique and, moreover, extremely ambitious. Here, there is nothing of the sort. I am not and I do not want to be Napoleon; nor do I wish to copy Caesar, let alone Iturbide. I regard such examples as unworthy of my reputation. The title of Liberator is superior to all those bestowed on human pride. Therefore, it cannot be degraded. What is more, our population is unlike the French in every way. The Republic has raised the country to fame and prosperity, and endowed it with laws and liberty. The magistrates of Colombia are neither Robespierre nor Marat. The danger ceased when hopes began; consequently, there is no reason for such a measure. Colombia is surrounded by republics and has never been a kingdom. A throne would strike terror by its aloofness as much as by its brilliance. Equality would be destroyed and the coloured population would lose all its rights with a new aristocracy. Lastly, I cannot be persuaded that the project communicated by

Guzmán is sound; and I also think that those who suggested it are of the same feather as the men who supported Napoleon and Iturbide in order to benefit from their prosperity and to forsake them in time of danger; or, if they are acting in good faith, believe me, they are scatter-brained or partisans of extreme opinions regardless of their form or principles.

In all frankness, I must say that this project is not to the advantage of you or me or the country. However, I am confident that, during the period designated for the reform of the Constitution, significant changes can be made in favour of basic conservative principles without breach of any of the most republican rules. I shall send you the draft Constitution I have drawn up for the Republic of Bolivia: you will find that it contains all the guarantees of stability and freedom, equality and order. Should you and your friends wish to approve my project, it would be highly advisable to write about it and commend it to public opinion. This is the service we can do the country; a service that will be appreciated by all the parties which are not extreme or, rather, which desire true liberty with true stability. Beyond that, I am not counselling any course that I would not wish for myself, but, if the people so desire and if you accept the national vote, my sword and my authority will be gladly employed in supporting and defending the decrees of the sovereign people. This declaration is as sincere as is the heart of your constant friend.

## 82

# Admiration for Washington

*On 25 May 1826, Bolívar wrote to George Washinton Parke Custis from Lima, thanking him for the gift of the medallion of the distinguished founder of the United States and the father of its freedom. Its dispatch was announced to Bolívar by General Lafayette.*

Sir,

Although I had learned from official documents of the glorious gift with which the son of the great Washington had chosen to honour me, I had not yet received the sacred heirloom of that man of freedom, nor the flattering letter from his worthy descendant. Today I touched this priceless present with my hands. The image of the first benefactor of the continent of Columbus, borne by the citizen hero General Lafayette and offered by the noble heir of that immortal family, was enough to reward the most illustrious deed by the greatest man in the universe. Shall I be worthy of such recognition? No; but I accept it with joy and gratitude which will be shared, as the venerable memento of the father of America will be treasured, by all generations to come in my country; for they shall be the last to belong to the New World.

I have the honour to be, sir, your most humble and obedient servant.

*Bolívar*

## 83

# Some thoughts on ways of governing free men in accordance with the principles adopted among educated peoples

*Speech to the Constituent Congress of Bolivia, regarded as one of his basic texts. It was accompanied by a draft Constitution which Bolívar had elaborated. It is dated Lima, 25 May 1826.*

Legislators!

As I submit to you the draft Constitution for Bolivia, I am overcome by embarrassment and apprehension because I am convinced of my inability to make laws. When I consider that the wisdom of all the centuries is still not enough to draft a fundamental law which is perfect, and that even the most enlightened legislator is the immediate cause of human unhappiness and brings derision, so to speak, on his divine mission, what am I to say of the soldier who, born among slaves and buried in the deserts of his native country, has seen nothing but prisoners in chains and companions in arms to break them? I, a Legislator! Your illusion and the commitment I have given you may well compete for preference here: I am not sure who will suffer most in this conflict—you, because of the evils you must fear from the laws you have asked me to draft, or I from the scorn to which you condemn me by your trust.

I have summoned all my strength to set forth my thoughts on ways of governing free men in accordance with the principles adopted among educated peoples, although the lessons of experience show only long periods of disaster, interspersed with short moments of good fortune. What guidelines shall we choose against the sombre background of these discouraging examples?

Legislators! Your duty calls you to withstand the assault of two redoubtable enemies who are fighting one another, and who will also attack you together. Tyranny and anarchy form a vast ocean of oppression around a tiny island of freedom, perpetually lashed by the violence of the waves and the hurricanes that are ceaselessly trying to submerge it. That is the sea which you are about to cross in a fragile boat whose pilot is so unskilled.

In the draft Constitution for Bolivia, provision is made for four political powers, one having now been added without changing the classical delimitation of each of the others. The electoral branch has been given powers which were not accorded to it in other governments which consider themselves among the most liberal. These powers very closely resemble those of the federal system. I thought it not only advisable and useful but also feasible to grant to the immediate representatives of the people the privileges most desired by the citizens of each department, province or district. Nothing is more important for a citizen than the election of his legislators, magistrates, judges and pastors. The electoral colleges in each province represent the needs and interests of the province and serve also to censure breaches of the law and abuses by magistrates. I may say with some degree of certainty that these representatives share the rights enjoyed by the separate governments of the federated states. In this way a new weight has been brought into the balance against the executive; and the government has acquired more guarantees, a more popular form and new attributes, so that it can be regarded as one of the most democratic of governments.

Every ten citizens appoint an elector; as a result the nation is represented by one-tenth of its citizens. Ability alone is required, and not the possession of property, in those who perform the august function of the sovereign power; but an elector must be able to write his ballot papers, sign his name and read the laws. He must profess a science or an art that ensures him an honest livelihood. There are no other disqualifications except crime, idleness and total ignorance. Intelligence and uprightness, not money, are the requirements for the exercise of the public power.

The legislative body is so composed that its parts are bound to be harmonious; it will not always be divided for want of an arbitrator, as often happens where there are only two chambers. As there are three in this case, any discord between two of them may be settled by the third and the matter may be examined by the two parties to the dispute and by one acting as a judge. Consequently, no useful law will remain without effect: at least it will have been considered once, twice or three times before being rejected. In all issues between two conflicting parties, a third will be appointed to settle the matter; and would it not be absurd if in the most imperative interests of society this provision, dictated by overriding necessity, were to be disregarded? The chambers will thus maintain between them the relations indispensable for preserving the unity of the whole, which will deliberate dispassionately and in the tranquillity of wisdom. Modern congresses, you will say, are made up of only two parts. This is because in England, which has served as the model, the gentry and the people had to be represented in two chambers; and, if the same was done in North America where there was no gentry, it may be supposed that the habit of being ruled by the English Government gave rise to this imitation. The fact remains that two deliberating bodies are bound to fight perpetually; that is why Sieyes wanted only one. A classic mistake!

The first chamber is the Chamber of Deputies and has the right to initiate laws concerning finance, peace and war. It has direct control over the branches administered by the executive with minimum interference from the legislature.

The senators prepare legal codes and ecclesiastical regulations and exercise control over the courts and public worship. The Senate also has to choose the prefects, district judges, governors, *corregidores* and all the lower officers in the Department of Justice. It proposes to the Chamber of Censors candidates for membership of the Supreme Court and for appointment as archbishops, bishops, prebendaries and canons. All matters relating to religion and legislation are the responsibility of the Senate.

The Censors exercise a political and moral authority not unlike that of the Areopagus of Athens and the Censors of Rome. They will be the government's prosecutors, to ensure that the Constitution and public treaties have been strictly complied with. I have made them responsible for the national hearing which is to decide whether administration by the executive is good or bad.

It is the Censors who protect morality, the sciences, the arts, education and the press. Theirs is the most serious and most dignified of functions.

They condemn to eternal scorn any usurpers of sovereign authority or notorious criminals. They honour the services and virtues of distinguished citizens. Their hands hold a sacred trust; therefore, their own probity must be without blemish and their lives without reproach. If they err, they will be tried, even for minor offences. I have entrusted the conservation of our sacred tablets to these priests of the law, because it is they who must accuse any person that profanes them.

The President of the Republic, in our Constitution, is like the sun which is fixed at the centre, and gives life to the universe. This supreme authority must be perpetual, because systems without hierarchies—more than any others—need a fixed point around which officials and ordinary citizens, and men and things, can revolve. 'Give me a fixed point,' said an ancient sage, 'and I shall move the earth.' For Bolivia, that point is the President for life. On him rests our entire order, though he has no powers to act. His head has been cut off so that no one can fear his intentions, and his hands are tied so that no one can be harmed by him.

## The presidency for life

The President of Bolivia shares the functions of the American executive, but with restrictions which are favourable to the people. His term of office is the same as that of the presidents of Haiti. For Bolivia I have taken the executive of the most democratic republic in the world.

The island of Haiti (pardon me this digression) was in a permanent state of insurrection. After trying to be an empire, a kingdom and a republic, and after experimenting with all known forms of government and a few more, it was forced to appeal to the noble Pétion for salvation. The people trusted him and the fate of Haiti was no longer in the balance. Once Pétion had been named life president with the power to choose a successor, neither the death of this great man nor the succession of a new president troubled the state in the slightest. Everything went smoothly under the worthy Boyer, in the tranquillity of a legitimate kingdom. This was convincing proof of the fact that a life president with the right to choose a successor is the most sublime inspiration in the republican order.

The President of Bolivia will be less dangerous than the President of Haiti, since the method of succession is safer for the good of the state. Furthermore, the President of Bolivia is deprived of all influence: he does not appoint either magistrates or judges, or ecclesiastical dignitaries, however minor. No such diminution of power has ever been suffered by any well-constituted government: it adds fetter upon fetter to the authority of a chief who will always find the whole people dominated by those who exercise the most important functions in society. The priests rule in matters of conscience, the judges in matters of property, honour and life and the officials in matters of all public acts. Since he relies for his dignities, fame and fortune on the people alone, the President cannot hope to involve them in his own ambitious designs. If in addition we bear in mind the considerations that spring naturally from the general opposition encountered by a democratic government at every stage of its administration, there seems every reason to believe that the usurpation of the public power is further from this government than from any other.

Legislators! Our present liberty will be indestructible in America. Think only of the savage nature of this continent, which in itself rejects the monarchic order, since deserts invite independence. Here there are no great noblemen and no great churchmen. Our riches were almost nothing and now are even less. Although the Church enjoys some influence, it is far from aspiring to domination and is content with preserving the influence it has. Without such support, tyrants cannot last; and if a few ambitious men persist in creating empires, Dessalines, Christophe and Iturbide can tell them what to expect. No power is more difficult to maintain than that of a new prince. Bonaparte, who defeated all armies, could not triumph over this rule, which is stronger than empires. And if the great Napoleon could not withstand the alliance of republicans and aristocrats, who in America will succeed in founding monarchies on a soil fired with the bright flames of freedom, which consumed the very structures that were intended to sustain those royal scaffolds. No, legislators! Do not fear the pretenders to crowns; crowns will be for their heads like the sword hanging over Damocles. The bold princes who rashly establish thrones on the ruins of freedom will instead build tombs for their own ashes, which will tell future ages how they set vain ambition above freedom and fame.

The constitutional restrictions on the President of Bolivia are the tightest known. He has the right only to appoint his civil servants for finance, peace and war, no more; and he commands the army. These are his only functions.

The entire administration is the province of the Ministry, which is responsible to the Censors and subject to close supervision by every legislator, magistrate, judge and citizen. Customs officials and soldiers, the only agents of this Ministry, are hardly the most likely to lend it popular appeal; and thus its influence will be negligible.

The Vice-President is, of all the officials, the one whose power is most restricted: he obeys both the legislative and the executive branches of a republican government. From the former, he receives laws and from the second he receives orders; and between these two barriers he has to walk along a narrow path bordered with precipices. In spite of these many disadvantages, it is preferable to govern in this way than by absolute rule. Constitutional barriers broaden political awareness and give firm hopes of finding the beacon which will guide us through the reefs on every side. They serve to protect us from the impulses of our passions, combined with the influences of foreign interests.

In the United States, the government has lately observed the practice of appointing the senior minister to succeed the President. Nothing can be more advisable, in a republic, than this method; it offers the advantage of placing at the head of the administration a person experienced in the management of the state. When he enters upon his functions, he is already trained, and brings with him the halo of popularity, and a wealth of experience. I have borrowed this idea and established it in law.

The President of the Republic appoints the Vice-President to administer the state and to succeed him in office. This provision avoids the need for elections, which produce that great scourge of republics—namely anarchy, the luxury of tyranny and the most immediate and terrible threat to popular governments. You will observe how great crises occur in republics, just as in legitimate kingdoms.

The Vice-President must be a man of complete probity since, unless the first magistrate chooses an upright citizen, he will fear him like an inveterate enemy and even suspect his secret ambitions. The Vice-President must strive to deserve, by his good services, the credit he needs to perform the highest functions and to hope for the great national reward, the supreme power. The legislative body and the people will demand ability and talent from this magistrate, and also blind obedience to the laws of freedom.

Heredity is what perpetuates the monarchic system and makes it almost general throughout the world; and is not the method I have just proposed for the succession of the Vice-President even more suitable? If hereditary princes were chosen for their worth and not by chance and if, instead of remaining idle and ignorant, they were to place themselves at the head of the administration, would they not be more enlightened monarchs and bring more happiness to their peoples? Yes, legislators, the monarchies which govern the earth have obtained their titles of approval from the heredity which makes them stable and the unity which makes them strong. Hence, although a sovereign prince may be a spoilt child, cloistered in his palace, brought up on adulation and led hither and thither by his every passion, this prince whom I might dare to call a mockery of a man rules the human race because he preserves the order of things and subordination among the citizens, with a firm hand and steady action. Legislators, these great advantages are all combined in the President for life and the hereditary Vice-President.

### True justice

The judicial power which I propose enjoys complete independence: nowhere does it have so much. The people nominate the candidates and the legislature selects the members of the courts. If the judicial power does not emanate from such a source, it cannot safeguard individual rights in all their purity. These rights, legislators, are the rights that constitute freedom, equality, security and all the guarantees of the social order. The true liberal constitution is contained in the civil and criminal codes, and the most awesome power is exercised by the courts through the mighty instrument of the law. Ordinarily the executive is no more than the repository of the common cause; but the courts are arbiters between the cases of individuals. It is the judicial power which determines how good or how bad the citizens are; and if there is freedom, if there is justice in the Republic, both are distributed by this power. Political organization sometimes is of scant importance, provided that the civil order is perfect and that the laws are complied with religiously and considered as inexorable as fate.

It was to be expected that, in keeping with the ideas of the day, we would prohibit the use of torture and confessions; and that we would put a limit on the prolongation of disputes in the intricate labyrinth of appeals.

The territory of the Republic is administered by prefects, governors, *corregidores*, justices of the peace and majors. I have been unable to include detailed provisions concerning the internal organization of these jurisdictions. However, I must recommend the Congress to adopt regulations concerning the administration of departments and provinces. Bear in mind, legislators, that nations consist of cities and villages, and that the happiness of the state lies in their well-being. You can never pay too much attention to good government of the departments. This is a key point in legislative science, but is all too often overlooked.

I have divided the armed forces into four units—the regular army, the navy, the national militia and the revenue patrol. The purpose of the army is to guard the frontier. God forbid it from turning its weapons against our citizens. The national militia is enough to maintain internal order. Bolivia has no long coasts and therefore does not need a navy: nevertheless, we must one day have both. The revenue patrol is preferable in every respect to a civil guard, a service more immoral than superfluous; consequently, it is in the interest of the Republic to protect its frontiers with regular forces and to use the revenue patrol to prevent smuggling.

I have taken the view that the Constitution of Bolivia should be revised periodically, as outlooks change. The formalities are described in the terms I deemed most appropriate.

The responsibility of civil servants is described in the Constitution of Bolivia in the most explicit terms. Without responsibility, without restraint, the state is chaos. I strongly urge the legislators to enact strong and definite laws on this important matter. Everyone talks of responsibility but pays only lip-service to it. There is no responsibility, legislators. The magistrates, judges and civil servants abuse their functions because the agents of the administration are insufficiently controlled; the victims, in the meantime, are the citizens. I would recommend a law prescribing an annual review of the manner in which each civil servant has discharged his responsibility.

The most perfect guarantees have been established. Civil liberty is true freedom. The others are nominal or carry little weight with the citizens. Personal safety, which is the aim of society, and the source of all other forms of safety, has been ensured. As for property, this will depend on the civil code which your wisdom will elaborate later, for the happiness of your fellow citizens. I have kept intact the law of equality; without it, all guarantees and all rights must perish. To it we must make our sacrifices. At its feet I have laid the infamy of humiliating slavery.

Legislators, slavery breaks every law. A law that preserves it would be the highest sacrilege. What grounds can there be for maintaining it? Considering this crime from every aspect, I cannot be persuaded that there is a single Bolivian so depraved as to wish to legitimize the most notorious violation of human dignity. One man owned by another! A man a piece of property! An image of God yoked like a draught animal! Tell us, where are the legal titles of the usurpers of man? Guinea has sent them to us, but Africa is devastated by fratricide and has nothing but crimes to offer. What law or power would be capable of condoning ownership of these victims, these relics of African tribes transplanted here? To hand on, to prolong, to perpetuate this crime with all the suffering it involves would be the most loathsome outrage. Basing a principle of ownership on the most fearsome misdeeds would be tantamount to undermining the elements of the law and perverting altogether the idea of duty. No one can violate the holy dogma of equality. Will there be slavery where equality reigns? Such contradictions would be an insult to our reason rather than to our justice: we would be considered insane rather than tyrannical.

If there were no Deity to protect innocence and freedom, I would prefer the lot of a noble lion, ruling the deserts and the forests, to that of a captive in the service of an infamous tyrant who, as an accomplice in his crimes, would provoke the wrath of Heaven. But no: God has destined man for freedom. He protects him so that he can exercise the divine function of free will.

## Further reflections on morality

Legislators! I shall now mention one article which my conscience obliged me to omit. In a political constitution, no specific religious faith should be prescribed because, according to the best doctrines on fundamental laws, such laws are the guarantees of political and civil rights, and, as religion affects none of those rights, it remains undefinable in the social order and belongs to the intellectual and moral domain. Religion gives man guidance in his home, at work and within himself: it alone has the right to examine his intimate conscience. Laws, on the contrary, deal with the surface of things: they apply only outside the citizen's home. This being so, can a state rule the consciences of its subjects, monitor the observance of religious laws and award prizes or punishment, when the courts are in Heaven, and when God is the judge? Only the Inquisition would be capable of replacing them in this world. Is the Inquisition to come back with its burning torches?

Religion is the law of conscience. Any law concerning religion cancels it out because, by forcing necessity upon duty, it robs faith—which is the basis of religion—of all its merit. Sacred precepts and dogmas are useful, enlightening and of metaphysical value. We should all profess them, but that duty is moral not political.

Moreover, what rights has man in this world with respect to religion? Those rights are in Heaven; here the court rewards merit and metes out justice according to the code dictated by the Legislator. Since all this belongs to divine jurisdiction, it seems at first sight to be sacrilegious and profane to mix our ordinances with the commandments of the Lord. So it is not for the legislator to prescribe religion; he must specify penalties for infringing laws, so that they are not mere advice. Without temporal punishments or judges to apply them, the law ceases to be the law.

Man's moral development is the legislator's primary intention; once that development has been achieved, man bases his morality on revealed truths and then professes in practice a religion, which is all the more effective since he has acquired it as a result of his own investigations. Parents cannot neglect their religious duty towards their children, either. Spiritual pastors are obliged to teach the science of Heaven. There is no more eloquent lesson in divine morality than the example given by the true disciples of Jesus; but morality cannot be commanded, and he who commands is no teacher, nor should force be used in giving advice. God and his Ministers are the authorities of religion, which works by exclusively spiritual means and instruments: but on no account can the national body do so, since it directs the public power for purely temporal purposes.

Legislators! As you see the new Bolivian Nation proclaimed, what noble, sublime and generous thoughts you must have! The entry of a new state into the society of the rest is an occasion for jubilation by the whole of mankind, because it increases the great family of peoples. So how great then must be the joy of its founders, and my own joy as I see myself compared with the most famous of the ancients—the Father of the Eternal City! This glory belongs by right to the creators of nations who, as their first benefactors, have earned immortal rewards; but my glory, in addition to being immortal, has the merit of being gratuitous, because it is unmerited. Where is the republic, where is the city I founded? Your generosity in naming a nation after me has surpassed all the services I have rendered; and it infinitely outweighs whatever good man may do us.

My despair increases as I contemplate the magnitude of your award because, even if I had exhausted the talents, the virtues and the very genius of the greatest of heroes, I should still be unworthy of the name you have chosen to take, my own! Shall I speak of gratitude when it can never succeed in expressing, however feebly, what I feel for your kindness which, like that of God, passes all understanding. Yes: only God had the power to call this land Bolivia. . . . What does Bolivia mean? A boundless love of freedom which, when your zeal had won it, could see nothing to match its worth. When your elation could not adequately reflect the depth of your feelings, you abandoned your own name and gave mine to future generations. This is without parallel in the history of the ages, and even in the history of selflessness. This act will show to generations still in the womb of Eternity that what you yearned for was the possession of your rights, the capacity to exercise political virtues, to acquire brilliant talents and to enjoy being men. This act, I say, will prove that you deserved to receive the great blessing of Heaven—the sovereignty of the people—the only legitimate authority of nations.

Legislators, you may be glad that you are presiding over the destinies of a republic which came into being crowned with the laurels of Ayacucho and will continue its happy existence under the laws dictated by your wisdom in the calm which followed the tempest of the war.

*Bolívar*

Lima, 25 May 1826

## 84

# On the Chamber of Censors

*In the draft constitution presented to the Constituent Congress of Bolivia, Bolívar once more raises the idea of a Moral Power, which he had proposed to the Congress of Angostura in 1819. This time he proposes a third legislative chamber rather than a fourth power.*

CHAPTER IV

*On the Chamber of Censors*

*Article 49.* Members of the Chamber of Censors shall satisfy the following conditions:
1. They must possess the qualities required of a senator.
2. They must be at least forty years of age.
3. They must never have been sentenced, even for minor offences.
   *Article 50.* The functions of the Chamber of Censors shall be:
   1. To ensure that the government complies with and enforces the Constitution and the laws and public treaties.
   2. To challenge before the Senate any violation of the Constitution or of the laws and public treaties by the executive.
   3. To request the Senate to suspend the Vice-President and Secretaries of State from their functions if the well-being of the Republic urgently so requires.

*Article 51.* The Chamber of Censors shall have the exclusive right to accuse the Vice-President and Secretaries of State before the Senate in cases of treason, extortion or flagrant violation of the fundamental laws of the state.

*Article 52.* If the Senate decides that an accusation made by the Chamber of Censors is well founded, a national hearing shall be held; if, on the contrary, the Senate rules in the negative, the accusation shall be transferred to the Chamber of Deputies.

*Article 53.* If two chambers are in agreement, the national hearing shall be opened.

*Article 54.* The three chambers shall then meet and, in the light of the documents presented by the Chamber of Censors, they shall decide by an absolute majority of votes whether or not there are grounds for prosecuting the Vice-President or the Secretaries of State.

*Article 55.* If it is decided at the national hearing that there are grounds for prosecuting the Vice-President or Secretaries of State, the latter shall automatically be suspended from their functions and the chambers shall transmit all the evidence to the Supreme Court of Justice, which shall have exclusive jurisdiction; its decision shall be enforceable without appeal.

*Article 56.* When the Chambers have declared that there are grounds for prosecuting the Vice-President and Secretaries of State, the President of the Republic shall propose to the assembled Chambers a candidate for the office of Acting Vice-President and shall appoint Acting Secretaries of State. If the first candidate is rejected by an absolute majority of the legislative body, the President shall nominate a second candidate. If the second candidate is rejected, a third candidate shall be nominated; and if the third candidate is also rejected, the Chambers shall elect by an absolute majority, and within twenty-four hours, one of the three candidates proposed by the President.

*Article 57.* The Acting Vice-President shall exercise his functions from that moment onwards until the outcome of the proceedings against the Vice-President is known.

*Article 58.* The cases in which the Vice-President and Secretaries of State are responsible collectively, and those in which they are responsible individually, shall be determined in a law proposed by the Chamber of Censors.

*Article 59.* The Chamber of Censors shall also:

1. Select, from lists of three candidates proposed by the Senate, members of the Supreme Court of Justice and persons to be appointed to vacant archbishoprics, canonries and prebends.

2. Draft all laws concerning the press and the economy, and also curricula and methods to be applied in public education.

3. Protect the freedom of the press and appoint the judges who are to hear final appeals against its decisions.

4. Propose regulations for promotion of the arts and sciences.

5. Grant national prizes and awards to persons deserving them for their services to the Republic.

6. Accord public honours to the memory of great men, and for the virtues and services of citizens.

7. Condemn to eternal opprobrium the usurpers of public authority, and the most dastardly traitors and infamous criminals.

*Article 60.* The Censors shall hold office for life.


## 85

# Honoured by learning

*A statement made to the full assembly of doctors of the ancient and distinguished University of San Marcos in Lima on 2 June 1826.*

As I crossed the threshold of this sanctuary of learning, I felt overwhelmed with respect and apprehension; and when I found myself already in the midst of the scholars of the celebrated University of San Marcos, I felt humbled among men who have grown old in the tasks of profound and useful meditation and have been raised with such justice to the high rank they hold in the sphere of learning. Though I am a person without knowledge and devoid of any merit, I have by your bounty been given a distinction which is normally the reward for whole years of unbroken study.

Gentlemen, I shall forever remember this honoured day in my life. I shall never forget that I belong to the Venerable Academy of San Marcos. I shall endeavour to bring myself closer to its worthy members and shall employ wherever moments are mine, after I have accomplished the duties to which I am now bound, in striving, if not to arrive at the peak you have attained, at least to copy you.

86

# 'With the passage of the centuries, perhaps a single nation . . . may cover the whole world'

*Memorandum for the Congress of Panama, the great event of Latin American unity. Bolívar contemplates the world from the standpoint of the Latin American compact.*

The Congress of Panama is to be attended by all the representatives of America and a diplomatic agent of the Government of His Britannic Majesty. This Congress seems destined to form the vastest, or most extraordinary, or strongest league which has ever appeared on earth to this day. The Holy Alliance will be inferior in power to this confederation, provided that Great Britain agrees to take part as a constituent member. Mankind would bestow a thousand blessings on this league of salvation; and America, like Britain, would reap a whole harvest of benefits. The relations of political societies would receive a code of public law in the form of universal rules of conduct.

1. The new world would consist of independent nations, linked by a common law which would determine their external relations and offer them stability through a permanent general congress.

2. The existence of these new states would receive new guarantees.

3. Spain would make peace out of consideration for England, and the Holy Alliance would recognize these newly created nations.

4. Internal order would be preserved between the different states and within each one of them.

5. None would be weak in respect of another; none would be stronger.

6. A perfect balance would be established in this truly new order of things.

7. The strength of all would contribute to assisting any one in need on account of an external enemy or anarchic factions within.

8. Differences of origin and colour would lose their meaning and power.

9. America would no longer fear that tremendous monster which devoured the island of Santo Domingo; nor would it fear the numerical preponderance of its original inhabitants.

10. Lastly, social reform would be achieved under the sacred auspices of liberty and peace; but England would necessarily have to take the balance of this scale into her hands.

Great Britain would doubtless derive considerable advantages from this arrangement.

1. Her influence in Europe would gradually increase and her decisions would become those of destiny.

2. America would serve as an opulent commercial dominion for her.

3. She would regard America as the centre of her relations between Asia and Europe.

4. Englishmen would consider the citizens of America as their equals.

5. Relations between the two countries would eventually become the same in both directions.

6. The British character and customs would be taken by Americans as normal objectives for their future existence.

7. With the passage of the centuries, perhaps a single nation—the federal nation—may cover the whole world.

Such ideas are being considered by certain Americans in high positions. They are eagerly awaiting the initiative of this project at the Congress of Panama, which may be the occasion to consolidate the union of the new states with the British Empire.


87

# A vast and comprehensive concept of a university

*From the new statutes for the University of Caracas, prepared in collaboration with the Rector, José María Vargas, and with the advice of José Rafael Revenga, Secretary-General to the government. Decree of 24 June 1827. This is the second longest legal text promulgated by Bolívar.*


## SIMÓN BOLÍVAR
### Liberator, President of Colombia, etc., etc.

Since it is important, for the fullest possible application of the Law of 18 March 1826 on the organization and regulation of public education, to adapt this law more satisfactorily to the climate, uses and customs of these departments; to provide for this Central University and for the studies pursued in it a building more suitable to the present time; and to endow them with more adequate funds by assigning for their support various properties and sources of income which are either used for other charitable works of lesser importance, or which would be totally exhausted if they continued to be used in the same way as they are at present:

I therefore, in exercise of the extraordinary powers entrusted to me, and having heard the views of the General Council and all the staff of the said University, and the opinions of several wise men and lovers of education,

Do decree as follows:

## CHAPTER I

*General Councils or Plenary staff meetings*

*Article 1.* General Councils shall be held in the University, consisting of the Rector, who will preside, and the Vice-Rector, doctors and lecturers. There shall be periodic elections as provided for in the corresponding articles of this Constitution. General Councils shall meet every month to deal with general business of the establishment which is not the responsibility of special councils, and to deliberate on the resolutions of the latter; and they shall meet also on days appointed by the Rector. On 20 December the General Council shall elect the six professors who make up the governing board; and in succeeding years it shall renew half the membership of the board. It shall be decided by lot who is to remain on the first occasion. Should a seat fall vacant, the General Council will fill it at its next meeting.

. . . . . . . . . . . . . . . . . . . . . . . . . . . . . . . . . . . . . .

*Article 12.* The Council meetings shall be conducted with the order and decorum proper to a body which has the obligation to mould the moral, political and literary habits of the youth entrusted to its guidance. The Rector shall in any case restore order by ringing a bell.

*Article 13.* The General Council may not revoke, alter or waive any law or resolution of the government: it shall be entitled only to promote and supervise their implementation, to consult with the Departmental Office and to request, through the Office, whatever it considers necessary for the improvements or reform of the University.

. . . . . . . . . . . . . . . . . . . . . . . . . . . . . . . . . . . . . .

*Article 18.* The General Council may not either resolve to use University funds for extraordinary expenses or for purposes other than those prescribed in this Constitution.

. . . . . . . . . . . . . . . . . . . . . . . . . . . . . .

CHAPTER IV

## The Rector

*Article 34.* The Rector shall be elected on 20 December every three years by the General Council from among the doctors of the university, whether or not they are professors, and whether they are still in office or retired. For electing the Rector from among the professors, an absolute majority is sufficient; for electing him from among the doctors, two-thirds of the votes will be needed. No one shall be absolved from voting unless he is a retired professor. The result of the election will be notified to the person elected on the same day by two members of the Electoral Body.

*Article 35.* When the whole University with its insignia is assembled and the student body is present, four members, two doctors and two lecturers, the most junior among them, shall go to his home and accompany him to the chapel, where he shall also be received at the entrance by the two most junior professors, together with the Secretary, who shall conduct him to the rectoral table and then sit in their respective seats. The person elected will kneel and swear the following oath on the Gospels: 'I [name] do swear and promise to observe and faithfully comply with the Constitution of the Republic and the academic regulations and laws, and to perform with all possible care the duties of the office of Rector to which I have been appointed.' When this act is concluded and he has been placed in his chair by the retiring Rector, he shall confirm the Vice-Rector in his post.

*Article 36.* Next, an oath of obedience to the Rector and Vice-Rector shall be sworn by the doctors, lecturers and all the students. No expense shall be incurred in this ceremony, and the outgoing Rector shall notify the Departmental Office, the Administration and the Executive Power of the Republic in an official letter.

*Article 37.* The Rector of the University shall remain in office for three years and shall supervise the observance of the academic laws, ensuring that they are properly complied with and carried out. The Vice-Rector, professors, officers and students shall be subordinate to the Rector. He shall accept no excuse for carelessness and negligence by those under his authority. For the professors, he shall have feelings of consideration as required by their posts. If they do not respond to this honourable treatment, he shall, in agreement with the Governing Board, decide on measures to oblige them to perform their duty; and, if this is not sufficient, the General Council shall take whatever course it thinks fit and shall be answerable to the Departmental Office for the measures taken, which may include dismissal and permanent deprivation of tenure in accordance with the laws governing education.

*Article 38.* Apart from the visits he makes to classes whenever he deems fit, the Rector shall nominate two students from each class every two months to inform him, under oath or not, according to his judgement, of the conduct of the professor.

. . . . . . . . . . . . . . . . . . . . . . . . . . . . . . . . . . . .

## The Vice-Rector

*Article 42.* There shall be a Vice-Rector who shall act as the Rector's deputy whenever he is absent; the Vice-Rector shall have the same powers and shall be elected by the General Council every three years, on the same day as the Rector, who shall confirm him in his post with the same formalities as are followed in the case of the Rector himself, and shall place him in the seat ordained for him in Article 221 concerning orders of precedence.

. . . . . . . . . . . . . . . . . . . . . . . . . . . . . . . . . . . .

CHAPTER VI

## Enrolment

*Article 50.* Bearing in mind that the most beautiful and refreshing season of the year in this capital occurs in the months of November and December and that it would be sensible to have holidays at this time, but that this is on the other hand the most appropriate season for anatomy and surgery classes, the academic year shall from now on begin on 1 September and the enrolment lists shall be opened on the preceding 5 August, every year, by an edict of the Rector affixed to the doors of the University. Those who wish to enrol in any class should do so, from that day onward until the last day of August, with the Secretary of the University who shall note, in the book marked 'Enrolments', the name of the student, his age, country, parents, guardians, or those who have immediate responsibility for him in this city, the date on which he enrolled and the class he is to follow. For this purpose, each student, when coming to enrol, shall be accompanied by his father or whoever is in charge of his education, so that the address of this person can be noted and the necessary relations established between the teachers and the parents of the students. The Secretary shall transmit all this information to the Vice-Rector so that he may note it in his confidential record, and he shall write it out also on the certificate of enrolment which he must give to each student to show to the professor; the latter will make the appropriate entry in his own book.

. . . . . . . . . . . . . . . . . . . . . . . . . . . . . . . . . . .

CHAPTER VII

*Students*

*Article 54.* Students are persons who, having enrolled in the University, undertake to pursue academic studies under the direction of the professor who conducts the class concerned. In the absence of such an undertaking, persons shall be judged to be 'merely attending lectures'. This concept means that no one is prevented from listening to a professor's lectures.

. . . . . . . . . . . . . . . . . . . . . . . . . . . . . . . . . . .

*Article 58.* Students must be punctilious in the performance of their duties.

. . . . . . . . . . . . . . . . . . . . . . . . . . . . . . . . . . .

*Article 60.* Students at the University may not enlist in armed forces of any kind, not even when these are called national or civil; and they may not engage in any occupation which will distract them from the academic career to which they are dedicated.

CHAPTER VIII

*University professorships and length of courses*

*Article 61.* In this University there shall be two professorships of Latin grammar, one of literature, one of ideology and metaphysics, one of general grammar, one of logic, and one of general and applied physics. There shall also be a professorship of mathematics, and one of geography and chronology, a professorship of ethics and natural law, four professorships of medicine, four of civil law and four of exact sciences.

. . . . . . . . . . . . . . . . . . . . . . . . . . . . . . . . . . .

*Article 85.* General and particular anatomy. A professor shall teach general and descriptive anatomy in the order which is most convenient. Anatomy lessons shall always be illustrated by demonstrations of organs or parts of the human body, which will be described. These shall be prepared in advance by an anatomy demonstrator, who shall be present to help the professor and shall be remunerated for his work. The wax models which exist, in some laboratories of schools of medicine may also be used, as well as organs preserved in spirits. But true anatomists can be trained only by dissecting human and animal bodies, in order to perfect themselves in comparative anatomy. Young students shall, therefore, after the first five months of their anatomy course, practise dissections and shall allocate sufficient time for these every day in the anatomy theatre, under the eye of the professor. The demonstrator shall teach them how to make incisions to expose the organs. Discipline and good order shall be observed in the laboratory; and care shall be taken to ensure that bodies are not thrown away but buried when they are no longer used.

*Article 86.* Physiology and hygiene. The physiology professor shall teach students the functions of the organs of the human body in its healthy state. After his students have acquired a basic knowledge of the other subjects taught in the school of medicine, he shall give lessons in hygiene. The same professor shall be responsible for teaching public hygiene and explaining to students the rules which must be followed by municipal authorities in order to prevent epidemic and contagious diseases in cities and military camps and on sea voyages, and also to prevent a disease from spreading once it has appeared, or to lessen its effect as far as possible.

. . . . . . . . . . . . . . . . . . . . . . . . . . . . . . . . . . . . . .

*Article 95.* Students enrolled in medical classes shall not only attend the courses mentioned in the foregoing articles, but shall also attend the first year of the French course and the academy of literature, when these have been established. In their second year, they shall attend the English course and the academy of physical and medical sciences; and they shall attend these in the four subsequent years, once they also have been established.

. . . . . . . . . . . . . . . . . . . . . . . . . . . . . . . . . . . . . .

*Article 100.* In the first year of the second two-year period, instruction shall be given in the Constitution of the Republic, and in political law and administrative science. In the second year, international law shall be taught. After completing these courses in civil and canon law, and after passing the examinations prescribed in this Constitution, they may receive the degree of Bachelor in either of the two faculties or in both. They shall remain in the University for a third two-year period during which, in the mornings of the first year, a professor shall lecture on the principles of universal legislation and civil and penal law, and on political economy in the second year. At the same time another professor shall lecture in the afternoons during the first year on civil and criminal proceedings in court, while in the second year students shall follow the course in forensic medicine, at the times appointed for the teaching of this course.

*Article 101.* During the third two-year period, those who wish to be lawyers shall receive instruction in pleading in court, and shall attend the language classes which have been established.

. . . . . . . . . . . . . . . . . . . . . . . . . . . . . . . . . . . . .

*Article 108.* Anyone may attend the classes in theology and may mention, either in Latin or in the vernacular, any difficulties or objections they may have; and it shall be the duty of the professor to resolve them.

. . . . . . . . . . . . . . . . . . . . . . . . . . . . . . . . . . . . .

*Article 117.* Each professor shall propose, for debate, subjects which he has taught up to the day of his debate, and he shall select two students, neither of whom may be excused, to support him morning and afternoon.

*Article 118.* The subjects chosen for the debates shall be those best suited for illustrating the progress made by young persons and the state of studies in the University.

*Article 119.* In public debates, no proposition may be defended which is contrary to the fundamental laws and liberties of the Republic, the Catholic faith and public morality and decency. Propositions shall be written in Spanish and in Latin, so that they may be argued in either of the two languages.

. . . . . . . . . . . . . . . . . . . . . . . . . . . . . . . . . . . . .

*Article 129.* From each class there shall be selected three students, who are, in the judgement of the Rector and the examiners, the most outstanding students; and, after they have been placed in order of merit in the light of the knowledge they have demonstrated, a record of their achievements shall be kept in a file closed and sealed by the Rector, to be published with the greatest solemnity and in the most imposing manner on 8 December, on the occasion of the feast of the Immaculate Conception, thus maintaining the custom of this great University and honouring the memory of Don Juan Agustín de la Torre, founder of the prizes for this institution. For this purpose, the Rector may annually withdraw from the treasury the amount which the Governing Board considers appropriate for spending on essential books, or on medals, with insignia or suitable inscriptions, which he shall distribute to those who have earned prizes for their industry. These medals may be worn on academic occasions. The Rector shall nominate a member of the University to delivery the customary oration in praise of learning.

*Article 130.* The presentation of awards after the general examinations shall not prevent any lovers of public education from offering other prizes on the same day, 8 December, whether these be for subjects which have already been taught in classes, or for other special subjects which cannot be taught at present but which some industrious students have read without prejudice to the courses they are obliged to follow in their own faculty. It will not be inappropriate, either, for other prizes to be offered and public examinations to be held on other occasions, such as the saints' days of the patron saints of the University.

*Article 131.* The institution of medals for good behaviour and industry, for all classes in Latin, which was initiated on 7 March 1825 and was later approved by a plenary staff meeting, will be retained as useful for moral purposes and conducive to progress in the instruction of students.

*Article 132.* The general vacation each year shall extend from the day on which the examinations in each faculty end in the month of July until the 1st day of September following. In addition, the vacation for grammarians shall extend from 12 August until 1 September; and apart from these periods, the students shall have no other vacations except public holidays, Christmas holidays, the whole of Easter week, and Thursdays in weeks when there is no public or religious holiday.

CHAPTER XI

*Degrees*

*Article 133.* The University, through the Rector, shall confer academic degrees or medals on those who, having followed the necessary courses, give public and certain proof of the knowledge and aptitude required for each degree. These degrees shall be qualifications for various civil and ecclesiastical purposes and the University shall continue to confer the degrees of bachelor, licenciate and doctor in canon and civil law and in medicine and theology, and the degrees of bachelor, licenciate and master in philosophy.

. . . . . . . . . . . . . . . . . . . . . . . . . . . . . . . . . . .

*Professors*

*Article 189.* From the day on which a suitable candidate is appointed to a chair, his duties and rights shall begin. Professors shall arrive in their classrooms punctually on all the days and at the times prescribed for teaching. They shall supervise the development, attendance and good conduct of their students, and shall set them an example by their good behaviour, and their punctual attendance at all functions, meetings, and ceremonies of the University they are required to attend.

. . . . . . . . . . . . . . . . . . . . . . . . . . . . . . . . . .

*Article 192.* The professors should be a model for the youths entrusted to their care: decency, decorum, urbanity, refined language—everything a teacher should embody whereby they might train good pupils with practical examples.

. . . . . . . . . . . . . . . . . . . . . . . . . . . . . . . . . .

*Article 196.* After twenty years of uninterrupted teaching in the same chair, professors shall be retired on full pay. The said period of twenty years shall be counted from the day on which each professor took possession of his chair either in his own right or by replacement, as long as he obtained it in open competition. All the chairs of Latin studies shall be regarded as one.

*Article 197.* A professor who has held various chairs over twenty years, either in his own right or by replacement, may retire on half pay and with the title of Professor Emeritus. If he has held the chairs for twenty-five years, he shall retire on two-thirds pay; and, if for thirty years, he shall retire on full pay with the title of Retired Professor of the chair which he has held longest. If he has spent the same time in two chairs, the professor himself shall choose which title pleases him most.

. . . . . . . . . . . . . . . . . . . . . . . . . . . . . . . . . .

*Article 199.* A professor who writes a basic work approved by the University and by the Departmental Office shall earn, for the purposes of his retirement, an amount of time to be determined by the Council on a sliding scale in accordance with the merit of the work, but in no case exceeding eight years; any professor who under the same conditions translates and prints a classical work for the use of the University, which must also be approved, shall earn only two years. The same professor may obtain these two bonuses once only. Any professor who after ten years of teaching suffers from ill-health and remains an invalid will be retired on one-third pay.

. . . . . . . . . . . . . . . . . . . . . . . . . . . . . . . . . .

CHAPTER XXII

*Feast days*

*Article 244.* The feast days of the Patron Saint Rosa of Lima, of the Conception of Our Lady and of the angelic doctor St Thomas, which have been celebrated by this University since it was built, shall continue to be celebrated, and the celebrations shall be paid for out of its funds and out of those of the Seminary as has been the case up to now; but, if the General Council wishes to celebrate any other feast day, it will be at the expense of its members. On all these feast days, the Doctors and Masters of the University assigned by the Rector must officiate and deliver addresses.

. . . . . . . . . . . . . . . . . . . . . . . . . . . . . . . . . . .

*Article 249.* On 10 November each year memorial services shall be held for deceased members of the University, in accordance with the bequest of a private person, which has been accepted by a plenary session of the Council. Professors will be chosen by preference to say mass and deliver the funeral oration but if none are available, the Rector will appoint other persons.

CHAPTER XXIV

*Income and expenses of the University, and its assets and liabilities*

*Article 250.* The income of the University shall be as follows:
    1. The sum of 200 pesos annually which the Treasury of this city has contributed since 1592 to the two chairs of rhetoric, and 100 pesos each for lesser chairs, which payments are to be continued in accordance with article 72 (1) of the Education Law of 18 March 1826.

. . . . . . . . . . . . . . . . . . . . . . . . . . . . . . . . . . .

    7. Capital left by benefactors to endow a chair, but which has not yet been duly recognized and possessed by the University.
    8. Income from the religious foundations of Chuao, after they have fulfilled their obligations to provide alms for the poor, for candles and other purposes of public worship.
    9. Income from the religious foundations of Cata, together with those from the estate of Miranda and others added to it after its foundation, less any obligations such as those which are principally recognized, i.e. the stipend of the priest at Cata and annual

contributions for festivals, altars and alms for the poor, and the amount owed to the steward and administrators, if such a debt is legally proved before the properties are rented.

10. The income from the sugar-cane plantation and mill, known as Concepción, in the administrative district of Tácata, which belonged to the Canary Islander José Antonio Sánchez Castro and was assigned to the University by decree dated 16 May 1827. The collection and distribution of this income and of the income referred to in the two previous paragraphs, and also the care of the properties and intervention in their administration or leasing, shall be the responsibility of the Administrator of the University, subject to the decisions of the plenary session of the Council.

11. The annual income remaining from Indian reservations, after deduction of the endowment for the primary schools which are to be established in these villages.

. . . . . . . . . . . . . . . . . . . . . . . . . . . . . . . . . . . . . .

*Article 251.* The expenses of the University shall consist of:

1. The ordinary expenses to pay the salaries of fifteen professors which, at the rate of 400 pesos per annum, amount to 6,000 pesos. Professors from whose income deductions are made, since they are subject to certain obligations, shall be compensated for these deductions so that they receive their salary of 400 pesos in its entirety. One hundred pesos shall be paid for the annual expenses of the Secretariat, twenty-five as gratuity for the Master of Ceremonies, ten pesos monthly as gratuity for the anatomy demonstrator during the months when he helps in the demonstrations of this science, and 600 pesos for the two beadles, 300 annually to each. Fifty-one pesos and four-and-a-half reals shall be paid for the festivals of the Patron Saints, and seventy-five pesos and four reals for the anniversary of deceased members of the University; finally, administrative expenses shall be paid in accordance with Article 266.

2. The sum of 2,000 pesos which the University is to contribute, when it is in possession of its income, to help the college for girl students.

3. Major extraordinary expenses approved by the plenary session of the Council with the agreement of the Departmental Director of Studies, and minor items of expenditure ordered by the Rector and agreed by the Governing Board.

4. Expenses which may arise in connection with the anniversaries of deceased Doctors and Masters, and expenditure on annual prizes.

. . . . . . . . . . . . . . . . . . . . . . . . . . . . . . . . . . . . . .

CHAPTER XXVII

*Academies*

*Article 276.* The University shall gradually constitute other chairs and establishments, as its funds permit. It shall try to form as soon as possible the Academy of Emulation, divided into four sections, respectively for literature and *belles-lettres*, natural sciences, political science and ethical and ecclesiastical studies. Each of these, within the first two months following its establishment, shall draw up regulations for its internal organization and for the most efficient promotion of its studies; and, with the Rector's advice, it shall approve or revise such regulations, having regard to the fact that the general good calls for the section dealing with medicine to be organized as soon as possible.

. . . . . . . . . . . . . . . . . . . . . . . . . . . . . . . . . . . . . .

*Article 280.* With regard to public instruction, the functions of the Faculty of Medicine, Surgery and Pharmacy shall be:

1. To promote theoretical and practical study of the medical sciences by any means within their power and which their various concerns may suggest.

2. In the establishment of the Academy of Emulation, to improve as much as possible the section relating to medical sciences, and ensure that the young students receive all necessary teaching, especially on the practical side, in private academic sessions.

3. To ensure that, as soon as possible, a complete course is prepared and published on the branches of medical science which are to be taught in this school of medicine. Such a course shall take into account the local climate and the constitution and illnesses of the inhabitants of these countries, and, in addition to containing the best teaching by the leading authorities and explaining the latest discoveries, it shall be of the appropriate brevity for schools.

. . . . . . . . . . . . . . . . . . . . . . . . . . . . . . . . . . . . . .

*Article 287.* The Faculty of Medicine shall be entrusted with:

1. Promoting in this district, by means of representations to courts and other authorities, compliance with the laws regarding doctors, surgeons, pharmacists, chemists' shops and the sale of drugs.

2. Proposing to Health Councils the most suitable measures or regulations, in the light of the climate and circumstances of the country, for maintaining public health or restoring it after outbreaks of illness.

3. Formulating and publishing details of the most appropriate cures when there are epidemic or contagious diseases.

4. Publishing details of methods for protecting the people from the most common or endemic diseases of these countries, such as certain skin diseases, goitre, elephantiasis, and other illnesses which occur in the various climates, and for curing those who suffer from them.

*Article 288.* The Medical Faculty shall try to form a collection of all articles on the subject of medicine relevant to the three kingdoms—animal, vegetable and mineral.

*Article 289.* The Secretary of State and Secretary General of my Office shall be entrusted with communicating this decree to whomever it may concern.

Headquarters of the Liberator in Caracas, 24 June 1827.

*Simón Bolívar*

For the Liberator President,
Secretary of State and Secretary General
of His Excellency,
*J. R. Revenga*

<br>

88

# Anyone who illegally appropriates taxes and other assets of the state, 'however small the amount', shall incur the penalty of death and confiscation

*During his last visit to his native country, Bolívar concerned himself with public administration in Venezuela, and issued an important code for the Public Treasury. With regard to sanctions against corrupt officials, he reaffirmed his usual exemplary severity in these rules decreed in Caracas on 8 March 1827.*

CHAPTER II

*Penalties for Treasury officials and others who defraud the state of its income*

*Article 194.* Any individual who illegally appropriates taxes and other assets of the state, removing them from its coffers or from the power of revenue officials, by force or secretly, however small the amount, shall incur the penalty of death and confiscation of all his property, if he has no children, and confiscation of one-third and one-fifth, if he has children. He shall also pay the costs of the proceedings and return the amount taken.

*Article 195.* If it is discovered that the Treasurer, the Principal or Deputy Administrator, or any other Treasury employee has stolen from the coffers or from the revenues he manages any sum, however small it may be, he shall incur the same penalty of death solely on the word of three reliable witnesses, and on presumptions or indications which confirm this.

*Article 196.* Any revenue official who, through indulgence or culpable neglect, allows the revenues of the state to be appropriated shall, if it is proved that he took part in the appropriation in the manner referred to in the above article, incur the penalty of death.

*Article 197.* If the official has not taken part in the appropriation but has connived at it, he shall incur the penalty of ten years in prison and dismissal from his post and shall be barred in perpetuity from holding any other Treasury post. An announcement to this effect shall be published in the newspapers; and the Treasury shall be entitled to repayment of the amount appropriated. If the offender repay it, the property of his guarantor shall be distrained up to the amount of his guarantee.

*Article 198.* Any Treasurer, Administrator or revenue official who, as a result of omission, negligence or ineptitude, permits the appropriation of taxes due to the state, however great or small the sum may be, shall, without prejudice to the penalty to be imposed on the appropriator, be dismissed from his post, barred in perpetuity from obtaining another post, and imprisoned in accordance with the decree dated 23 November 1826 concerning the responsibility of employees. An announcement of the penalty shall be published in the newspapers, and the state shall be reimbursed from his own property, or from that of his guarantor up to the amount of the guarantee, for the damage or prejudice which has occurred.

. . . . . . . . . . . . . . . . . . . . . . . . . . . . . . . . . . . .

*Article 201.* A Treasurer or Administrator who does not produce his accounts in the first three months of the following year to the Tribunal of Accountancy or to the Principal Accountant's Office for Tobacco, shall incur the penalty of dismissal from his post without any other procedures or formalities apart from the simple proof that he has failed to do so.

. . . . . . . . . . . . . . . . . . . . . . . . . . . . . . . . . . . .

*Article 207.* Any Head of Department who, after being reprimanded twice by the Administrator for failing to attend his office from 8 a.m. until 2 p.m., does not mend his ways, shall incur a fine of half his monthly salary; and this penalty shall be re-imposed if his absences continue, until he is brought to trial and the penalty for negligence imposed on him.

. . . . . . . . . . . . . . . . . . . . . . . . . . . . . . . . . . .

*Article 212.* Any revenue official, whether civil or military, shall be obliged to offer every possible help and co-operation in order to discover and disclose any fraud being committed against the state. Omission or negligence shall be subject to the penalties prescribed in this decree and to those specified in the other decree dated 23 November 1826 regarding the responsibility of employees.

*Article 213.* Any citizens living in the four departments covered by this decree, whether or not they are employees in any branch, shall report, denounce or prevent any fraud, illegal appropriation or fault they may discover in the handling and collection of state funds, by informing the Administrators or any other officials who are by this decree granted authority and jurisdiction over the business of the Treasury, which authority may not be contested.

*Article 214.* They may also report such offences by means of the printed word, describing in as much detail as possible the fraud or embezzlement which has come to their knowledge, so that it can be investigated.

. . . . . . . . . . . . . . . . . . . . . . . . . . . . . . . . . . .

*Article 235.* Whenever the prescribed period for continuous work in any office is not sufficient to keep the business up to date, it shall be extended as long as necessary, since an employee cannot be considered to have done his duty if his business is not always up to date and if in addition he makes no effort to use every means in his power to increase revenue without increasing the burden on taxpayers.

. . . . . . . . . . . . . . . . . . . . . . . . . . . . . . . . . . .

89

# A decree organizing the
# Central University of Quito
# as well

*Bolívar's reforming spirit reached out also to the University of Ecuador. Amongst other innovations he decided that the Quechua language of the Andean Indians should be studied as well as major European languages. Decree promulgated on 6 November 1827 in Bogotá.*

## SIMÓN BOLÍVAR
### Liberator President, etc., etc.

In view of the need to organize the Central University of Quito, to determine the number of chairs it is to have, and to fix the salaries to be paid to its staff,

And having heard the report of the Departmental Directorate of Studies in Quito, and that of the Directorate General,

I have decided to decree as follows:

*Article 1.* The Rector of the University of Quito shall receive an annual salary of 500 pesos, the Vice-Rector 400, the Secretary 300, the first beadle of the University 200 pesos and the under-beadle 150 pesos.

*Article 2.* Two hundred and fifty pesos shall also be paid out of the income of the University of Quito to the secretary of the Departmental Director of Studies, for the purpose of defraying office expenses.

*Article 3.* In the faculty of literature and *belles-lettres* there shall be the following chairs: one for French and English; two for Latin combined with Spanish grammar; one for the Quechua language, and one for literature, *belles-lettres* and bibliography, which shall be entrusted to the University librarian, who shall be obliged to pay for an assistant. The first three chairs shall receive 300 pesos each; the chair of Quechua shall be entrusted to one of the Dominican friars of the province of Quito, in accordance with the law; and the librarian, in this capacity and as professor, shall receive a salary of 500 pesos annually.

*Article 4.* In the faculty of philosophy and natural sciences, there shall be the following chairs: one for mathematics, to which will be added the teaching of the principles of geography and chronology; one for general, applied and experimental physics; one for ideology and metaphysics, general grammar and logic, ethics and natural law; and one for natural history in its three kingdoms and chemistry. Each of these chairs shall receive 300 pesos annually.

*Article 5.* In the faculty of medicine there shall be the following chairs: one for general, applied and pathological anatomy, which shall have an anatomy demonstrator; one for physiology and hygiene, nosology and pathology; one for therapy and pharmacy; and, finally, one for medical and surgical clinical training and forensic medicine. Each of these professors shall receive 300 pesos annually, and the demonstrator 200.

*Article 6.* In the faculty of law there shall be a chair for the principles of universal law, civil and penal legislation; one for political public law, international law, the constitution and science of administration; another for history and the institutions of Roman civil law and national law; another for political economy; and, finally, another for ecclesiastical history and the history of the Councils. Each of these chairs shall receive 300 pesos annually.

*Article 7.* In the faculty of theology there shall be a chair for the foundations of religion, theological doctrine and studies in defence of religion; one for sacred writings and another for the institutions of dogmatic and ethical theology. The two first chairs shall receive 300 pesos annually, and the third shall be entrusted to the schoolteacher of Quito Cathedral in accordance with the law of public education.

*Article 8.* The aforementioned salaries shall be paid from the revenues which the University of Quito has hitherto received, some of which were assigned to it by the 1826 law and some of which, in accordance with that law, are paid by the government. These salaries shall be increased as the University's income is augmented and the Departmental Directorate of Studies shall report in due course when the increase has occurred and in what proportion.

*Article 9.* Since the professors are due to begin their courses on 2 January next, the Administrator of Ecuador shall be authorized, on the proposal of the Departmental Directorate of Studies, which shall hear reports from the Governing Board of the University, to nominate acting professors for the various university courses. These acting professors shall occupy the chairs for the time considered necessary in the opinion of the Governing Board and the Departmental Director of Studies. When it is judged that there are adequate numbers of candidates for the chairs and that studies will not suffer thereby, announcements shall be made and the chairs shall be filled by open competition in accordance with the law and the regulations governing education.

*Article 10.* The Administrator of Ecuador shall be authorized, on the proposal of the Departmental Director of Studies, to issue in accordance with the law and the organic regulations governing education any measures he considers fitting for the complete establishment of the University. Such measures may be put into effect without prior consultation of the Executive Power, to which the Administrator shall report later on the steps he has taken.

The Secretary of State for Internal Affairs shall be charged with the execution of this decree.

Done in the Government Palace, Bogotá, on 6 November 1827.

*Simón Bolívar*

The Secretary of State for Internal Affairs,
*José Manuel Restrepo*

<br>

90

# Description of the troubles of Colombia

*A heart-breaking summary of the severe crisis in Colombia. A distressing account of a great work unfulfilled. Important message to the Ocaña Convention, from Bogotá, 29 February 1828.*

TO THE REPRESENTATIVES OF THE PEOPLE
AT THE NATIONAL CONVENTION

Fellow citizens,

I congratulate you on the honour which the nation has bestowed on you by entrusting you with its high destiny. As the legal representatives of Colombia, you are invested with the highest powers. I also share in the great happiness by returning to you the authority which had been placed in my weary hands. Persons well loved by the people now possess the sovereign powers, the supreme rights, as delegates of the omnipotent nation of which I am both a subject and a soldier. In what more worthy hands could I leave the president's staff and the general's sword? I bid you to dispose freely of these symbols of command and glory for the benefit of the cause of the people, without any thought of personal considerations which might turn you aside from perfect reform.

Since it is my duty to inform you of the situation of the Republic, I must regretfully give you a description of its troubles. Do not think the terms I use are exaggerated, or that they have emerged from some dismal house of mysteries. I have simply copied them in the light of known scandal. Taken together, they may seem ideal to you; but if that were so, would Colombia have called upon you now?

Measures to remedy the afflictions of the country have already been started, and the elected representatives are now gathered together to examine them. Your task, indeed, is as difficult as it is glorious; and although the obstacles have been somewhat diminished by the fortunate circumstance that you are, now, able to address a united and obedient Colombia, I must tell you that we owe this inestimable advantage only to the hopes which have been placed in the Convention, hopes which demonstrate the national confidence in you and the weight you bear on your shoulders.

A brief survey of our history is enough to demonstrate the causes of our decline. Colombia, which knew how to give itself life, lies lifeless. Once identified with the cause of the people, it no longer considers duty as the only rule for its well-being. Those who, during the struggle, were content with their poverty and did not run up a foreign debt of 3 million, have now had to burden themselves with debts, shameful in their consequences, in order to maintain peace. Colombia, which, faced by hosts of oppressors, breathed only self-respect and virtue, seems now to be insensitive to the national disrepute. Colombia, which used to think only of grievous sacrifices and meritorious services, is now concerned with its rights and not its duties. The nation would have perished if some residue of public spirit had not urged it to cry out for a remedy and halted it on the brink of the grave. Only a terrifying danger, it seems, has induced us to try to alter the fundamental laws; only this peril has placed itself above the passion we professed for appropriate and legal institutions, whose bases obtained for us our long-desired emancipation.

I would not add anything to this gloomy picture, unless the post I occupy obliged me to inform the nation of the practical deficiencies of its laws. I know that I cannot do this without exposing myself to sinister interpretations, and that ambitious thoughts will be read behind my words. However, since I have never refused to dedicate my life and my reputation to Colombia, I consider that I am obliged to make this last sacrifice.

I must declare it: our government is in essence badly constituted. Fogetting that we had only just thrown off the yoke of oppression, we allowed ourselves to be dazzled by aspirations superior to those which the history of all ages shows to be compatible with human nature. On other occasions we have mistaken the means and attributed our misfortunes to the fact that we did not keep close enough to the deceitful guide who left us behind on the journey; and we closed our ears to those who tried to follow the order of things and compare the various parts of our Constitution with each other, and to compare the whole Constitution with our education, customs and inexperience, in order to prevent us from being swept into a stormy sea.

Our various powers are not distributed in the manner required by the form of our society and the welfare of our citizens. We have made the Legislature the only sovereign body, when it should have been no more than a member of the sovereign body. We have made the Executive Power subordinate to it, and given it a much larger role in general administration than legitimate interest allows. To make matters worse, all our strength has been placed in the force of will, and all our weakness in the movement and actions of society.

The right to present bills has been left exclusively to the Legislature which, by its nature, is far from knowing the realities of government and is purely theoretical.

The discretion granted to the executive to object to laws is ineffective, since its opposition offends the sensitivity of the Congress. The latter can insist and win by the vote of one-fifth, or less than one-fifth, of its members; and this leaves no means of avoiding harm.

Since the Secretaries of State are not allowed free entry into our parliament to explain or account for the motives of the government, not even this resource remains to enlighten the Legislature in cases where some resolution is opposed. A great deal of trouble could have been avoided if a certain time had been required or a certain proportion of votes—considerably more than that which is now prescribed—had been needed to pass laws opposed by the Executive.


*Criticisms of the legislation and of the system*

It will be seen that our already very unwieldy code of law, instead of leading to happiness, offers obstacles to its progress. Our laws seem to have been made by chance; they do not form a whole, they lack method, classification and legal language. They are opposed to each other, confused, sometimes unnecessary and even contrary to their own purposes. There is no lack of examples of times when it was essential to check destructive and contagious vices by rigorous provisions: but the laws enacted with this intent have proved to be much less adequate than the old ones, since they indirectly protect those vices which they were supposed to prevent.

In aiming at perfection, we introduced representation on a scale which our capacity does not yet allow. By squandering this great function, we have degraded it; and, in some provinces, it seems to be a matter of indifference and even somewhat dishonourable to represent the people. From this has arisen in part the disrepute into which the laws have fallen; and what happiness can discredited laws produce?

The Executive Power in Colombia is not the equal of the Legislature, nor is it master of the judiciary. It has become a weak arm of the supreme power, in which it does not participate as much as it should, because Congress interferes in its natural functions with regard to the administrative, judicial, ecclesiastical and military branches. The government, which should be the fountainhead and driving power of the public will, has to look for this outside its own resources and has to lean on others who should be subordinate to it. The government should be the centre and the driving force, although the impetus of movement should not come from it. Having been deprived of its proper nature, it has fallen into lethargy, which is disastrous for the citizens, and which leads to the ruin of institutions.

The weaknesses of the Constitution with regard to the Executive are not confined to these defects. Just as important as those already mentioned is the lack of responsibility of the Secretaries of State. Since responsibility is assigned exclusively to the chief of the administration, its effect is nullified. Harmony and method between the different branches are not ensured, and guarantees of observance of the law are reduced. Greater care will be taken in administration when ministers have real moral responsibility which should certainly be assigned to them. There will then be more powerful incentives for them to seek the common good. Punishment, which unfortunately is sometimes deserved, should not be the seed of greater ills, the cause of major disturbances or the origin of revolutions. Responsibility in a man elected by the people will always be illusory unless he accepts it voluntarily or, contrary to all probability, lacks the means to override the law. On the other hand, this responsibility can never be made effective unless the cases in which it is incurred have been defined and the penalty determined.

Everyone observes with surprise the contrast presented by the Executive which has too great a degree of strength and, at the same time, extreme weakness. It has been unable to repel invasion from abroad or to contain attempts at sedition, unless it has resorted to dictatorship. The Constitution itself, convinced of its own shortcomings, has assumed many of the functions which it avariciously withheld from the Executive. Thus, the Government of Colombia is either a paltry source of well-being or a devastating torrent.

In no other nation has the power to pass sentence been so highly enthroned as it is in Colombia. Considering the manner in which the powers are constituted among us, it cannot be said that the functions of the body politic of a nation are confined to wishing and executing its will. A third supreme agent has been added, as if the capacity to decide what laws apply to specific cases were not the principal duty of the Executive. In order to ensure that those entrusted with deciding this question are not unduly influenced, they have been left entirely separate from the Executive, of which by their nature they should be an integral part; and although the Executive has been entrusted with continuous supervision of the prompt and correct administration of justice, this duty has been assigned to it without providing it with the means to discover when its intervention might be timely, or stating to what point it should go. Even its power of choosing suitable people has been restricted.

Not satisfied with this exaltation of the judiciary, we have, in later laws, given absolute supremacy to the civil courts over military trials. This is contrary to the uniform practice of centuries; it is derogatory to the authority given by the Constitution to the President, and destructive of the discipline which is the basis of an army of the line. Later laws on the judicial function have extended the right of judgement to a point it should never have reached? As a result of the procedural laws, law-suits have become complicated. Everywhere new local courts and tribunals have been set up, and the miserable people whom they entrap and sacrifice for the benefit of the judges are crying out for reform. On many occasions higher courts, consisting almost exclusively of laymen, have decided whether the law is correctly or incorrectly applied. The Executive has heard plaintive claims against the cunning or prevarication of judges, and has had no means of punishing them; it has seen the public treasury suffering from the ignorance and malice of the courts, and has been unable to apply a remedy.

The accumulation of all the administrative branches in the hands of the local agents of the Executive in the departments increases its importance, because the Administrator, the head of the civil order and internal security, is overburdened with the administration of the national revenue, supervision of which needs many individuals merely to prevent its deterioration. Although this accumulation of powers may appear to be convenient, it is not, except in the case of the military authority which, in maritime departments, should be combined with the civil authority, and the latter separated from the revenue authorities so that each of these branches may serve the people and the government in a satisfactory manner.

The town councils, which would be useful as counsellors to provincial governors, have scarcely fulfilled their proper functions. Some of them have dared to arrogate to themselves the sovereignty which belongs to the nation, others have encouraged sedition. Nearly all the new ones have undermined rather than promoted the provisioning, the improvement and the general welfare of their respective towns. Such corporations are no use for the purposes for which they were intended: they have made themselves distasteful for the taxes they collect, and for the trouble they give to those chosen to sit on them, and also because in many places there is no one to replace them. What makes them most invidious is the obligation for citizens to hold the office of magistrate for a year, in which they must employ their time and their fortune and frequently compromise their responsibility and even their honour. It is not rare for certain individuals to leave their homes and go into self-imposed exile, to avoid being nominated for these troublesome offices. And if I am to say what everyone thinks, there would be no more popular decree than one abolishing town councils.

### Insecurity, misery and laxity

There is no general police law, or even the shadow of one. The result of this is a state of confusion—or, more accurately, a mystery—for officials of the Executive, who find themselves dealing one by one with individuals who are unmanageable without a diligent and effective police force, which could place every citizen in immediate contact with government agents. In consequence, administrators encounter many difficulties in ensuring that the laws and regulations in all branches of their office are complied with.

Once calm and security—the only desires of the people—had been destroyed, it was impossible for agriculture to remain even in its former deplorable state. Its ruin has contributed to that of other sectors of industry; it has demoralized the rural economy and reduced the sources of income, and everything has been plunged into unmitigated misery. In some districts the people have regained their primitive independence since, once they have lost their possessions, nothing binds them to society and they have even become its enemies. Foreign trade has followed the same path as the country's industry. I would even say that it is barely sufficient to provide us with basic requirements. The frauds favoured by the laws and judges, followed by numerous bankruptcies, have caused loss of confidence in a profession which is based solely on credit and good faith. And what trade can there be without exchange and profits?

Our army was once the model for America and the glory of freedom: its obedience to the law, to the magistrature and to the general public seemed to belong to the heroic days of republican virtue. It wore its weapons for cover, since it had no uniforms; dying of want, it fed on the spoils of the enemy, and without ambition breathed only love for its country. These generous virtues have been eclipsed to a certain degree by the new laws enacted to regulate and protect it. The soldier shares in the violent changes which have disturbed society, and no longer retains his devotion to the cause he saved and a healthy respect for his own scars. I have mentioned the disastrous consequences that must have arisen from subjecting the army to civil courts, whose doctrine and decisions are fatal to the strict discipline, passive submission and blind obedience which form the basis of military power, the support of the whole of society. The law which allows a soldier to marry without permission from the government has harmed the army considerably in mobility, strength and spirit. There was good reason for not seeking recruits among heads of households; now, contravening this rule, we have made fathers of families of the soldiers. One major contribution to the relaxation of discipline has been the abuse publicly heaped on commanders by their subordinates. Declaring arbitrary detention to be a correctional punishment is tantamount to establishing human rights by decree, and spreading anarchy among soldiers who are most cruel and also most terrible when they become demagogues. Dangerous rivalries between the civil and the military powers have been promoted by newspaper articles and by discussions in the Congress, the army no longer being considered as the liberator of the country, but as the executioner of liberty. Was this the recompense due for such grievous and sublime sacrifices? Was this the reward reserved for heroes? The scandal has even reached the point of inciting hatred and rancour among soldiers from different provinces, for whom neither unity nor strength exist.

I would prefer not to mention the leniency with which military crimes are treated in this dreadful time. Every legislator is completely aware of the gravity of this wicked indulgence. What army will be worthy, in future, of defending our sacred rights, if crime is punished by rewarding it? And if glory no longer belongs to loyalty, and courage to obedience?

Since 1821 when we began to reform our financial system, everything has been an experiment; and the last one has left us more disillusioned than those which went before. The lack of energy in the administration, in each and every one of its branches, the general desire to avoid payment of taxes, the remarkable disloyalty and carelessness of the tax collectors, the creation of unnecessary posts, the small salary they carry, and the laws themselves have conspired together to destroy the exchequer. Several times we have thought of checking this evil by invoking the action of the courts; but the courts, in appearance the protectors of innocence, have absolved the complaining taxpayer and indicted the collector, while the slow and dilatory action of the judges has not allowed time for the Congress to issue new laws; and this weakens government action even more. The Congress has still not established supervisory bodies to handle major sources of income. It has still not examined, not even provisionally, the investment of the funds for which the government is trustee.

The continued absence in Europe of the person who, by orders issued in 1823, must account for the millions owed on the loan contracted and ratified in London; the expulsion of the commercial attaché we had in Peru, who was organizing the recovery of the subsidies we paid to that Republic; and, finally, the wasteful distribution of national property—all this has forced us to debit to the national account the sums which we would otherwise have received. The Colombian exchequer has, then, reached such a critical point that it cannot honour our commitments to the generous foreigner who has lent us funds, trusting in our good faith. The army is not receiving half its pay; and, apart from Treasury employees, others are suffering the same misfortune. I blush to admit it, and I hardly dare tell you, that the nation is bankrupt and that the Republic is pursued by a formidable army of creditors.

In describing the chaos surrounding us, it seems almost superfluous to speak of our relations with the other nations of the world. These relations prospered when our military glory was great, and our citizens prudent, thus inspiring confidence that our civil organization and social well-being would reach the high level that Providence had indicated. Progress in foreign relations has always depended on the wisdom of the government and the agreement of the people. No nation ever made itself esteemed, except by making use of these advantages; none ever made itself worthy of respect unless it was fortified by unity. And Colombia in discord, despising her laws, ruining her credit, what encouragement can she offer for her friends? What guarantees does she have to keep even those she has? Retrograde steps, instead of advances in the civil state, inspire only disdain. She has already been provoked and insulted by an ally who would not exist without our magnanimity. It is your deliberations which have to decide whether friendly nations, who may already repent of having recognized us, are now to erase our name from the list of peoples which compose the human race.

## The country's anguished appeal

Legislators! Great and arduous is the task which the will of the nation has entrusted to you. Save us from the difficulties in which our fellow citizens have placed us, and save Colombia. Look into the depths of the hearts of your constituents. There you will see the prolonged anguish they are suffering. They are sighing for security and peace. 'A firm, powerful and just government' is the cry of the country. Look at the country, standing on the ruins of the desert left by despotism, pale with fright, weeping for 500,000 heroes who died for her, whose blood sprinkled in the fields gave birth to her rights. Yes, legislators, the dead and the living, the tombs and the ruins, demand guarantees from you. And I, sitting now in the home of a simple citizen, and lost among the crowd, recover my voice and my right, I who am the last to call for the end of society, I who have made a religion of country and freedom, I must not now be silent in such a solemn moment. Give us a system of government in which the law will be obeyed, the magistrature respected, the people free—a government which prevents transgressions of the general will and the commands of the people.

Consider, legislators, that energy in the public power is the safeguard against individual weakness, the threat which deters the unjust, and the hope of society. Consider that the corruption of nations arises from the leniency of the courts and the impunity with which crime is committed. Understand that without power there is no virtue; and, without virtue, the Republic will perish. Understand, finally, that anarchy destroys freedom and that unity preserves order.

Legislators! In the name of Colombia I beg you with repeated prayers to give us, in the image of the Providence you represent as arbiters of our destinies—to give us, for the people, for the army, for the judges and for the administrators, laws which are inexorable!

Bogotá, 29 February 1828                                        *Simón Bolívar*

91

# Lessons for a soldier of the country

*Remarks by Luis Perú de Lacroix in his* Diario de Bucaramanga. *Entries for 8 and 15 May 1828, recounting what the Liberator said and did, and showing Bolívar as a teacher of manners.*

8. In the morning Lieutenant Freire, one of my staff officers, arrived from Pampa. I had sent for him by order of the Liberator, to help in the secretary-general's office. His Excellency asked him various questions regarding General Fortoul, and Freire gave him to understand that he had not arrived at Pamplona in a very contented frame of mind. When the officer had left, the Liberator said to me that he should come to supper every day at his table and that I should tell him so. After lunch, His Excellency set to work with his private secretary.

. . . . . . . . . . . . . . . . . . . . . . . . . . . . . . . . . . . . .

15. When lunch was over we all accompanied the Liberator to Mass, and afterwards we went with him to visit the priest. While His Excellency was sitting at the street door he saw passing by the officer Freire (the one of whom I spoke on the eighth of this month), and he asked me why he had not come to sup at his table. I answered that Freire through shyness and lack of custom would be very embarrassed by this and feel out of place, and that therefore I had not told him to do so. He then asked me about the behaviour of the said officer and I told him that it was good. 'Then,' His Excellency continued, 'you will tell him from me that he should come to sup with me today.' I obeyed the order although with some misgiving, since I knew that Freire, who had been promoted only a short while before from sergeant to sublieutenant, still had the manners of a soldier and, it may be said, the behaviour of the guardhouse which would make him ridiculous at the table of the President of the Republic. Freire arrived at the stated time and the Liberator himself indicated where he should sit, and His Excellency saw by his attitude that this officer had no manners. During supper it happened that General Soublette said: 'Lieutenant Freire, please pass me' this or that; and then the Liberator observed to the General that he should call him Officer. There was another incident; in order to help himself from a dish which was some way away from him, Freire got up from his seat and, stretching his body and arms, helped himself from the dish on to his own plate. The Liberator then said to him: 'Officer, do not trouble to serve yourself in that way when a dish is not within your

reach, but ask the man nearest to it, since that is less work.' After supper the Liberator said to me: 'Your staff officer is bit of a country bumpkin; however, let him come to lunch and supper every day; we will lick him into shape and teach him manners.'

---

92

# An affirmation of republican principles and a categorical observation concerning the United States

*In the middle of Colombia's grave political crisis, the Liberator wrote on 5 August 1829 from Guayaquil to Colonel Patrick Campbell, the Chargé d'Affaires of Great Britain in Bogotá. It is this letter that contains the phrase: 'The United States, which seems destined by Providence to plague America with misery in the name of liberty'.*

Dear Colonel and friend:

Thank you for your kind letter of 31 May from Bogotá.

I must begin by thanking you for the many kind things you have said in your letter about Colombia and myself. How many times have you deserved our gratitude? I am embarrassed when I consider what you have thought, what you have done, since you have been among us to support the country and the glory of its leader.

The English minister resident in the United States does me too much honour when he says that he has hope only for Colombia because there is a Bolívar here. But he does not know that Bolívar's physical and political being is very weak and soon to die.

What you have kindly told me regarding the project of nominating a European prince to succeed me in my authority is not new to me, since something of the sort had been communicated to me with no little mystery and some embarrassment, since they know what I think.

I do not know what to say to you about this idea, which involves a thousand difficulties. You should know that, on my part, there would be none, since I am determined to hand over power at the next Congress; but who could mollify the ambition of our leaders and the fear of inequality in the lower classes? Do you not think that

England would be jealous if the choice fell on a Bourbon? And how much opposition would there be from all the new American states, and from the United States, which seems destined by providence to plague America with misery in the name of liberty? It seems to me that I can already see a general conspiracy against this poor Colombia, already too much envied by as many republics as America now has. Every press will be set in motion calling for a new crusade against the accomplices of the betrayal of freedom, the Bourbon lovers and the violators of the American system.

In the south the Peruvians will light the flame of discord, in the Isthmus the Guatemalans and Mexico, and in the Antilles the Americans and liberals from all sides. Santo Domingo would not remain inactive and would call upon its brothers to make common cause against a prince of France. Everyone would turn into enemies and Europe would do nothing to support us, because the New World is not worth the expense of a Holy Alliance. At least, we have some motive for thinking thus, in view of the indifference with which it has watched us undertake and struggle for the emancipation of half the world, which will soon be the most productive source of European prosperity.

Finally, I am far from opposing the reorganization of Colombia in accordance with institutions tested in wise Europe. On the contrary, I would be infinitely pleased and would rally my forces to help in a task which might be described as a task of salvation, and which might be undertaken, not without difficulty, were we to be supported by England and France. With this powerful help we would be capable of anything, but without it, no. Therefore, I reserve my final judgement until we know what the Governments of England and France think about this change of system and choice of a royal family.

I assure you, my worthy friend, with the greatest sincerity, that I have told you my entire thoughts and have held nothing back. You may use my comments as seems best for your duty and for the well-being of Colombia. These are my views, and in the meantime accept the heartfelt affection of your humble and obedient servant.

*Bolívar*

93

## An offering to culture

*Words spoken to the Rector of the University at the political function which took place on 24 June 1928 when the Liberator entered Bogotá from Bucaramanga, after the dissolution of the Ocaña Convention, and when he took power as demanded by the people.*

Sir,

I would it had pleased Heaven to allow me to spread the light of truth and of learning to the minds of all, so that we might not stray from the path of virtue, nor fall into the shadow of error and ignorance. But unfortunately the state of things has not permitted me to do so. However, I say that I would like nothing better in future than to direct these young shoots of life, these citizens who will be the inheritors of our rights, our liberty and our independence, so that they may preserve these precious possessions by their virtues, their knowledge and enlightenment. From now on I shall direct my steps to the teaching of the people and of its children.

94

## With Mexico he will continue to support the cause of unity

*During the critical period of the 'Dictatorship', Bolívar—for the last time—states his integrationist views. He declares his confidence that Mexico will join Colombia in this mighty undertaking of Latin American unity. Message to General Guadalupe Victoria, President of Mexico, dated 14 August 1828, from Bogotá.*

Republic of Colombia

### SIMÓN BOLÍVAR

Liberator President, etc., etc.

*To our great and good friend, faithful ally and confederate, President of the United States of Mexico, Guadalupe Victoria.*

Dear and good friend and faithful ally,

It is not possible for the great American Assembly, to which for our part we have designated Mr Pedro Gual and Mr Miguel Santamaría as plenipotentiaries, to meet before the treaties drawn up in the Isthmus have been ratified, since these must serve as the basis for its operations; and, since this ratification will now not take place in Peru, according to information we have received, and it will not be easy to ratify the treaty in the Central American Republic in view of its state of turmoil, we have decided on our part to postpone the meeting of this Assembly and to recall our plenipotentiaries.

Colombia will never cease working towards the American Confederation which would be of so much benefit to all the nations of this continent, to ensure their independence, and to unify their politics by making their relations closer; and, if she may count on the efforts of her sister ally and confederate, the Republic of the United States of Mexico, she will certainly propose the meeting of plenipotentiaries in better days and in happier circumstances, in order to deal with our common interests. Fortunately, this meeting is not necessary to maintain existing relations, which will never be broken, between our respective countries since these are founded on existing treaties and our unalterable desire that our friendship and alliance shall be firm, perpetual and eternal if possible.

Mr Gual will let Your Excellency know our feelings in favour of your States and our constant desire to support their independence and promote their content and happiness.

Bogotá, 14 August 1928                                    *Simón Bolívar*
Secretary for Foreign Affairs,
*Estanislao Vergara*

95

# For the scientific protection and exploitation of the forestry resources of the nation

*For the conservation and care of the natural resources of the nation, responsibilities were assigned to the Faculties of Medicine in Caracas, Bogotá and Quito. Decree promulgated on 31 July 1829 in Guayaquil.*

SIMÓN BOLÍVAR
Liberator of Colombia and Peru etc., etc.

Considering:

1. That the forests of Colombia, whether they be public or private

property, contain great wealth, both in the wood itself for all kinds of building and in the dyes, quinine and other substances useful to medicine and the arts;

2. That everywhere there is over-exploitation of wood, dyes, quinine and other substances, especially in the forests belonging to the State, causing them great damage;

3. That, to avoid this, it is necessary to issue regulations to protect effectively both public and private properties against any violation whatever;

And having seen the reports sent to the Government on the matter and having heard the opinion of the State Council, I decree that:

*Article 1.* Provincial governors shall designate in each district, through the judges at law or persons enjoying their confidence, the uncultivated land belonging to the Republic, providing written evidence of its demarcation and its particular products such as precious woods, medicinal plants and other useful substances, and shall file one copy of this information and send another to the prefecture.

*Article 2.* They shall immediately publish notices in each district stating that no one may remove from the uncultivated, or state, lands any precious woods or wood suitable for building merchant ships, without written permission from the provincial governor concerned.

*Article 3.* These permits shall not be issued without payment; but a fee shall be charged for them, on a sliding scale to be decided by the governors with the help of experts, thus establishing a regulation for this purpose which shall be submitted to the prefect for approval.

*Article 4.* Anyone who removes from state forests quinine, precious woods, or woods for use in building, without the required permit, or who exceeds the limits prescribed for him, shall incur a fine of 25 to 100 pesos, payable into public funds; he shall also pay, at a just rate to be decided by experts, for what he has removed or damaged.

*Article 5.* The prefects of maritime departments shall take particular care to ensure that the wood in state forests is preserved, especially wood which may be of use to the national navy, and that only what is necessary, or what may be sold with profit to the Treasury, is removed.

*Article 6.* Provincial governors shall prescribe simple rules suited to local circumstances to ensure that the exploitation of wood, quinine or dyes shall be undertaken in an orderly manner, so that their quality may be improved and greater profits obtained from their sale.

*Article 7.* Wherever there are quinine trees and other substances useful to medicine, a board of inspectors shall be set up, and the prefect concerned shall assign to the Board such territories as he thinks fit. This board shall consist of at least three persons, of whom one must be a doctor wherever this is possible. The members of the Board shall be nominated by the prefect, on the proposal of the governor, and shall remain in their posts as long as they conduct themselves satisfactorily.

*Article 8.* Anyone who wishes to extract quinine or other substances useful to medicine from forests belonging to the state or to private persons shall have his operations inspected by one or two commissioners nominated by the board of inspectors; their food, or daily allowances, shall be provided by the contractor or contractors.

The board and the commissioners shall ensure:

1. That the limits fixed in the permit to make cuts on quinine trees and to extract other substances useful to medicine are not exceeded;

2. That extraction and preparation are affected in accordance with rules to be laid down by the Faculties of Medicine in Caracas, Bogotá and Quito, in a simple set of instructions which they are to prepare in order to avoid the destruction of plants producing the said substances, and to explain how the substances are to be prepared and packed, etc., so that they may obtain the best price and repute in the trade.

*Article 9.* In ports where a Board of Inspectors has not been set up, the inspection referred to in the previous article shall be undertaken by intelligent persons nominated for this purpose by the Governor; the quality of the quinine, or the purpose for which it is intended, should be noted in their report. In the absence of proof that this requirement has been met, customs officials shall not accept certificates to register these articles; and if it is found that they are mixed with other bark or substances, or if they have not been sufficiently refined, this shall also be noted and the governor or customs officer shall be informed so that shipment may be prevented.

*Article 10.* The Faculties of Medicine at Caracas, Bogotá and Quito, as well as the prefects of departments, shall send their reports to the government, proposing means of improving the extraction, preparation and marketing of quinine and of other substances contained in the Colombian forests, which are useful to medicine or for the arts, and shall make all the necessary suggestions for the growth of this important branch of public wealth.

The Minister, Secretary of State for Internal Affairs, shall be charged with the execution of this decree.

Issued at Guayaquil on 31 July 1829.

*Simón Bolívar*

For His Excellency the Liberator President of the Republic,
The Secretary General,
*José D. Espinar*

96

# Mining policy, law and science

*From the decree signed in Quito on 24 October 1829, which constitutes the basis for existing legislation on mining and hydrocarbon extraction in Venezuela, where oil, iron and gas have been nationalized and the subsoil belongs to the nation.*

## SIMÓN BOLÍVAR
### Liberator President of the Republic of Colombia, etc., etc.

Considering:

1. That mining has been abandoned in Colombia, despite the fact that it is one of the chief sources of public wealth;

2. That in order to promote mining, it is necessary to repeal some earlier provisions which have been the source of frequent litigation and dissension among miners;

3. That ownership of mines must be protected against any infringement and against the ease with which it can be interfered with or lost;

4. Finally, that it is important to promote scientific knowledge of mining and mechanics, and also to spread the spirit of partnership and enterprise, so that mining may reach the high degree of perfection needed for the prosperity of the state,

I decree as follows:

CHAPTER I

*Discovery, ownership and abandonment of mines*

*Article 1.* In accordance with the law, mines of any kind belong to the Republic, whose government cedes the ownership and possession of them to citizens who apply for them, on the conditions laid down in the mining laws and regulations, and on the further conditions specified in this decree.

*Article 2*. For the title deed of any mine containing metal or precious stones, the appropriate duties must be paid and, in addition, 30 pesos must previously have been paid into the provincial treasury concerned. These charges shall create a fund to pay for the establishment of a chair of mining and mechanics, which will be set up in every mining province, where possible; no Treasury official shall use this fund, under penalty of replenishing it at his own cost.

. . . . . . . . . . . . . . . . . . . . . . . . . . . . . . . . . . . . . .

*Article 13*. . . . [Sole paragraph]. Provincial governors shall send to the Minister of the Interior every six months samples from new mining discoveries, labelled to show which mine they are taken from; and these samples shall be placed in the National Museum. Provincial governors shall also encourage owners of old mining seams, alluvial gold and other metals and precious stones to send samples from their mines, also to be placed in the National Museum. Each governor shall try to collect, within a year, samples from all the mines in his province.

. . . . . . . . . . . . . . . . . . . . . . . . . . . . . . . . . . . . . .

*Article 38*. Until suitable regulations are formulated for the mines and miners of Colombia, the mining regulations of New Spain, issued on 22 May 1803, shall be observed provisionally, with the exception of the part dealing with the mining court and mining judges, and anything which may be contrary to existing laws and decrees shall not be observed either.

The Minister, Secretary of State for Internal Affairs, shall be entrusted with the execution of this decree.

Issued in Quito, on 24 October 1829.

*Simón Bolívar*

For His Excellency, the Secretary General,
*José Domingo Espinar*

97

# 'Independence is the only good we have obtained at the cost of all others'

*A moving message addressed by Bolívar, at the end of his public career, to the Constituent Congress of Colombia—called 'The Admirable Congress'—in Bogotá on 20 January 1830.*

Fellow citizens!

Permit me to congratulate you on the convening of this Congress which, on behalf of the nation, is about to carry out the noble duties of legislator.

Great and arduous is the task of creating a people just emerging from oppression through anarchy and civil war, and not prepared in advance to receive the healthy reform to which it aspires. But the lessons of history, the examples of the old and new worlds and the experience of twenty years of revolution should serve as beacons to guide you through the darkness of the future; and I flatter myself that your wisdom will rise to the point of being able to dominate with vigour the passions of some, and the ignorance of the multitude, consulting, as often as necessary, the enlightened reasoning of sensible men, whose goodwill is an invaluable aid in resolving questions of high politics. Moreover, you will also find worthy advice to follow in the very nature of our country, which includes the heights of the Andes and the torrid banks of the Orinoco. Examine it in all its extent, and you will learn from it, from the infallible teacher of men, what laws the Congress must pass for the happiness of Colombians. Our history will tell you much, and our necessities more, but the cries of our sorrow for the lack of rest and certain freedom will be even more persuasive.

How happy the Congress will be if it can give Colombia the joy of these supreme benefits, for which it will merit the greatest of blessings!

Since the Congress has been summoned to prepare the basic code to rule the Republic, and to nominate the high officials to administer it, it is the duty of the government to inform you of the knowledge possessed by the respective ministries concerning the present situation of the state, so that you may enact laws in a manner befitting the nature of things. It is for the presidents of the Council of State and the Ministerial Council to report to you on their work during the last eighteen months. If this work has not fulfilled the hopes we had of it, it has at least overcome the obstacles placed in the way of administration by the troubled circumstances of war abroad and internal upheavals—evils which, thanks to Divine Providence, have now abated in favour of mercy and peace.

I bid you to lend your sovereign attention to the origin and course of these disturbances.

The disorders which unfortunately occurred in 1826 obliged me to come back from Peru, despite the fact that I was resolved not to accept the principal constitutional office, to which I had been re-elected in my absence. Called back urgently to re-establish harmony and avoid civil war, I could not refuse my services to my country, from which I had received that new honour and unmistakeable proofs of confidence.

## The 'Dictatorship'

The national representatives began to consider the causes of the discord which disturbed the minds of the people; and, convinced that these still existed and that radical measures were needed to deal with them, they bowed to the necessity of bringing forward the meeting of the great Congress. This body was established when factional feeling was at its height; and for the same reason it was dissolved without its members being able to agree on the reforms they were considering. Seeing that the Republic was threatened with complete collapse, I was again obliged to support it in such a crisis; and, if national feeling had not immediately arisen to concern itself with its own preservation, the Republic would have been torn apart by the hands of its own citizens. It wished to honour me with its confidence, a confidence that I had to respect as the most sacred law. When my country was about to perish, could I hesitate?

The laws, which had been violated by the clash of arms and the dissensions of the people, lacked force. Already the legislative body had decreed, knowing the necessity, that an assembly should be convened to reform the Constitution; and already, at last, the Congress had unanimously declared that reform was most urgent. Such a solemn declaration, together with those which had preceded it, constituted a formal judgement against the political system of Colombia. In opinion, and in fact, the Constitution of 1811 had ceased to exist.

The situation of the country was dreadful, and my own situation was even more dreadful, because it put me at the mercy of opinions and suspicions. However, I was not held back by the damage to a reputation acquired in a long history of service, during which similar sacrifices had been necessary and frequent.

The crucial decree which I issued on 27 August 1828 should have convinced everyone that my most ardent desire was to unburden myself of the insupportable weight of a power without limits, and that the Republic should again be constituted by its representatives. But scarcely had I begun to exercise the functions of supreme leader when warring elements sprang up with violent passion and criminal ferocity. An attempt was made on my life, and civil war broke out. Encouraged by this example, and in other ways, the Government of Peru invaded our southern departments with intent to conquer and seize them. I do not base my remarks, fellow citizens, on simple conjecture: the facts, and the documents accrediting them, are authentic. War was inevitable. The army of General La Mar was defeated in Tarqui in the most splendid and glorious manner by our arms; and its remnants were saved only by the generosity of the victors. Despite the magnanimity of the Colombians, General La Mar started the war again, trampling the treaties underfoot, and opened hostilities on his side, whilst I responded by inviting him to make peace again. But he vilified us and outraged us with insults. The department of Guayaquil was the victim of his extravagant pretensions.

Deprived of a navy, cut off by winter floods and other obstacles, we had to wait for a favourable season to re-take the ground. In the meantime a national trial, as it was called by the Peruvian supreme leader, vindicated our conduct and freed our enemies of General La Mar.

The political attitude of Peru having thus changed, the path of negotiation was made easier for us and we recovered Guayaquil by an armistice. Finally, the peace treaty was signed on 22 September, putting an end to a war in which Colombia defended its rights and its dignity.

I congratulate myself, with the Congress and the nation, for the satisfactory result of the negotiations in the south, both for the ending of the war and for the unmistakeable signs of goodwill we have received from the Peruvian government, which has nobly confessed that we were provoked to war by evil intentions. No government has ever satisfied another as the Peruvian Government has satisfied ours, and its magnanimity deserves the highest esteem from us.

## Internal struggles and justice

Fellow citizens! Peace was concluded with the moderation which was to be expected amongst brother nations, which should not use against each other the arms dedicated to liberty and mutual preservation; and we were also lenient with the unhappy people in the south who allowed themselves to be drawn into civil war, or were led astray by our enemies. I am happy to tell you that not one drop of blood has tarnished the vengeance of the law in ending our domestic strife; and although a brave general and his followers fell on the field of death, their punishment came from the hand of the Most High, when our own hand would have offered the mercy with which we have treated those who survived. All enjoy freedom in spite of their misconduct.

The country has suffered too much from these upheavals, which we shall always remember with sorrow. But, if anything can allay our grief, it is the consolation we have that no part in their origin can be attributed to us and that we behaved so generously to our adversaries when they were in our power. We certainly regret the sacrifice of some criminals on the altar of justice; and although a parricide does not merit clemency, many of them—and perhaps the most cruel—yet received it from my hands.

Let this vision of horror which it has been my misfortune to show you serve as an example; let it serve us in the future like those terrible blows that Providence has the habit of dealing us throughout our lives as punishment. It is for the Congress now to pick sweet fruit from this bitter tree, or at least to move away from its poisonous shadow.

If I had not had the honour to convene you to represent the rights of the people so that, in accordance with the wishes of your electorate, you may create or improve our institutions, this would have been the place to inform you of the conclusions drawn from twenty years dedicated to the service of the country. But I must not even hint to you what all citizens have a right to ask of you. Everyone may, and indeed everyone must, express their opinions, their fears and their wishes to those we have summoned to cure a society ailing with turmoil and weakness. Only I am prevented from performing this civic duty since, as I summoned you and gave you your authority, I am not allowed to influence your counsels in any way. Moreover, it would be inopportune to repeat to the people's chosen representatives what Colombia has publicly written in letters of blood. My only duty is to submit without reservation to the code and administrators you are to give us; and my only aspiration is that the will of the people shall be proclaimed, respected and carried out by its delegates.

To this end I have made arrangements for everyone to state their opinions in complete freedom and security, the only limits being those prescribed by order and moderation. And so it has happened, and you will find in the petitions brought for your consideration the simple expression of the people's will. All the provinces are waiting for your resolutions: everywhere the meetings held for this purpose have been marked by orderliness and respect for the authority of the Government and the Constituent Congress. The only thing to be regretted is the excesses of the Caracas council, which your prudence and wisdom must also judge.

### Final resignation

I fear with some reason that you will doubt my sincerity when I speak to you of the office of the chief magistrate who is to preside over the Republic. But the Congress must be persuaded that its honour should not allow it to think of me for this post, and my honour should not allow me to accept it. Would you by chance return this precious faculty to him who has demonstrated it to you? Would you dare, without diminishing your reputation, to give me your votes? Would that not be tantamount to my nominating myself? An act so ignoble is as far from your thoughts as it is from mine.

Bound, as you are, to constitute the government of the Republic from persons within and outside the membership of your own body, you will find distinguished citizens to occupy the presidency of the state with glory and advantage. All, all my fellow citizens enjoy the inestimable good fortune of seeming innocent in the eyes of suspicion; only I am branded as aspiring to tyranny.

Free me, I pray you, from the insults awaiting me if I continue to occupy a post which is never far from the reproach of ambition. Believe me, the Republic now needs a new chief magistrate. The people want to know if one day I will cease to rule them. The new American states watch me with a certain anxiety which may one day bring Colombia misfortunes such as the war with Peru. Even in Europe there are some who fear that my behaviour discredits the splendid cause of freedom. Ah! How many plots and wars we have endured in the assaults on my authority and my person! These blows have caused suffering to the people, whose sacrifices would have been unnecessary if Colombia's legislators had not, from the beginning, forced me to bear a burden which has crushed me more than the war and all its calamities.

Fellow citizens, show yourselves worthy of representing a free people by putting aside any idea that I consider myself necessary to the Republic. If one man is necessary to keep a state in being, that state should not exist and in the end would not exist.

The chief magistrate you choose will, no doubt, be a peacemaker at home, a bond of brotherhood, a consolation for the defeated factions. All Colombians will close ranks around this fortunate mortal: he will embrace them in the arms of friendship and make a family of citizens of them. I will obey this legally appointed chief magistrate with the most cordial respect: I will follow him as if he were the angel of peace. I will support him with my sword and all my strength. It will all add energy, respect and obedience to the man you choose. I swear it to you, legislators; I promise it in the name of the people and the Colombian army. The Republic will be happy if, on accepting my resignation, you designate as president a citizen beloved of the nation. The nation will go under if you insist on my governing it. Listen to my pleas; save the Republic; save my glory which is that of Colombia.

Dispose of the presidency which I respectfully leave in your hands. From today I am no more than a citizen armed to defend the country and obey the government; my public functions have ended for ever. I solemnly and formally abdicate the supreme power which the national vote had conferred on me.

You are from every province; you are the finest citizens; you have served in every public post; you know matters of local and general interest; you lack nothing to regenerate this failing Republic in every branch of its administration.

You will allow my last act to be my recommendation to you to protect the holy religion we profess, the source of abundant blessings from Heaven. The national treasury calls for your attention, especially the system of tax collection. The public debt, the cancer of Colombia, claims its most sacred dues from you. The army, which has so much right to national gratitude, needs radical reorganization. Justice demands codes capable of defending the rights and the innocence of free men. Everything is needed to create it, and you must lay the foundation of prosperity by establishing the general bases of our political organization.

Fellow citizens! I am ashamed to say it: independence is the only good we have obtained at the cost of all others. But it opens the door for us to regain the others under your sovereign auspices, with all the splendour of glory and freedom.

Bogotá, 20 January 1830

*Simón Bolívar*

## 98

# Brazil is a 'powerful guarantee' of the independence of the American republics

*Reply to Louis Souza Díaz, Envoy Extraordinary and Minister Plenipotentiary of His Majesty the Emperor of Brazil. Bogotá, 30 March 1830.*

Sir,

The mission with which you have been entrusted by His Majesty the Emperor of Brazil to the Government of Colombia fills me with satisfaction, because it will establish a bond of friendship between both nations. The Empire of Brazil, recently created by your illustrious monarch, is one of the most powerful guarantees received by the American republics in the course of their independence. Since your sovereign has set a fine example by voluntarily submitting to the most liberal constitution, he has become worthy of the applause and admiration of the world.

The esteem you have shown me on behalf of His Majesty the Emperor of Brazil is too flattering, and I would be failing in my duty if I did not recognize it as a sign of his benevolence; and I beg you, sir, to inform His Majesty of the feelings with which the Colombian Government wishes to cultivate the most friendly and close relations with Brazil.

When His Majesty chose such a distinguished person as yourself for the post of Minister Plenipotentiary to our Republic, he gave the clearest proof of the consideration he bears towards us. Therefore, your stay here will be a new incentive that will ensure for ever the most perfect friendship between our neighbouring and sister nations.

99

# A most painful farewell

*On the road from Bogotá to the shores of the Caribbean, on his way
into exile, the Liberator wrote from Turbaco—on 26 May 1930—his
last letter to the Grand Marshal of Ayacucho, his loyal partner and
lieutenant, Antonio José de Sucre. Barely nine days later, on 4 June,
Sucre was foully murdered. This crime of political passion was a
mortal blow to Bolívar.*

*Turbaco, 26 May 1830*

TO HIS EXCELLENCY GENERAL SUCRE

Dear General and good friend,

Your kind letter—you do not give the date—in which you take
leave of me has filled me with emotion, and if it cause you pain to
write it, what can I say? I, who am leaving not only my friend, but
also my country! You say very truly that words cannot express the
feelings of the heart in circumstances like these. Forgive me, then,
the lack of words and accept my very best wishes for your prosperity
and happiness. I shall forget you when the lovers of glory forget
Pichincha and Ayacucho.

You will be pleased to know that on the way here from Bogotá
I have received many marks of esteem from the people. This department in particular has been outstanding. General Montilla has
behaved like a perfect gentleman.

My affectionate regards to your wife. I assure you that nothing
is more sincere than the affection with which I sign myself, my dear
friend, your

*Bolívar*

100

# 'You must all work for the inestimable good of the Union ... My last wishes are for the happiness of my country'

*A final statement of forgiveness and patriotism. The last proclamation of the Liberator, seven days before his death on 17 December 1830.*

## SIMÓN BOLÍVAR
Liberator of Colombia, etc., etc.

### TO THE PEOPLE OF COLOMBIA

Colombians,

You have seen my efforts to establish freedom where tyranny reigned before. I have worked disinterestedly, losing my fortune and even my peace of mind. I stepped down from power when I realized that you mistrusted my impartiality. My enemies abused your credulity and trampled on what was most sacred to me, my reputation and love of freedom. I have been the victim of my persecutors, who have brought me to the door of the tomb. I forgive them.

As I leave you, my affection tells me that I should declare my last wishes. I aspire to no glory other than the consolidation of Colombia. You must all work for the inestimable good of the Union, with the people obeying the present government to free themselves from anarchy, with the ministers of religion addressing their prayers to Heaven, and with the soldiers using their swords to defend the guarantees of society.

Colombians! My last wishes are for the happiness of my country. If my death can help to end dissension and to consolidate the Union, I shall go peacefully into my grave.

Hacienda de San Pedro, in Santa Marta, 10 December 1830. 20th year of Independence.

*Simón Bolívar*

# CHRONOLOGY

## 1773
*1 December:* Marriage in Caracas of Colonel Don Juan Vicente de Bolívar y Ponte to Doña Concepción Palacios y Blanco.

## 1777
*10 November:* Birth of María Antonia de Bolívar y Palacios.

## 1779
*21 May:* Birth of Juana Marí de Bolívar y Palacios.

## 1781
*30 May:* Birth of Juan Vicente de Bolívar y Palacios.

## 1783
*24 July:* During the night of 24/25 July, birth in Caracas of Simón José Antonio de la Santísima Trinidad de Bolívar y Palacios (Simón Bolívar).

## 1786
*19 January:* Death of father.

## 1792
*6 July:* Death of mother.

## 1795
*23 July:* Runs away from the home of his guardian, Dón Carlos Palacios, to live with his sister, María Antonia.

## 1798
*4 July:* Commissioned as a second lieutenant.

## 1799
*19 January:* Travels to Spain. *2 February:* Veracruz. *February/March:* Visits

Mexico City. *20 March:* Leaves Veracruz; stops at Havana. *31 May:* Lands in Spanish port of Santoña. *10 June:* Madrid.

## 1800
*30 September:* Decides to marry María Teresa Rodríguez del Toro.

## 1801
*20 March:* Receives passports and joins his fiancée in Bilbao.

## 1802
*January:* Goes to Bayonne, on his way to Paris. Attends the peace celebrations at Amiens. *March/April:* Returns to Spain. *26 May:* Married in Madrid. *June:* Returns with his wife to Venezuela.

## 1803
*22 January:* Death of María Teresa. *23 October:* Gives power of attorney to his brother, Juan Vicente; leaves immediately for Spain. *December:* In Cadiz.

## 1804
Arrives in Madrid at the beginning of the year. *April/May:* Travels to Paris. *18 May:* Coronation of Bonaparte at Saint Cloud. *September:* In Paris meets the scholar Alexander von Humboldt and the physicist Aimé Bonpland. *2 December:* Attends Napoleon's coronation by the Pope.

## 1805
*6 April:* Leaves for Italy, with Simón Rodríguez and Fernando Toro. *26 May:* Attends the coronation of Napoleon in Milan and the great military review on the plain of Monte Chiaro, near Castiglione. From Milan he travels to Venice, Ferrara, Bologna, Florence, Perugia and Rome. *15 August:* Swears on the Aventine Hill to free his country. *3 September:* Climbs Vesuvius with Humboldt and the French physicist Gay-Lussac. *December:* Returns to Paris.

## 1806
*September:* Travels to Hamburg. *October:* En route to Venezuela, via the United States.

## 1807
*1 January:* Lands in Charleston. Visits Washington, Philadelphia, New York and Boston. *April/May:* Returns to La Guaira. *June:* Caracas. *2 September:* Settles on his estate at San Mateo.

## 1808
Conspiratory meetings at the 'Cuadra Bolívar', on the outskirts of Caracas.

## 1809

*28 July:* Appointed Chief Justice of Yare.

## 1810

*19 April:* The revolution of Venezuela against the colonial order breaks out; in Caracas, a Supreme Council is formed. Bolívar, confined to his property in Aragua, does not take part in the movement. *May:* The Supreme Council promotes him Colonel. *10 June:* Leaves for London on diplomatic mission, with Luís López Méndez and Andrés Bello. *10 July:* Lands at Portsmouth. In London, makes contact with Miranda. *July/August:* Meetings with Lord Wellesley, British Foreign Secretary. *21 September:* Sails for La Guaira, via Trinidad. *7 December:* Back in Caracas, reports on his mission.

## 1811

*January–June:* Regulary attends meetings of the Sociedad Patriótica. *4 July:* Declares himself in favour of full independence. *5 July:* Congress declares Venezuela's independence. *20 July:* Miranda marches to put down the insurrection of Valencia. Bolívar leads the Aragua batallion. *13 August:* Bloody battle of Valencia. *15 August:* Arrives in Caracas with news of the victory of the patriots.

## 1812

*26 March:* The Caracas earthquake; historic and impassioned speech. *4 May:* Takes command of Puerto Cabello. *30 June:* Uprising of the Fort of San Felipe against the patriots. *6 July:* Takes flight on the brig *Celoso*. *24 July:* Miranda surrenders to Monteverde. *30 July:* A group of officers, Bolívar among them, arrests Miranda in La Guaira; Monteverde's troops arrest the leading patriots; Bolívar goes into hiding. *1 August:* Goes to Caracas. *26 August:* Acquires passport to leave the country. *27 August:* Leaves La Guaira for Curaçao, where he arrives *1 September*. *October:* Goes to Cartagena, from where, on *27 November*, he writes to the Congress of New Granada pleading for the protection of his countrymen. *15 December:* Composes and signs the Cartagena Manifesto. *21 December:* Is appointed Major and begins the River Magdalena campaign.

## 1813

*February:* Victories in Cúcuta. *14 May:* Beginning of the Campaña Admirable ('Admirable Campaign'). *23 May:* Hailed as Liberator in Mérida. *15 June:* Proclaims, in Trujillo, the Guerra a Muerte ('War to the Death'). *7 August:* Enters Caracas. The Municipality names him General of the patriot forces and confers on him the title of Liberator. *8 August:* Announces, to the Congress of New Granada, the re-establishment of the Republic of Venezuela. *5 December:* Battle of Araure. *29 December:* Returns to Caracas.

## 1814

*2 January:* Gives account of his actions before the Popular Assembly meeting in Caracas. *February/March:* Fighting in San Mateo. *15 June:* Defeated in La

Puerta. *7 July:* Directs and supervises the mass emigration of the people of Caracas to the east of the country. *7 September:* Makes public his Carúpano Manifesto. *8 September:* Leaves Carúpano for Cartagena, where he arrives on *19 September. 24 November:* Appears before the Congress of New Granada, in Tunja. *27 November:* The Government of New Granada promotes him to Major General; under its orders, he subdues Cundinamarca and brings it into the Granadine Union.

## 1815

*23 January:* General of the Confederation of New Granada. *9 May:* Sails to Jamaica, arriving in Kingston on *14 May. 6 September:* Writes the Jamaica Letter. *10 December:* Escapes assassination. *18 December:* Sails for Cartagena. Informed of its surrender, he changes course and goes to Haiti. *25 December:* Lands at Les Cayes.

## 1816

*2 January:* Meeting with Pétion; prepares the Les Cayes Expedition. *7 February:* The exiled patriots acclaim him as Supreme Leader. *31 March:* Leaves with his men for Margarita Island. *2 May:* Fighting off the island of Los Frailes; boarding of the brig *Intrépido. 3 May:* Lands on Margarita Island. *7 May:* An assembly of patriots confirms his nomination as Supreme Leader. *2 June:* Decrees, in Carúpano, the freedom of the slaves. *June/July:* The Ocumare disaster. *22 August:* Mutiny breaks out against him; escapes being killed. *23 August:* Sails for Haiti. *21 December:* Jacmel expedition. *31 December:* Lands in Barcelona.

## 1817

*3 April:* Arrives at the Orinoco River. *4 July:* Escapes capture by jumping into the lagoon of Sacacoima. *17 July:* The Republican forces enter the Orinoco region. Bolívar occupies Angostura. *10 October:* Promulgates the Law on Land distribution to soldiers. *16 October:* Execution of Piar by firing-squad. *30 October:* Founds the State Council.

## 1818

*22 January:* Assembles all Guayana troops on the island of La Urbana on the upper Orinoco. *31 January:* Meets with Páez at the Cañafístola Ranch. *February/March:* Fighting on the plains. *17 April:* Surprised at Rincón de los Toros; escapes assassination. *5 June:* Arrives at Angostura. *15 August:* Announces to the people of New Granada that they will soon be free. *1 October:* Expounds the country's political and military situation to the State Council, and his plan for calling a meeting of Congress. *22 October:* Calls elections for deputies.

## 1819

*15 February:* Opens the Congress at Angostura with a historic speech. *March/April:* Fighting on the plains of Apure. *23 May:* Council of war in the village of Setenta; describes his plan to cross the Andes and take the Royalist rearguard by surprise. *27 May:* Undertakes the *Campaña Libertadora de Nueva Granada* (the Campaign for the Liberation of New Granada). *5 July:* Crosses the plateau of Pisba with his army. *25 July:* Battle of Pantano de Vargas. *7 August:* Battle of Boyacá; the independence of New Granada is sealed. *10 August:* Enters Santa Fe de Bogotá in victory. *20 September:* Returns to Venezuela. *11 December:* Arrives in Angostura. *17 December:* Congress declares the founding of the Republic of Colombia and elects him president. *24 December:* Leaves for New Granada.

### 1820

*5 March:* Arrives in Bogotá. *22 March:* Travels to Cucuta to prepare the Venezuelan campaign. *6 July:* Morillo proposes an armistice to him; a truce is arranged. *21 September:* Writes to Morillo from San Cristóbal; operations recommence. *1 October:* He takes Mérida. *7 October:* Enters Trujillo. *21 November:* More peace talks. *27 November:* Talks with Morillo in Santa Ana; they sign the Tratado de Armisticio y Regularización de la Guerra (Treaty of Armistice and the Proper Conduct of the War).

### 1821

*10 January:* Returns to Bogotá. *1 March:* Fighting with Venezuela recommences. *17 April:* Announces breaking of the Armistice. *24 June:* Battle of Carabobo; the Independence of Venezuela becomes a certainty. *23 August:* From Trujillo, he communicates the victory of Carabobo to General San Martín and offers his collaboration in the liberation of Peru. *7 September:* Congress, in the Villa del Rosario of Cúcuta, elects him President of the Republic, and he arrives there on *29 September* from Maracaibo. *2 October:* Assumes the presidency of the Republic. *4 October:* Prepared to free the southern departments of the country, he asks the Congress to tell him what his duties are as President at the head of the army. *9 October:* Receives plenipotentiary powers from the Congress. *11 October:* Leaves for Bogotá; prepares for the Southern Campaign.

### 1822

*2 January:* Arrives in Cali. *7 April:* Defeats Royalists at Bomboná. *24 May:* Sucre wins battle of Pichincha; the independence of Ecuador is sealed. *16 June:* Enters Quito to an enthusiastic welcome; meets Manuela Sáenz. *13 July:* Arrives in Guayaquil. *27 July:* Talks with San Martín.

### 1823

*February:* Invites Chile and Buenos Aires to co-operate simultaneously in destroying the royal army in South America. *1 March:* Riva Agüero, President of Peru, asks him for 4,000 soldiers. *15 March:* Notifies Lima that he will send two divisions of 3,000 men each. *14 May:* The Congress of Peru calls him. *2 August:* Receives permission from the Congress of Colombia to go to Peru. *7 August:* Sails from Guayaquil to El Callao; arrives *1 September.*

*10 September:* The Congress of Peru confers upon him supreme military authority.

## 1824

*1 January:* Very ill in Pativilca. *15 January:* Answers Mosquera with a resounding 'I shall be victorious' when asked by him what he will do in the face of the enormous obstacles surrounding him. *1 February:* The Congress of Peru names him Dictator. *8 March:* Establishes his headquarters in Trujillo; decrees general mobilization so that 'not a straw will remain unused throughout the free territory'. *26 March:* Installs the Supreme Court of Justice. *8 April:* Orders the distribution of land among the Indians. *1 May:* Founds the University of Trujillo. *15 July:* Gathers his troops in Pasco. *28 July:* The Congress of Colombia withdraws the plenipotentiary powers it had granted him and removes him from the command of the army. *2 August:* Reviews his troops: 6,000 Colombians and 3,000 Peruvians, in Sucre's opinion the best army that had yet been organized in America; historic proclamation. *6 August:* Fights the battle of Junín. *24 October:* Receives notice that his powers have been revoked; delegates to Sucre all his powers as General-in-Chief of the Colombian troops in Peru and takes over the supreme command of the war as Dictator of Peru. *7 December:* Occupies Lima. The same day convenes the Amphictyonic Congress of Panama. *9 December:* Battle of Ayacucho: independence of Peru and America. *22 December:* Resigns the Presidency of Colombia.

## 1825

*10 February:* Gives an account of his leadership to the Congress of Peru; resigns the Dictatorship. The Congress re-affirms its trust in him and appoints him to the supreme political and military command of the country with the title of Liberator. *1 April:* Establishes the Council of Government. *11 April:* Official visit to the southern departments. *16 May:* Calls together the deputies of upper Peru. *15 June:* Arrives in Cuzco. *4 July:* Decrees the distribution of land among the Indians, abolishes the title and authority of the Indian chiefs and frees the natives from compulsory personal service. *8 July:* Creates, in Cuzco, the Teachers' College and School for Studies in Sciences and Arts. *5 August:* Arrives in Puno. *6 August:* Signing of the act of independence, and creation of the Republic of Bolivia. *18 August:* Triumphant entry into La Paz; is granted supreme powers. *20 September:* Leaves for Potosí. *10 October:* Receives the Argentine envoys, Alvear and Diaz Vélez. *26 October:* Raises the flags of Colombia, Argentina and Peru on the peak of Potosí. *1 November:* Goes to Chuquisaca, capital of the new state, arriving on *3 November. 26 November:* Calls elections for the General Assembly. *8 December:* Decrees that the administration of justice should be free of charge; orders the construction of roads. *11 December:* Decrees the creation of primary schools and schools for orphans, schools for the sciences and arts, and a military academy in Chuquisaca; orders that the property, rights, income and activities of the chaplaincies should fall to the state for educational expenditure. *14 December:* Orders that land should be distributed to the Indians. *15 December:* Creates the Law Court of La Paz. *22 December:* Exempts the Indians from all taxation. *24 December:* Creates an Economic Society for the study, exploration and exploitation of the country's natural resources. *29 December:* Delegates high command to Sucre.

### 1826

*10 January:* Leaves Chuquisaca for Lima. *7 February:* Lands in Chorrillos. *6 March:* Rejects Páez's monarchist plans. *25 May:* Sends his draft constitution for Bolivia and his introductory speech to Sucre. *22 June:* Meeting in Panama of the Amphityonic Congress. *3 August:* Sends circular to northern departments dealing with reforms of the Cúcuta Constitution. *16 August:* Peru adopts the Bolivian Constitution. *1 September:* Summoned by his countrymen, he delegates the supreme command of Peru to Santa Cruz and the ministers of the cabinet and returns to Colombia. *3 September:* Sails from El Callao for Guayaquil, arrives on *12 September,* and is warmly welcomed. *28 September:* Goes up to Quito. *5 October:* Continues his journey to Bogotá where he arrives *14 November,* taking over the presidency on *23 November. 25 November:* Once more delegates his official powers to Vice-President Santander—except in the Venezuelan departments, over which he reserves for himself the exclusive exercise of Executive Power—and goes to put down the secessionist rebellion led by Páez. *30 November:* The Council of Government, in Lima, proclaims him President-for-Life of Peru. *17 December:* From Maracaibo, he calls on the conspirators to lay down their arms. *23 December:* Writes conciliatory letter to Páez from Coro. *31 December:* Arrives in Puerto Cabello.

### 1827

*1 January:* Declares general amnesty and names Páez to take over the civil and military authority of Venezuela. *4 January:* Goes to Valencia to meet Páez; public demonstration of obedience and submission by the latter to the Liberator. *12 January:* Caracas receives him in jubilation. *6 March:* Falls out with Santander. *6 April:* Asks Sucre to accept the Presidency-for-Life of Bolivia. *6 June:* The Congress rejects his resignation sent in February and invites him to assume his office again. *19 June:* In Caracas, he announces his march towards the South of the Republic to re-establish order, subverted in Guayaquil by a separatist movement fomented by Peru. *24 June:* Decrees the new Statutes of the University of Caracas. *5 July:* Sails from La Guaira bound for Bogotá, via Cartagena. *10 September:* Arrives in Bogotá and takes command.

### 1828

*14 March:* Travels to Bucaramanga; on *31 March* establishes his centre of operations there. *May:* From Bucaramanga, he follows the debates in the

Convention. *9 June:* Goes to Bogotá. *11 June:* Convention of Ocaña dissolved. *13 June:* Popular assembly in Bogotá annuls the mandate of the deputies and gives all power to Bolívar. *24 June:* Arrives in Bogotá and takes command as Dictator-President. *27 August:* Issues the decree constituting his government. *20 September:* Creates the Council of State. *25 September:* Escapes unharmed from dramatic attempt on his life. His already delicate health suffers. *24 December:* Calls a Constituent Assembly for January 1830. *28 December:* Delegates command to the Council of Ministers and travels south.

1829

*23 January:* Arrives in Popayán on his way to Quito. *26 February:* Sucre defeats the Peruvians at Portete de Tarqui. *28 February:* Signing of the Treaty of Girón. *17 March:* Bolívar arrives in Quito. *21 July:* Colombia retakes Guayaquil; the Liberator is acclaimed. *10 August:* Falls ill. *22 September:* Peace treaty with Peru. *20 October:* Returns to Quito and continues towards Bogotá on *29 October. 22 November:* From Popayán, he disapproves the cabinet's monarchist plans and reaffirms his republican intentions.

1830

*15 January:* Enters Bogotá. *20 January:* Establishes the Constituent Assembly; offers to resign the Presidency. The Assembly declares itself powerless to consider it. *1 March:* Appoints Domingo Caicedo as interim President of the Republic, gives him command and withdraws to Fucha, outside the capital. *27 April:* Offers once more to resign the Presidency. *8 May:* Ill, leaves Bogotá to go into exile, intending to sail from Cartagena to Europe. *24 June:* Arrives in Cartagena. *1 July:* Receives news of the assassination of Sucre. *2–5 September:* Bogotá, Cartagena and other cities ask him to return to the Presidency. *25 September:* Makes public his decision not to return to the supreme office. *2 October:* Leaves Cartagena and travels to Santa Marta. *15 October:* Stops at Soledad; his health worsens. *8 November:* Arrives in Barranquilla. *1 December:* Puts in at Santa Marta. *6 December:* Dón Joaquín de Mier, Spanish nobleman, lodges him in his country house at San Pedro Alejandrino. *10 December:* Receives the last rites and dictates his final proclamation. *11 December:* Signs his will, written the night before. *14 December:* His condition worsens. *16 December:* Delirious; his last hours are long and painful. *17 December:* Dies, at seven minutes past one in the afternoon.

# GEOGRAPHICAL
# GUIDE

*Angostura:* Town in Venezuela, on the south bank of Orinoco at the narrowest point of the river. Now Cuidad Bolívar.

*Apure, San Fernando de:* Town in Venezuela, on the right bank of the Apure River, on the southern plains.

*Babahoyo:* Town, province and river of Ecuador.

*Barcelona:* Town in eastern Venezuela, near the Caribbean and on the banks of the Neverí River.

*Barichara:* Colombian town in Department of Galán, in the eastern part of the country.

*Barinas:* Town and province in the western plains of Venezuela.

*Bogotá:* Capital of the Republic of Colombia, called, during the colonial and independence periods, Santa Fe de Bogotá, and also Santafé or Santa Fe.

*Boyaca:* Colombian village where the Liberator won the famous battle of the same name which secured the independence of New Granada.

*Bucaramanga:* Colombian town where the Liberator resided, in 1828, during the meeting of the Convention of Ocaña.

*Caracas:* Capital of Venezuela, 20 kilometres from the Caribbean coast and 922 metres above sea-level; in the central-northern region of the country.

*Cartagena de Indias:* Colombian port on the Caribbean, famous for its fortifications that protected it against pirates during the colonial period.

*Carupano:* Town and port on the eastern coast of Venezuela.

*Chancay:* Province and town of Peru.

*Chimborazo:* Highest point in Ecuador: 6,272 metres.

*Chuquisaca:* Important town in Bolivia, presently called Sucre.

*Cucuta:* Colombian town, near border with Venezuela. Also called El Rosario, Villa del Rosario and El Rosario de Cúcuta.

*Cundinamarca:* Province of Colombia and old name of New Granada.

*Curaçao:* Dutch island in the Caribbean, off the Venezuelan coast.

*Cuzco:* Historic city of Peru in the Andes, the ancient and famous capital of the Empire of the Incas.

*Guayana:* Province and region in the south of Venezuela, on the right bank of the Orinoco River and extending to the Essequibo River.

*Guayaquil:* Port on the Guayas River, on the Pacific Coast. The most heavily populated city in Ecuador.

*Huamachuco:* Municipality and town of Peru.

*Huamanga:* Province of Peru; its capital is Ayacucho.

*Ibarra:* Town in Ecuador, north-east of Quito and 2,628 metres above sea-level.

*Ica:* Town in Peru, south-east of Lima.

*Kingston:* Capital of Jamaica, in the Caribbean.

*Lima:* Important metropolis, capital of the Vice-royalty of Peru and the Republic of Peru. Near the Pacific coast.

*Magdalena, La:* Suburb of the city of Lima and name of the residence which the Liberator occupied there.

*New Granada:* Viceroyalty in the northern part of South America, with both Pacific and Caribbean coastlines. Capital: Bogotá. Now Colombia.

*Ocaña:* Colombian town, in the Andean highlands.

*Panama:* City on the isthmus of the same name, the narrowest part of the American continent, between the Pacific and Atlantic Oceans.

*Pasco:* Department of Peru.

*Pativilca:* Town, river and district of the province of Chancay on the Peruvian coast.

*Potosí:* City in Bolivia, capital of the department of the same name. Altitude: 4,040 metres.

*Puerto Caballo:* Important port and fortress in the central-western region of Venezuela.

*Quito:* Capital of the Republic of Ecuador, 2,800 metres above sea level.

*Rosario de Cúcuta, El:* See Cúcuta.

*Río de la Plata (River Plate):* Viceroyalty created by Spain in the territories of present-day Argentina, Uruguay, Paraguay and Bolivia.

*San Carlos:* Town in the western plains of Venezuela.

*San Mateo:* Town in the Valley of Aragua, in the centre of Venezuela.

*Santa Marta:* Colombian port, on the Caribbean.

*Socorro, El:* Town and municipality in south-western Colombia.

*Trujillo (Venezuela):* Town in the Andean highlands.

*Tulcan:* Ecuadorian town north-east of Quito. 2,745 metres above sea level.

*Urubamba:* River, province and town of the department of Cuzco, in Peru.

*Valencia:* Important Venezuelan town in the vicinity of Sabana de Carabobo and Puerto Cabello.

# BIBLIOGRAPHICAL
# NOTE

The written works of Simón Bolívar, from which the present anthology is drawn, are both extensive and varied. Letters, speeches, proclamations, laws, decrees and an assortment of documents all embody his thought. These works are being constantly re-printed and re-edited. The names of Daniel Florencio O'Leary, Francisco Javier Yanes, Cristóbal Mendoza, José Félix Blanco, Ramón Azpúrua and Vicente Lecuna should be mentioned among the most important compilers and disseminators of Bolívar's writings.

The most significant collections of documents on this subject are:

*Memorias del General O'Leary*, originally published in thirty-two volumes, between 1879 and 1888, in Caracas.

*Documentos para la historia de la vida pública del Libertador*, compiled by José Félix Blanco y Ramón Azpúrua, published in fourteen volumes between 1875 and 1877, in Caracas.

Both collections were ordered by President Antonio Gúzman Blanco. New editions were made of *Memorias del General O'Leary*, in thirty-four volumes, in 1981, in Barcelona (Spain) by GRAFESA, and of *Documentos para la historia de la vida pública del Libertador*, in fifteen volumes, made in 1978 and 1979 in Caracas by LITETECNIA. The new editions were ordered on 27 February 1979 and 9 July 1977, respectively, by President Carlos Andrés Pérez, for the Bicentenary of the Liberator.

The accomplished Bolivarian historian, Don Vicente Lecuna, compiled eleven volumes of *Cartas del Libertador* (Letters of the Liberator), a volume of *Proclamas y discursos del Libertador* (Proclamations and Speeches by the Liberator), another of *Papeles de Bolívar* (Papers of Bolívar), and two more of *Documentos referentes a la creación de Bolivia* (Documents Concerning the Creation of Bolivia). The thirteen volumes of the first three compilations—with notes by Doctor Lecuna and the collaboration of Esther Barret de Nazaris—were partially brought together in two volumes, on rice paper, of *Obras completas de Simón Bolívar*, originally published in 1947 with numerous re-printings.

The Sociedad Bolivariana de Venezuela, under commission by the national government, in compliance with a decree by President Rómulo

Batancourt, recently published an exhaustive edition of Bolívar's works with the title *Escritos del Libertador* (Writings of the Liberator). By June 1981, fourteen volumes of this masterly and definitive collection had been brought out.

The Sociedad Bolivariana also published three volumes of *Decretos del Libertador* (Decrees of the Liberator), 1961.

The John Boulton Foundation, under the guidance of the highly reputed historian, Professor Manuel Pérez Vila, published an important body of Bolívar-related documents, discovered in recent research, in one volume: *Cartas del Libertador* (Letters of the Liberator), Vol. XII, 1959. The Vicente Lecuna Foundation, on its part, published for the first time an equally valuable collection: *Correspondencia del Libertador* (Correspondence of the Liberator), 1974.

An essential document for a proper understanding of Bolívar is the *Diario de Bucaramanga* (Bucaramanga Diary), written by Luis Peru de Lacroix; it has been widely published.

Among the many volumes of documents mentioned above are to be found the one hundred pieces included in this anthology: *Simón Bolívar: The Hope of the Universe*.

# BIOGRAPHICAL
# NOTES

*Alvear, Carlos M. de* (1788–1852). Argentine general and politician; friend and collaborator of the liberator, José de San Martín.

*Arboleda, José Rafael* (1795–1831). Colombian writer and politician, renowned for his brilliance, culture and human qualities.

*Bello, Andrés* (1781–1865). Born in Caracas; one of America's foremost humanists.

*Bolívar, Fernando* (1810–1898). Venezuelan; nephew to Simón Bolívar; educated in the United States.

*Bonpland, Aimé* (1773–1858). French naturalist and explorer; friend of Bolívar from 1804; collaborated with Humboldt.

*Briceño Mendez, Pedro* (1794–1835). Venezuelan soldier and politician; a close deputy and trusted assistant to the Liberator, eventually marrying into his family.

*Campbell, Patrick.* British colonel; was Commercial Representative of Great Britain to the Government of the Republic of Colombia.

*Cullen, Henry.* British subject residing in Falmouth (Jamaica); friend and correspondent of Bolívar.

*Diaz Velez, José Miguel.* Argentine diplomat; accompanied Alvear on the mission to Bolívar in 1825.

*D'Evereux, John.* Irish general; distinguished volunteer in the British Legion.

*Humboldt, Alexander von* (1769–1859). German natural scientist. Distinguished for his scientific work and the quality and range of his studies of America.

*Lacroix, Luis Peru de* (1780–1837). A talented Frenchman; Colonel of Colombia; became Bolívar's intimate friend and was author of the *Diario de Bucaramanga* (Bucaramanga Diary).

*Lancaster, Joseph* (1778–1838). British educator, inventor of the system of mutual instruction, in which a teacher could, with the help of 'monitors' chosen from among the pupils, supervise as many as 1,000 students.

*Lopez Mendez, Luis* (1758–1841). Venezuelan politician and diplomat; accompanied Bolívar on the mission to London in 1810; resided in

England for many years and played a key role in securing British volunteers for the Independence Wars.

*Nariño, Antonio* (1765–1823). Distinguished Colombian thinker, soldier and politician; precursor of Independence.

*O'Higgins, Bernardo* (1776–1842). Renowned Chilean patriot and soldier. Outstanding figure in the history of his country.

*Paez, José Antonio* (1790–1873). Well-known Venezuelan soldier and politician; active over a very long period of time. Famous for his military record in the Llanos.

*Palacios, Esteban* (1767–1830). Uncle and godfather of Simón Bolívar, perhaps his most dearly loved relative.

*Penalver, Fernando* (1765–1837). Venezuelan politician, deputy and conscientious man of state. Intimate and trusted friend of Bolívar.

*Pétion, Alexandre* (1770–1818). Great figure of Haitian history.

*Pueyrredon, Juan Martin* (1776–1850). Famous Argentine politician; governed his country for several years; friend of San Martín and Bolívar.

*Renovales, Mariano* (1774–1819). Spanish soldier who at one time planned to serve American independence.

*Rodriguez de Francia, José Gaspar* (1766–1840). Important Paraguayan politician; governed his country despotically for twenty-six years.

*Rodriguez, Simón* (1771–1854). Venezuelan philosopher, educator and intellectual; the most influential of Simón Bolívar's teachers.

*Saenz, Manuela* (1797–1856). Worthy woman of Quito; faithful companion and mistress to Bolívar from 1822 onwards.

*Salias, Vicente* (1782–1816). Venezuelan doctor, poet and journalist; a heroic revolutionary idealist.

*San Martín, José de* (1778–1850). Famous liberator of Argentina, Chile and Peru; notable soldier and politician.

*Santander, Francisco de Paula* (1792–1840). Important Colombian soldier and politician; was Vice-President of the Republic and was active in government over a long period of time.

*Soublette, Carlos* (1789–1870). Distinguished Venezuelan soldier and politician.

*Souza Diaz, Luis.* Envoy Extraordinary and Minister Plenipotentiary of His Majesty the Emperor of Brazil to the Government of Colombia in 1830.

*Sucre, Antonio José de* (1795–1830). Distinguished Venezuelan soldier and politician; the most intimate and best-loved of Bolívar's deputies; one of the greatest figures in the history of Latin America.

*Victoria, Guadalupe* (1786–1843). Mexican patriot and politician; was President of Mexico from 1824 to 1829.

*Washington Parke Custis, George.* Adopted son of George Washington.

*White, Guillermo* (died 1834). Venezuelan of English origin; highly esteemed friend of Simón Bolívar.

*Wilson, Robert* (1777–1849). Distinguished British soldier and parliamentarian; friend of Bolívar and of the revolution of independence; father of his aide-de-camp, Belford Wilson.

# INDEX TO
# THE ANTHOLOGY